PLATFORM 5 EUROPEAN

C000004530

SWIS RAILWAYS

LOCOMOTIVES RAILCARS AND TRAMS

SECOND EDITION

The complete guide to all Locomotives, Railcars and Trams of the Railways of Switzerland

Chris Appleby

Published by Platform 5 Publishing Ltd., Wyvern House, Sark Road, Sheffield S2 4HG, England.

Printed in England by Hubbard Print, Dronfield, Sheffield.

ISBN 1 872524 90-7.

2

Rhätische Bahn Class Ge4/4II No. 614 SCHIERS arrives at Bergun with a St. Moritz–Chur train during December 1993.

Eric Sawford

CONTENTS

Front Cover Photograph: The Bern–Lötschberg–Simplon Railway operates a fleet of modern Class 465 Bo–Bo locomotives which are the same as the SBB Class 460. Here 460 003-2 is seen in May 1996 at Frutigen with a Basel–Milano EC train. **Regis Chessum**

Rear Cover Photograph: Brig–Visp–Zermatt ABDeh8/8 2041 'BRIG' at Brig on 19/09/94. **Brian Leighton**

INTRODUCTION TO SECOND EDITION

Unlike the rest of Europe, a large proportion of the Swiss railway system is privately-owned by nearly 60 separate companies varying in length from 381 km down to just 294 metres! This book contains full details of all locomotives and railcars of the Swiss Federal Railways, the Bern Lötschberg Simplon Railway Group and the Rhätische Bahn, together with information on the stock of the numerous private railways.

Since the first edition of this book was published, Swiss railways have continued to modernise their fleets, and very few pre-war locomotives and railcars remain in use, although some have been added to the historic fleets or privately preserved. The computer renumbering scheme continues to be adopted slowly by the SBB and has now been extended to cover most standard gauge railways. Although a few lines have closed and others are under threat, the MThB has expanded into Germany and is to take over the operation of an SBB line! Such events may become more common in future where the cantons put services out to tender.

LANGUAGES

Switzerland is a country with four official languages. The most widely spoken is German, with a large French-speaking area in the west of the country and Italian being spoken in the areas south of the Gotthard and Bernina passes. The fourth language, Romantsch, is spoken in parts of Canton Graubunden in the south-east. The national timetable uses all languages as appropriate to each table; this system has been adopted in this publication for place names. It should be noted that some towns are bilingual, Biel/Bienne (German/French) being the best-known example.

The official use of three languages in the areas where the Federal Railways operate requires it to display an official name in each of the three languages:

German:	Schweizerische Bundesbahnen	SBB
French:	Chemins de Fer Fédéraux	CFF
Italian:	Ferrovie Federali Svizzere	FFS

The Romantsch – Viafers Federalas Svizras (VFF) – appears only in the timetable, which also has an introduction in English.

Swiss Federal Locomotives and coaches are either lettered "SBB CFF FFS" on both sides or "SBB CFF" on one side and "SBB FFS" on the other. Their controls are labelled in German, French and Italian.

In this publication, the initials "SBB" are used throughout.

TICKETS

Apart from the ordinary single and return tickets (the cost of a return being less than twice the single fare for journeys of about 40 km), numerous concessions are available, usually through the purchase of "passes" or "cards".

The Swiss Pass gives unlimited travel on most major railways, boats, the transport systems of 24 cities and most postbuses together with a reduction on many privately-owned funiculars and mountain railways. The current prices are : four days – £110 second class, £166 first class, 8 days – £138 second, £198 first, 15 days – £162 second, £232 first and 1 month – £220 second, £322 first.

The Swiss Card provides a transfer from the point of entry into Switzerland to the holder's destination and back and a 50% reduction on other tickets purchased. It is valid for 1 month and costs £74 second class and £89 first. In fact, the first and last days are effectively rover tickets, giving the enthusiast opportunities limited only by the timetable, his or her ingenuity and stamina. The Swiss Transfer Ticket is similar but omits the 50% reduction, costing £52 second class and £78 first.

Regional Passes can be obtained covering 8 different areas. The length of validity (7 days or 15 days) and class of travel available varies according to the area. Day, family and half-fare cards are also available and the latter two can be used to obtain a reduction on the cost of regional passes.

The prices quoted are correct at January 1997. Full details of all these tickets and other facilities are available from:

Swiss National Tourist Office, Swiss Centre, New Coventry Street, London, W1V 8BB, England.

CLASSIFICATION OF SWISS MOTIVE POWER

All Swiss railways use a standard classification system for their motive power. It should be noted that separate systems are used for locos and railcars; hence it is possible for a loco and a railcar to have the same classification.

PREFIX LETTERS (Locomotives)

R   Max speed more than 110 km/h
A   Max speed 85 to 110 km/h
B   Max speed 70 to 80 km/h
C   Max speed 60 to 65 km/h
D   Max speed 45 to 55 km/h
E   Shunting loco
G   Narrow gauge loco

½ H   Rack fitted loco (combined with above if
½   rack & adhesion)
½ O   Open wagon body
½ T   Tractor
½ X   Departmental vehicle (some of these
½   are ex-railcars)
½

PREFIX LETTERS (Railcars)

Note: Further prefixed by R if max speed is more than 110 km/h.

A   1st class accommodation
B   2nd class accommodation
D   Baggage compartment

½ S   Saloon vehicle
½ Z   Postal compartment
½

SUFFIX LETTERS (All motive power)

a   battery powered
e   Electric powered
em   Electric & diesel powered (i.e. an electro-diesel)
h   Rack fitted (only used with railcars & tractors); if this precedes the a, e or m then the unit is pure rack; if it follows, the unit is rack & adhesion
m   Diesel or petrol powered
r   Restaurant vehicle
rot   Rotary snowplough
t   (only used with X in the form of Xt) Self propelled departmental vehicle, but not a loco (e.g. a self propelled crane or snowplough)

NUMBERS

These indicate the number of powered and total number of axles, e.g.
4/4 = all 4 axles powered (e.g. BoBo)
3/6 = 6 axles of which 3 are powered (e.g. 2Co1)

SUB-CLASS INDICES

To differentiate between classes with otherwise similar classifications, small Roman numbers are used, e.g. Re4/4^I, Re4/4^{II} etc.

All the above are combined as required to give full classifications, e.g.

Ae6/6   Co–Co electric loco, max speed 85–110 km/h
Be4/6   1B–B1 electric loco, max speed 70–80 km/h
ABDe4/4   Bo–Bo electric railcar, 1st, 2nd & baggage accommodation

The above system is now being replaced by new computer numbers. The classification letters are retained, but the 'fraction' numbers are replaced by a three digit class number. The system originally only included the SBB itself but has since been expanded to incorporate most of the standard gauge private railways. This has caused some new computer numbers to be changed! See the section on SBB numbering system for further details.

ACKNOWLEDGMENTS

We would like to thank all who have helped with the preparation of this book, especially Messrs. B. Garvin and M.R. Taplin, various members of the Locomotive Club of Great Britain, various officials and staff of the SBB and all who submitted photographs.

LAYOUT OF DATA

For each class of vehicles technical and historical information is given followed by a list of individual vehicles arranged as follows:

(1) Number.
(2) Previous number in parentheses (if any).
(3) Livery code (if applicable) – in bold condensed type.
(4) Column notes (if applicable).
(5) Code for depot allocation.
(6) Name (if any).

BUILDERS

The following builder codes are used in this publication:
(All are in Switzerland, unless stated otherwise)

ABB	ASEA Brown Boveri, Baden & Zürich Oerlikon.
ACEC	Ateliers de Constructions Électriques de Charleroi, Belgium.
ACMV	Ateliers de Constructions Mécaniques SA, Vevey.
AEG	Allgemeine Elektrizitäts Gesellschaft, Berlin, Germany.
ALIOTH	Elektrizitätsgesellschaft Alioth, Münchenstein.
ASPER	Viktor Asper AG Maschinenbau, Küsnacht.
BBC	AG Brown Boveri & Cie, Baden.
BBC (M)	Brown Boveri & Cie, Mannheim, Germany.
BEIL	Martin Beilhack Maschinenfabrik, Rosenheim, Germany.
BIBUS	Bibus Hydraulik AG, Zumikon.
BL	Anciens Etablissements Brissonneau & Lotz, Creil, France.
BREDA	SA Ernesto Breda, Milano, Italy.
BšH	Bühler SA, Officine Meccaniche, Taverne.
BšS	Büssing Fahrzeug und Motorenbau, Braunschweig, Germany.
CAT	Caterpillar, Peoria, Illinois, USA.
CEG	Chemins de Fer Electriques de la Gruyère (predecessor of GFM).
CEM	Cie Electro Méchanique, Le Havre, France.
CET	Carminati e Toselli, Milano, Italy.
CFD	Chemins de Fer Départmenteaux, Montmirail, France.
CGV	Compagnie Générale de Villefranche sur Saone, France.
CMR	Constructions Mécaniques SA, Renens.
CUM	Cummins Engine Corporation, Columbus, Indiana, USA.
DBZ	Daimler Benz AG, Stuttgart, Germany.
DIEMA	Diepholzer Maschinenfabrik (Fr. Schöttler GmbH), Diepholz, Germany.
DMG	Daimler Motoren Gesellschaft, Stuttgart, Germany.
DZ	Klöckner Humboldt Deutz AG, Köln, Germany.
FFA	Flug und Fahrzeugwerke AG, Altenrhein.
FORD	Ford Motor Company, Detroit, Michigan, USA.
FUCHS	H. Fuchs Waggonfabrik AG, Heidelberg, Germany.
GANG	Gangloff Carrosserie AG, Bern.
Gm	Gmeinder & Co GmbH, Maschinenfabrik Mosbach, Germany.
GM	General Motors AG, Biel.
GSEG	Gewerkschaft Schalker-Eisenhütte, Gelsenkirchen, Germany.
HEN	Henschel Werke AG, Kassei, Germany (now part of ADtranz).
HESS	Hess AG, Carrosserien, Bellach SO.
HÜR	H. Hürlimann Tractorenwerke, Wil SG.
IEG	Compagnie de l'Industrie Électrique, GenŠve.
JMR	J. Meyer AG, Rheinfelden.
JUNG	Arn. Jung Lokomotivfabrik GmbH, Jungenthal bei Kirchberg an der Sieg, Germany.
KM	Krauss Maffei AG, München, Germany.
KRON	L. Kronenberger & Söhne, Luzern.
KRUPP	Fried Krupp Maschi nenfabriken, Essen, Germany.
LISTER	R & A Lister & Co Ltd., Dursley, Glos., UK.
LMG	Lübecker Maschinenbau AG, Werk Dorstfeld, Germany.
LÜTHI	Eduard Lüthi, Worb.
MaK	Maschinenbau Kiel GmbH, Kiel, Germany (Now Krupp MaK).
MAN	Maschinenfabrik Augsburg-Nürnberg AG, Germany.

MAYBACH	Maybach Motorenbau, Friedrichshafen, Germany.
MB	Mercedes Benz, Berlin Marienfeld, Germany.
MFO	Maschinenfabrik Oerlikon, Zürich Oerlikon (now part of ADtranz).
MOY	Gaston Moyse, La Corneuve, France.
MTU	Motoren und Turbinen Union GmbH, Friedrichshafen, Germany.
MWM	Motoren Werke Mannheim, Germany.
NEN	Martin Nencki AG, Fahrzeugbau und Hydraulik, Langenthal.
OK	Orenstein & Koppel AG, Dortmund, Germany.
PER	Perkins Engines Ltd., Peterborough, UK.
PETER	Konrad Peter, Maschinenfabrik, Liestal.
PFING	Pfingstweid AG, Zürich.
PLEI	Paul Pleiger Maschinenfabrik, Blankenstein, Germany.
POY	Moteurs Poyaud, Surgères, France.
Puch	Puch Werke.
RACO	Robert Aebi & Co AG, Regensdorf.
RC	Regazzoni Costruzioni, Lugano.
REG	Officine Meccaniche Italiane Reggiane, Reggio d'Emilia, Italy.
REN	R,gie Nationale des Usines Renault, Billancourt, France.
RIET	AG vormals J.J. Rieter, Wintherthur.
RING	F. Ringhoffer Werke AG, Waggon & Tenderfabrik, Smichow bei Prag, Czechoslovakia.
ROBEL	Robel Maschinenfabrik, München, Germany.
RUHR	Ruhrthaler Maschinenfabrik, Mülheim, Germany.
SAAS	SA des Ateliers de Sécheron, Genève (now part of ADtranz)
SAU	AG Adolf Saurer, Arbon.
SCH	Christoph Schöttler Maschinenfabrik GmbH, Diepholz, Germany. (trade name 'Schöma')
SCIN	Scintilla AG, Zuchwil.
Siemens	Siemens AG, Werk Erlangen, Germany.
SIG	Schweizerische Industriegesellschaft, Neuhausen am Rheinfall.
SLM	Schweizerische Lokomotiv und Maschinenfabrik, Winterthur.
SSW	Siemens Schuckert Werke, Berlin, Germany.
STAD	Ernst Stadler AG, Fahrzeugbau, Bussnang.
STECK	Ferdinand Steck, Maschinenfabrik, Bowil.
SWG-A	Schindler Werk Gesellschaft – Altenrhein.
SWG-P	Schindler Werk Gesellschaft – Pratteln.
SWP	Schindler Waggon AG, Pratteln.
SWS	Schweizerische Wagons und Aufzügefabrik AG, Schlieren.
SZ	Gebrüder Sulzer AG, Winterthur.
TIB	Technomasio Italiano Brown Boveri, Milano, Italy.
TUCH	Gebrüder Tuchschmid AG, Frauenfeld.
U23A	Uzinele 23 August, Bucuresti, Romania.
VBZ	Verkehrsbetriebe der Stadt Zürich (Zürich Tramways).
VM	Stabilimenti Meccanici VM SpA, Cento Ferrara, Italy.
VOITH	J.M. Voith GmbH, Heidenheim, Germany.
VR	von Rollsche Eisenwerke, Gerlafingen.
VW	Volkswagenwerke, Wolfsburg, Germany.
WIND	Rheiner Maschinenfabrik Windhoff AG, Rheine, Germany.
ZÜR	Zürcher & Cie SA, St Aubin.

KEY TO MAPS
ON PAGES 8-11

Thick lines are standard
gauge (1435 mm)

Thin lines are narrow
gauge

— — SBB

——— BLS Group

——— Rhätische Bahn

} Miscellaneous Private Lines

——— DB

——— SNCF, FS or ÖBB

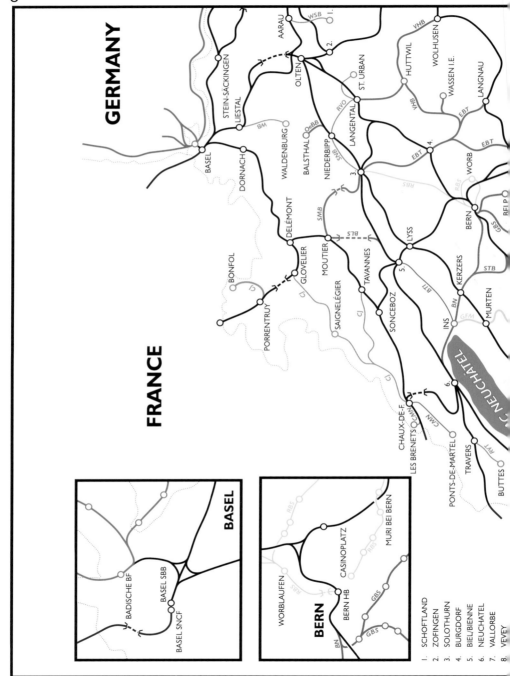

ITALY

FRANCE

LAC LEMAN
(LAKE GENEVA)

BRIENZ
GRINDELWALD
12.
13.
INTERLAKEN
LAUTERBRUNNEN
MURREN
JUNGFRAUJOCH
SPIEZ
THUN
BRIG
Simplon Tunnel
VISP
Lötschberg Tunnel
ST. NIKLAUS
ZERMATT
GORNERGRAT

ZWEISIMMEN
LENK
GSTAAD
MONTBOVON
CHÂTEAU-D'OEX
ROCHERS DE NAYE
DIABLERETS
BRETAYE
LEYSIN
BEX
ST. MAURICE
SION
LE CHÂBLE
ORSIÈRES
MARTIGNY
GIETROZ
CHÂTELARD
EMOSSON
CHAMPÉRY
CHAMINOX

ROMONT
BULLE
BROC
GRUYÈRES
PUIDOUX
PALÉZIEUX
BERCHER
MOUDON
ECHALLENS
LAUSANNE
ST-GINGOLPH
EVIAN

YVERDON
ORBE
L'ISLE
APPLES
BIÈRE
MORGES
LE PONT
LE BRASSUS
LA CURE
NYON
GENÈVE AÉROPORT
GENÈVE
EAUX VIVES

12. SCHYNIGE PLATTE
13. WENGEN
14. AIGLE

LAUSANNE

RENENS VD
LAUSANNE-CHAUDERON
LAUSANNE FLON
PULLY-NORD
OUCHY

10

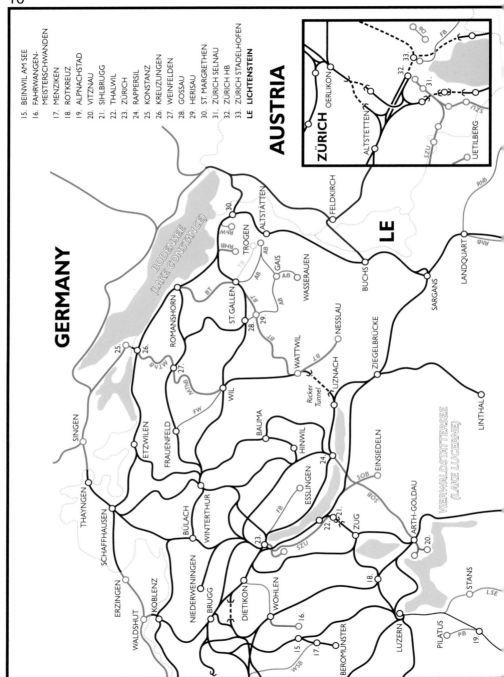

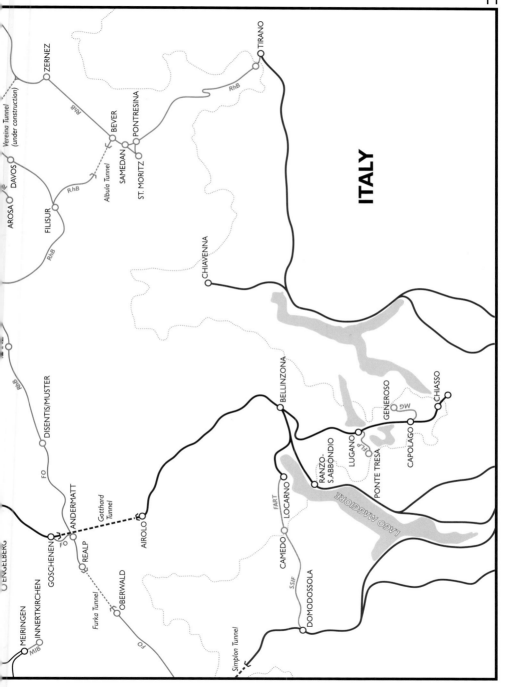

▲ Re 4/4 ¹ No. 10035 at Vufflens-la-Ville on a Lausanne to Neuchâtel service on 25th August 1994. The class was the first of the modern generation of SBB electrics and is now being withdrawn.

David A. Haydock

▼ Re 4/4 ¹¹ No. 11295 at Biberbrugg on 12th September 1995. The most numerous SBB class.

T.N. Hall

1. SWISS FEDERAL RAILWAYS

GENERAL

The SBB was formed in 1902 when most of the major private companies were nationalised, and a few other railways have been absorbed since. The SBB is now divided into 3 zones:

Zone I   Lausanne – covers the south west.
Zone II Luzern – covers the Basel to Chiasso line and branches.
Zone III Zürich – covers the north and east.

NUMBERING SYSTEM

Steam locomotives were numbered below 10000, and consequently when main line electric locomotives first appeared, they were numbered 10001 upwards. However, when railcars, shunting tractors and later diesel locomotives were purchased, they each had their own separate numbering systems, railcars in fact being initially numbered in the carriage series. This resulted in many duplicated numbers, and to eliminate these much renumbering occurred during the 1950s and 1960s. Although this eliminated duplicated numbers (except the Brünig line – see below), the result was a non too logical system, particularly in the case of the 8xxx and 9xxx series tractors which were numbered in these blocks when vacant numbers in the earlier series were exhausted.

The Brünig narrow gauge stock was for many years numbered in its own separate series, and although the tractors and electric locomotives did not duplicate numbers in the standard gauge series, the older motor baggage vans clashed with standard gauge tractors; recent renumbering has, however, eliminated this clash.

This number series is as follows:

1–	250	Electric tractors (traffic stock)
251–	399	Electro-diesel tractors (traffic stock)
401–	599	Diesel tractors (traffic stock)
601–	950	Diesel tractors (departmental stock)
951–	963	Electric tractors (departmental stock; all now withdrawn)
964–	979	Battery tractors (all are departmental)
980–	999	Diesel tractors (Brünig Line departmental stock)
1001–	1899	Electric railcars
1901–	1999	Electric locomotives (Brünig Line)
2001–	2999	Electric railcars
8001–	8399	Electric tractors (traffic stock)
8401–	8999	Diesel tractors (traffic stock)
9401–	9999	Diesel tractors (departmental stock)
10001–11999		Electric locomotives, max speed more than 80 km/h
12001–13999		Electric locomotives, max speed 70 to 80 km/h
14001–14999		Electric locomotives, max speed 60 to 65 km/h
15001–15999		Electric locomotives, max speed 45 to 55 km/h (all now withdrawn)
16001–16999		Electric shunting locomotives
17001–17999		Electro-diesel locomotives (being converted to diesels)
18001–18999		Diesel locomotives

Commencing in 1989, a new numbering system has been introduced for new classes. However, to date it has only been applied to existing classes where renumbering has been carried out, even lthough all have been allotted new class numbers. There is no indication of any intention to renumber existing stock except where major refurbishment has been carried out. The new scheme consists of seven digits, comprising a three digit class number, a three digit running number and a computer check digit. The scheme has been revised since it was first drawn up to incorporate all standard gauge private railways. This means all tractors delivered with new numbers will be renumbered! On the other hand, it is apparently no longer the intention to renumber pre-war main line locos, now all classed as museum stock. The system has also been expanded to include the standard gauge private railways which have adopted the system rather more enthusiastically than the SBB. The system operates as follows:

1st Digit:	0	Steam Loco or historic railcar
	1	Metre Gauge Loco (Brünig Line)
	2	Tractor
	3	Electric Loco (3 powered axles)
	4	Electric loco (4 powered axles)
	5	Electric Railcar
	6	Electric Loco (6 powered axles)
	7	Departmental Stock (self-propelled, but not a loco e.g. crane or tamper)
	8	Diesel Loco
	9	Electric Shunting Loco

2nd Digit:	0	Express Stock (Railcars only)
	1–6	Sub Class Index (Bogie Electric Locos)
		Type of Electric Railcar
		No. of Powered Axles (Diesel Locos)
	7–8	Not used
	9	Used in lieu of / on rigid frame electric locos (but in practice, not used)

3rd Digit: Used to differentiate between classes with identical 1st & 2nd digits. However, in some cases indicates the following:

| | 2–4 | 2, 3, or 4 voltage loco or railcar |
| | 5–8 | stock owned by Private Railways. |

4th to 6th Digits: Generally the last 3 digits of the old number, but with many exceptions.

SBB Stock with computer numbers is detailed at the end of each section.

ELECTRIFICATION & GAUGE

The SBB is electrified on the 15 kV 16 $^2/_3$ Hz system, the only exceptions being a few lines in border areas where the systems of neighbouring countries are used. All SBB electric stock can only operate on the above system unless stated otherwise. The SBB is standard gauge (1435 mm) except the Brünig Line from Luzern to Interlaken which is 1000 mm.

SBB DEPOTS

Code	Main Sheds	Sub-Sheds
Zone 1 (Lausanne)		
BN	Bern	Fribourg
		Thun
BI	Biel/Bienne	Chaux de Fonds
		Delémont
		Neuchâtel
BR	Brig	–
GE	Genève	–
LS	Lausanne	Payerne
		St Maurice
		Vallorbe
Zone II (Luzern)		
BE	Bellinzona	Chiasso (a)
BS	Basel	Kleinhünigen
		Muttenz
CH	Chiasso (a)	–
ER	Erstfeld	–
LZ	Luzern (b)	Arth Goldau
		Beinwil
		Zug
MR	Meiringen	Luzern (n.g.) (b)
OL	Olten	–

Zone III (Zürich)

RS	Rorschach	Buchs
		Chur
		Romanshorn
		Sargans
		St. Gallen
WT	Winterthur	Oberwinterthur
		Schaffhausen
		Wil
ZU	Zürich	Brugg
		Limmattal
		Rapperswil

(a) There are two depots in Chiasso; the main line depot is a sub-shed of Bellinzona and a separate tractor depot has its own allocation.

(b) Separate standard and narrow gauge depots exist in Luzern; a few tractors are allocated to the n.g. shed.

In addition to the above, many stations and other locations have small sheds housing one or more shunting tractors; often these belong to the permanent way or other engineer's departments.

SBB WORKSHOPS

Six workshops are responsible for the repair and overhaul of SBB motive power.

Bellinzona	Electric locos (Re4/4^{II}, Re4/4^{III}, Re6/6, Ae6/6, Re460).
Biel	All diesel locos; also diesel engines from Tem series tractors.
Meiringen	All metre gauge stock (Brünig Line)
Olten	All diesel tractors (this is the old works near the station; the new works some distance away is purely a carriage and wagon facility).
Yverdon	Electric locos (Re4/4^{I}, Re4/4^{II}, Re460).
	All electric shunters.
	All electric tractors (including electrical parts from Tem series).
Zürich	Electric locos (Re450).
	All electric railcars.

LIVERIES

Until 1984, most line electric locomotives and railcars were painted dark green, while diesels and shunters were reddish-brown. Since 1984, a red livery has been adopted for locomotives (except for the new 450 class), while new railcars are blue and cream. A number of non-standard liveries also exist, but several of these will disappear in the near future. The various liveries are shown in the lists using the following letter codes:

A Overall Advertising. Several Re460 class have been so treated.
B Brown (the original electric loco livery, a few 'museum' locos have been restored to this livery).
D Dark Red (applied to new railcars in the late 1960s, only the RABDe12/12 class remains in this livery).
C Special blue & yellow livery for Pridoux–Chexbres service.
E Eurocity (2-tone grey; the former TEE railcars are now in this livery).
G Dark Green (the standard livery for most electric locomotives and railcars prior to 1984).
L Dark Green/Red ends (some railcars have red ends to improve visibility).
N NPZ (Neue Pendel Zug), blue and grey with red ends. The new livery for local trains.
O Orange/Grey ('Swiss Express') livery, applied to Mark III coaching stock and some Re4/4^{II} locos during the 1970s).
P Reddish-Brown. (The standard livery for shunters and tractors until 1984).
R Red. (the current standard locomotive livery). (tractors in red livery are not shown as such due to lack of information).
S S-Bahn (blue with red ends, applied only to the new 450 class for the Zürich S-Bahn services).
V Violet/Yellow (applied to the prototype RABDe8/16 class; neither the class nor the livery were perpetuated).
Y Yellow (a few tractors used as works pilots are in this livery).

▲ RAe 2/4 No. 1001 at Bern on 23rd May 1996. This 'Red Arrow' railcar is used on charter work.
Brian Leighton

▼ BDe 4/4 No. 1631 at Brig on a Simplon local services. These railcars are being withdrawn.
David A. Haydock

1.1. SHUNTING TRACTORS

The SBB operates a large number of tractors for light shunting duties. Those numbered between 1 and 599 and in the 8000 series belong to the traffic department and are mainly used in station goods yards where they are driven by station staff. Those numbered between 601 and 999 and in the 9000 series are in departmental use, the greatest number being allocated to the permanent way department, with others being used by the overhead line and signals departments and as depot and works pilots. In addition to the depot allocation, the station at which each tractor is based is shown since these change infrequently. Those shown as 'reserve' are used to cover for others under maintenance or in works.

CLASS Te^{II}   B

Built: 1967–9.
Builder-Mech. Parts: SLM/Tuchschmid.
Builder-Elec. Parts: MFO.
Traction Motors: 1 single phase axle suspended with side rod drive.
One Hour Rating: 120 kW.
Maximum Tractive Effort: 33 kN.
Driving Wheel Dia.: 950 mm.
Weight: 22 tonnes.
Overall Length: 6.7 m.
Max. Speed: 60 km/h.
New Class No.: 211.0.

Number	Depot	Station	Number	Depot	Station
61	LS	Montreux	80	RS	Gossau
62	LS	*Reserve*	81	WT	Wald
63	BN	*Reserve*	82	RS	Sulgen
64	GE	Nyon	83	WT	Uster
65	BI	*Reserve*	84	WT	Rüti
66	BI	Gorgier-St Aubin	85	WT	Andelfingen
67	BI	*Reserve*	86	ZU	Rapperswil
68	BN	Gümligen	87	ZU	Stäfa
69	LZ	*Reserve*	88	WT	Weesen
70	OL	Münchenstein	89	ZU	*Reserve*
71	BE	Rivera-Bironico	90	WT	Uznach
72	LZ	Malters	91	RS	*Reserve*
73	OL	Resevre	92	WT	Frauenfeld
74	BS	Sissach	93	RS	Erlen
75	CH	Melide	94	WT	Sirnach
76	LZ	*Reserve*	95	RS	Schwanden
77	RS	Stein am Rhein	96	WT	*Reserve*
78	RS	Oberriet	97	RS	Buchs
79	RS	*Reserve*			

CLASS Te^{III}   B

Built: 1941–9.
Builder-Mech. Parts: SLM.
Builder-Elec. Parts: SAAS.
Traction Motors: 1 single phase axle suspended with side rod drive.
One Hour Rating: 250 kW.
Maximum Tractive Effort: 72 kN.
Driving Wheel Dia.: 1040 mm.
Weight: 28 tonnes.
Overall Length: 6.6 m.
Max. Speed: 60 km/h.
New Class No.: 212.1.

Number	Depot	Station	Number	Depot	Station
122	WT	Eglisau	124	BN	*Reserve*
123	LS	Moudon	125	OL	*Reserve*

▲ Te ^{II} No. 97 at Buchs on 3rd August 1994 is typical of the later electric tractors.   **T.M. Wallis**

▼ Tm ^{III} No. 916 on Bellinzona Depot on 1st August 1994. This class is used on shed and works pilot duties.   **T.M. Wallis**

126	OL	Dottikon-Dintikon	133	LS	Chavornay
127	OL	*Reserve*	134	BI	Travers
128	LS	Bex	135	WT	Bauma
130	BI	*Reserve*	136	WT	Uzwil
131	ZU	Siebnen-Wangen	138	WT	Bazenheid
132	OL	Othmarsingen			

CLASS Te^{III}

Bo

Built: 1965–6.
Builder-Mech. Parts: SLM.
Builder-Elec. Parts: MFO.
Traction Motors: 2 single phase axle suspended.
One Hour Rating: 245 kW.
Maximum Tractive Effort: 67 kN.
Driving Wheel Dia.: 950 mm.
Weight: 28 tonnes.
Overall Length: 6.64 m.
Max. Speed: 60 km/h.
New Class No.: 212.0.

Number	Depot	Station	Number	Depot	Station
139	OL	*Reserve*	160	WT	Koblenz
140	LZ	*Reserve*	161	ZU	Reichenburg
141	OL	*Reserve*	162	BI	Lyss
142	WT	Konolfingen	163	BR	Gampel-Steg
143	LZ	Langnau	164	WT	*Reserve*
144	WT	Rekingen	165	ZU	Glarus
145	RS	Heerbrugg	166	BN	Konolfingen
146	LS	Aigle	167	BI	Glovelier
147	BI	Kerzers	168	BI	Moutier
148	LS	Palézieux	169	BN	Düdingen
149	LS	Avenches	170	ZU	Thalwil
150	BN	Münsingen	171	ZU	Ziegelbrücke
151	BI	Murten	172	LS	Puidoux-Chexbres
152	OL	*Reserve*	173	LS	Martigny
153	OL	*Reserve*	174	BE	Ambri-Piotta
154	OL	*Reserve*	175	BS	Stein-Säckingen
155	LS	*Reserve*	176	LZ	*Reserve*
156	BI	*Reserve*	177	WT	*Reserve*
157	BE	Locarno	178	LZ	Sins
158	ZU	Wädenswil	179	LS	Vevey
159	RS	St Gallen Winkeln			

CLASS Tem^I

B

This class, and the following Tem^{II} and Tem^{III} classes are electric tractors fitted with a diesel engine to enable them to shunt non-electrified sidings.

Built: 1950–7.
Builder-Mech. Parts: Tuchschmid (SBB Yverdon *).
Builder-Elec. Parts: BBC/MFO.
Traction Motors: 1 single phase axle suspended with side rod drive.
One Hour Rating: 90 kW (electric), 50 kW (diesel).
Weight: 15 tonnes.
Maximum Tractive Effort: 36 kN (electric), 31 kN (diesel)
Driving Wheel Dia.: 950 mm.
Overall Length: 5.87 m.
Max. Speed: 60 km/h.
Engine: Saurer C615D 65 kW.
New Class No.: 220.

Number	Depot	Station	Number		Depot	Station
251	LS	*Reserve*	253	*	WT	Märstetten
252	BI	*Reserve*	254	*	WT	*Reserve*

255	OL	Dulliken		267	BE	Claro
256	OL	Aarau		268	WT	Bürglen
258	BI	*Reserve*		270	RS	*Reserve*
259	ER	Flüelen		271	RS	Walenstadt
260	OL	*Reserve*		272	LZ	Cham
261	WT	Pfäffikon		273	OL	*Reserve*
262	LS	*Reserve*		274	BI	Le Locle-Col des Roches
263	ZU	Unterterzen		275	BI	Les Verrières
265	RS	Amriswil				

CLASS Tem^{III}   B

Built: 1967.
Builder-Mech. Parts: SLM/Tuchschmid.
Builder-Elec. Parts: MFO.
Traction Motors: 1 single phase axle suspended with side rod drive.
One Hour Rating: 120 kW (electric), 60 kW (diesel).
Weight: 26 tonnes.
Maximum Tractive Effort: 33 kN.
Driving Wheel Dia.: 950 mm.
Engine: Saurer C615D 85 kW.
Overall Length: 6.7 m.
Max. Speed: 60 km/h.
New Class No.: 221.

Number	Depot	Station		Number	Depot	Station
276	ZU	*Reserve*		288	OL	Safenwil
277	RS	St Gallen St Fiden		289	OL	*Reserve*
278	ZU	Dübendorf		290	OL	Hunzenschwil
279	WT	*Reserve*		291	OL	Lenzburg
280	WT	Wetzikon		292	OL	Roggwil-Wynau
281	WT	Wattwil		293	RS	Hauptwil
282	BS	Frick		294	OL	Aarburg Oftringen
283	ZU	Zürich Wollishofen		295	BI	Tavannes
284	ZU	*Reserve*		296	OL	*Reserve*
285	RS	Döttingen-Klingnau		297	BI	Colombier
286	RS	Lachen		298	BI	*Reserve*
287	ZU	Meilen				

CLASS Tem^{II}   Bo

Built: 1954–62.
Builder-Mech. Parts: SLM (ACMV*).
Builder-Elec. Parts: BBC/SAAS (SAAS *).
Traction Motors: 2 single phase axle suspended.
One Hour Rating: 260 kW (electric), 95 kW (diesel).
Weight: 32 tonnes.
Maximum Tractive Effort: 59 kN (electric), 64 kN (diesel)
Driving Wheel Dia.: 1040 mm.
Overall Length: 7.29 m, 7.04 m*, 7.35 m†.
Max. Speed: 60 km/h.
Engine: SLM 12BD11 145 kW, (Saurer CV1D 145 kW*).
New Class No.: 222.

Number		Depot	Station		Number	Depot	Station
321	*	BE	Cadenazzo		333	OL	*Reserve*
322	*	CH	Mendrisio		334	WT	Etzwilen
324		BN	Ostermundigen		335	RS	*Reserve*
325		RS	Horn		336	RS	Romanshorn
326		BI	*Reserve*		337	ZU	*Reserve*
328		BS	Münchenstein		338	LS	Villeneuve
329		BN	Schmitten		339	WT	*Reserve*
330		BI	Biel Mett		340	WT	Frauenfeld
331		OL	Langenthal		341	BS	Laufenburg
332		LZ	Zug		342	RS	Salez-Sennwald

343		WT	Neuhausen	355	† BS	Lausen
344	†	ZU	Wallisellen	356	† ZU	Glattbrugg
345	†	ZU	Pfäffikon	357	† ZU	Bonstetten-Wettswil
346	†	ZU	Zürich Tiefenbrunnen	358	† LZ	Sursee
347	†	ZU	Affoltern am Albis	359	† OL	Herzogenbuchsee
348	†	RS	Kreuzlingen Hafen	360	† OL	Solothurn
349	†	OL	*Reserve*	361	† BE	Giubiasco
350	†	LS	Estavayer-le-Lac	362	† RS	St Gallen
351	†	LS	*Reserve*	363	† WT	Dielsdorf
352	†	OL	Zofingen	364	† BR	Sion
353	†	BE	*Reserve*	365	† LS	Bussigny
354	†	BS	Rheinfelden			

CLASS Tm^I (Tm †)   B

Built: 1957–65.
Builder: RACO (CMR *).
Engine: SLM 6VD11 66 kW.
    SLM 4VD111 44 kW (†).
    Deutz F6L413 90 kW (a).
    Deutz 87 kW (b).
    VM 90 kW (c).
Transmission: Mechanical.
Maximum Tractive Effort: kN.
Driving Wheel Dia.: 600 mm.
Weight: 10 tonnes (13 tonnes a, b, c).
Overall Length: 5.190 m.
Max. Speed: 45 km/h (50 km/h *, b, c).
New Class No.: 230.4 (230.0 *).

Originally all fitted with SLM engines, many of these tractors have been rebuilt with Deutz or VM engines since 1971.

Number	Depot	Station	Number	Depot	Station
401	†	Olten Works	453	b OL	Grenchen Süd
407	ZU	Horgen	454	c OL	Oberentfelden
409	ZU	Mühlehorn	455	c OL	Egerkingen
410	ZU	*Reserve*	456	OL	Wynigen
412	ZU	*Reserve*	457	b LZ	Gisikon-Root
414	LZ	*Reserve*	458	ZU	Horgen-Oberdorf
416	LS	Allaman	459	OL	Rupperswil
417	* LS	*Reserve*	460	BE	Biasca Works
422		Olten Works	462	*c OL	*Reserve*
423	BS	Stein Säckingen	463	*b LZ	*Reserve*
425	BE	*Reserve*	464	*b LZ	Sempach-Neuenkirch
429	WT	*Reserve*	465	*b LZ	Reinach
430	WT	*Reserve*	466	* WT	Kemptthal
431	WT	Müllheim-Wigoltingen	467	*c RS	Alstätten
432	WT	Stammheim	468	*c WT	Rafz
434	WT	Bütschwil	469	b RS	Bischofszell Nord
436	WT	*Reserve*	470	a ZU	Netstal
437	WT	Aadorf	471	a RS	*Reserve*
439	c ZU	Näfels-Mollis	472	b ZU	Flums
440	WT	Wil	473	a WT	Niederwenigen
441	b RS	Romanshorn	474	c WT	Ramsen
442	b ZU	Linthal	475	a WT	Bubikon
443	ZU	*Reserve*	476	b WT	Oberwinterthur
445	a WT	Winterthur Wülfingen	477	a WT	Marthalen
446	b ZU	Rümlang	478	b WT	Steckborn
447	b RS	Mels	480	c RS	Ermatingen
448	WT	Eschenz	481	a BE	Osogna-Crescia
449	a ZU	Nieder-Durnen	482	CH	*Reserve*
450	a RS	Flums	484	b LZ	Eschenbach
451	WT	*Reserve*	486	b LZ	Steinhausen
452	b OL	*Reserve*	487	c OL	*Reserve*

488	a	BE	Lavorgo	500	c	OL	Solothurn
489		LS	Croy-Romainmôti	501		ZU	Uetikon
490	c	LS	St Triphon	503	a	RS	*Reserve*
491	b	LS	Martigny	505	a	WT	Hüntwangen-Wil
492	c	BI	St Ursanne	506		RS	Rheineck
493	a	BI	*Reserve*	507	b	BN	Wichtrach
494	b	LS	*Reserve*	508	b	BI	Courtelary
495	a	BI	*Reserve*	509	b	BI	Court
496	c	BI	*Reserve*	510	*	BI	*Reserve*
497	b	BI	Les Hants Geneveys	511	*b	BI	*Reserve*
498	c	BI	Boncourt	512	*b	GE	*Reserve*

CLASS Tm^{II}   B

Built: 1950–68.
Builder: RACO.
Engine: Saurer C615D 70 kW.
Transmission: Mechanical.
Maximum Tractive Effort: kN.
Driving Wheel Dia.: 600 mm.
Weight: 10 tonnes.
Overall Length: 5.240 m.
Max. Speed: 45 km/h.
New Class No.: 230.6.

These tractors have a cabin for 4 personnel, and a platform for carrying tools and materials.
* Fitted for snowplough use.

Number		Depot	Station	Number		Depot	Station
601			Yverdon Works	642	*	RS	St Gallen
602		OL	Olten	643		BN	Bern
603		BS	Muttenz	645	*	BI	St Imier
604		LZ	Luzern	646	*	BR	Brig
605		OL	Solothurn	647		BS	Muttenz
608		ZU	Zürich	648		BE	Airolo
610		RS	Sargans	649		OL	Lenzburg
611		RS	Romanshorn	650		OL	Burgdorf
612		ZU	Zürich	651		LZ	Emmenbrücke
613		ZU	Brugg	653		OL	Olten
614	*	BI	Neuchâtel	654		BS	Muttenz
615		WT	Bülach	655		ER	Erstfeld
616	*	WT	Winterthur	656		BE	Bellinzona
617	*	ZU	Rapperswil	658		CH	Vedeggio
618	*	WT	Wil	659		LZ	Rotkreuz
619		LS	Puidoux-Chexbres	660		BE	Airolo
620	*	BI	St Imier	662		WT	Wil
621	*	BI	Neuchâtel	663		RS	Romanshorn
622	*	BI	Neuchâtel	664		RS	Romanshorn
623	*	OL	Dulliken	665		RS	Sargans
624		LZ	Luzern	666		BI	Neuchâtel
625		ER	Erstfeld	667		BI	Biel
626	*	LZ	Konolfingen	669		GE	Genève
627		OL	Olten	670		BN	Bern
628		BS	Basel	671		BN	Thun
629	*	LZ	Arth Goldau	672		LS	Bussigny
630	*	ZU	Ziegelbrücke	673		BE	Giubiasco
631	*	ZU	Pfäffikon	674		LZ	Zug
632		ZU	Zürich	675		OL	Burgdorf
633		ZU	Brugg	676		BE	Airolo
634		RS	Gossau	677		OL	Lenzburg
635	*	ZU	Rapperswil	678		BS	Muttenz
637	*	RS	Chur	679		GE	Genève
638		ZU	Zürich	680		WT	Frauenfeld
640	*	LS	Cossonay	681		RS	St Gallen
641	*	BI	Delémont	682		ZU	Zürich

683	ZU	Zürich		757	ZU	Wetzikon
684	ZU	Zürich		758	ZU	Zürich
685	ZU	Rapperswil		759	BN	Fribourg
686	BI	Biel		760	BR	Brig
687	LZ	Zug		761	LS	Lausanne
688	GE	Genève		762	LS	Yverdon
689	BN	Kerzers		763	LS	Yverdon
690	BR	Brig		764	OL	Dulliken
691	BI	Neuchâtel		765	OL	Olten
692	LS	Lausanne		766	OL	Solothurn
693		Olten Works		767	BE	Rivera
694	BS	Laufen		768	OL	Dulliken
695	LS	Payerne		769	CH	Chiasso
696	OL	Solothurn		770	LZ	Sursee
697	LZ	Emmenbrücke		771	BS	Muttenz
698	BS	Basel		772	LZ	Luzern
699	LZ	Zug		773	BI	Biel
700	BS	Muttenz		774	BI	Biel
701	BE	Airolo		775	LS	Nyon
703	CH	Vedeggio		776	BI	Delémont
704	BN	Bern		777	BI	Neuchâtel
705	ZU	Brugg		778	BI	Biel
706	ZU	Zürich		779	BR	Sion
707	WT	Winterthur-Grüze		780	LS	St Maurice
708	WT	Winterthur-Grüze		781	LS	Kerzers
710	* LS	Fribourg		782	BN	Thun
711	LS	St Maurice		783	BI	Biel
712	BI	Delémont		785	CH	Chiasso
713	BN	Fribourg		786	BN	Bern
714	BN	Fribourg		787	LZ	Luzern
715	OL	Brittnau		788	CH	Chiasso
716	BS	Muttenz		789	LZ	Luzern
717	OL	Solothurn		790	OL	Dulliken
718	BN	Bern		791	LZ	Rotkreuz
719	BN	Bern		792	ZU	Brugg
720	BN	Bern		793	ZU	Wallisellen
721	LS	Bussigny		794	ZU	*Reserve*
722	LS	Renens		796	WT	Schaffhausen
725	CH	Chiasso		797	RS	Gossau
726	LZ	Arth Goldau		798	BR	Sion
728	OL	Dulliken		800	RS	Sargans
730	ER	Erstfeld		801	WT	Schaffhausen
731	LS	Payerne		802	ZU	Zürich Altstetten
732	LS	St Maurice		803	RS	St. Gallen
733	BI	Biel		804	OL	Burgdorf
736	BI	Neuchâtel		805	BE	Giubiasco
737	OL	Solothurn		806	BN	Bern
738	OL	Olten		807	LS	Lausanne
739	BS	Basel		808	OL	Olten
740	LZ	Langnau		809	GE	Genève
741	OL	Olten		810	ZU	Brugg
742	GE	Genève		811	GE	Genève
743	ZU	*Reserve*		812	BI	Biel
744	ZU	*Reserve*		813		Biel Works
745	LZ	Konolfingen		815	WT	Schaffhausen
746	BR	Sion		816		Biel Works
748	LS	Bussigny		817	OL	Olten
749	LS	Bussigny		818	OL	Olten
750	BR	Sion		819	BR	Brig
751	LZ	Luzern		820	LS	Puidoux-Chexbres
752	OL	Langenthal		822	BI	Delémont
753	LZ	Zug		823	BI	Neuchâtel
754	ZU	Stein-Säckingen		824	ZU	Zürich
755	RS	Sargans		825	ZU	Zürich
756	ZU	Dietikon		826	LS	St Maurice

827	CH	Chiasso	842	BE	Bellinzona
830	BI	Neuchâtel	843	ER	Erstfeld
831	BN	Fribourg	844		Olten Works
832	BI	Kerzers	845	LZ	Emmenbrücke
833	GE	Genève	846	BS	Liestal
834	BI	Neuchâtel	847	OL	Langenthal
835	LS	Bussigny	848	ZU	Zürich
836	BR	Brig	849	ZU	Rapperswil
837	BN	Bern	850	ZU	Brugg
838	BN	Bern	851	ZU	Zürich
839	LS	Puidoux-Chexbres	852	RS	Gossau
840	BS	Muttenz	853	RS	Romanshorn
841	LZ	Zug			

CLASS Tm   B

A departmental tractor originally numbered 404 in traffic stock.

Built: 1958.
Builder: RACO.
Engine: SLM 4VD111 44 kW.
Transmission: Mechanical.
Maximum Tractive Effort: kN.
Driving Wheel Dia.: 600 mm.
Weight: 10 tonnes.
Overall Length: 5.19 m.
Max. Speed: 45 km/h.
New Class No.: 230.0.

Number	Depot	Station	Number	Depot	Station
893	LS	Lausanne			

CLASS Tm[III]   B

Diesel-electric tractors for use as shed and works pilots.

Built: 1958-66.
Builder-Mech. Parts: SLM.
Builder-Elec. Parts: BBC.
Engine: SLM 12BD11 145 kW.
Transmission: Electric.
Maximum Tractive Effort: 92 kN.
Driving Wheel Dia.: 950 mm.
Weight: 28 tonnes.
Overall Length: 6.540 m.
Max. Speed: 30 km/h.
New Class No.: 231.0.

Number	Depot	Station	Number	Depot	Station
901	BR	Brig	913	OL	Olten
902		Biel/Bienne Works	914	LZ	Luzern
903		Chur Works	915	ER	Erstfeld
904		Bellinzona Works	916		Bellinzona Works
905	BS	Basel	917	ZU	Zürich Works
906		Yverdon Works	918	LS	Lausanne
907		Zürich Works	919	BN	Bern
908	ZU	Zürich	920	GE	Genève
909	WT	Winterthur	921	GE	Genève-Praille
910	RS	Rorschach	922	LS	Lausanne-Terrasse
911	CH	Chiasso	923	BI	Biel
912	BS	Basel	924	OL	*Reserve*

CLASS Tm   B

This tractor is fitted with exhaust filtration equipment for use on work inside tunnels.

Built: 1964.
Builder: Kronenberg.
Engine: GM 62306-RD 170 kW.
Transmission: Hydro-mechanical.
Maximum Tractive Effort: kN.
Driving Wheel Dia.: 900 mm.
Weight: 35 tonnes.
Overall Length: 7.520 m.
Max. Speed: 35 km/h.
New Class No.: 232.0.

Number	Depot	Station	
940	LZ	Luzern		

CLASS Ta   B

This assortment of battery tractors of six widely differing designs are used as works pilots.

New Class No.: 200 (978 = 201).

No.	Date	Builder	Hourly Rating	Weight	Length	Max. Speed	Location
966	1987	Stadler	4 kW	7 t.	2.85 mm	10 km/h	Olten Works
968	1977	SBB Yverdon	4 kW	6.5 t.	2.85 mm	10 km/h	Yverdon Works
969	1911	SBB Olten	4 kW	7 t.	3.30 mm	10 km/h	Yverdon Works
972	1914	SBB Olten	4 kW	7 t.	3.30 mm	10 km/h	Yverdon Works
974	1965	SBB Zürich	4 kW	6.5 t.	3.32 mm	10 km/h	Zürich Works
975	1971	Stadler	4 kW	6.5 t.	2.85 mm	10 km/h	Zürich Works
976	1971	Stadler	4 kW	6.5 t.	2.85 mm	10 km/h	Bellinzona Works
978	1913	AEG	145 kW	24 t.	8.40 mm	25 km/h	Bellinzona Works

Note: 1000-2004 are electric railcars. See next section.

CLASS Te^{IV} Bo

These tractors incorporate electrical equipment recovered from withdrawn De4/4 class railcars.

Built: 1980.
Builder-Mech. Parts: Tuchschmid.
Builder-Elec. Parts: BBC.
Traction Motors: 2 single phase axle suspended.
One Hour Rating: 480 kW.
Maximum Tractive Effort: kN.
Driving Wheel Dia.: 1040 mm.
Weight: 34 tonnes.
Overall Length: 7.7 m.
Max. Speed: 60 km/h.
New Class No.: 214.

Number	Depot	Station		Number	Depot	Station
8201	LS	Lausanne		8203	LS	Yverdon
8202	LS	Romont				

CLASS Tm^{IV} B

In addition to the hydraulic transmission, these tractors have a 2 ratio gearbox giving a maximum shunting speed of 30 km/h.

Built: 1970–8.
Builder: SLM.
Engine: MAN R8V 16/18 280 kW.
Transmission: Hydraulic.
Maximum Tractive Effort: kN.
Driving Wheel Dia.: 1040 mm.
Weight: 30 tonnes.
Overall Length: 7.67 m.

Max. Speed: 60 km/h.
New Class No.: 232.1.

* Purchased 1994 from Sulzer, Winterthur.

Number	Depot	Station	Number	Depot	Station
8751	LS	*Reserve*	8775	OL	Oberbuchsiten
8752	BE	Airolo	8776	ER	Göschenen
8753	LS	Cossonay	8777	RS	*Reserve*
8754	CH	Chiasso	8778	BI	Reuchenette-Péry
8755	OL	Wildegg	8779	BN	Thun
8756	OL	Dagmergellen	8780	GE	Nyon
8757	OL	*Reserve*	8781	BN	*Reserve*
8758	RS	Bischofszell Nord	8782	BI	Biel
8759	ZU	Regensdorf-Watt	8783	BI	Delémont
8760	ZU	Killwangen	8784	BI	Aarberg
8761	ZU	Otelfingen	8785	ZU	Zürich Seebach
8762	WT	Bülach	8786	OL	*Reserve*
8763	ZU	Siggenthal-Würenling	8787	ZU	*Reserve*
8764	ZU	Buchs-Dallikon	8788	ZU	*Reserve*
8765	ZU	Regensdorf-Watt	8789	OL	Rothrist
8766	WT	Rielasingen	8790	OL	*Reserve*
8767	ZU	Dietikon	8791	BE	Taverne-Torricella
8768	WT	Hinwil	8792	OL	Wangen bei Olten
8769	ZU	Kloten	8793	RS	*Reserve*
8770	ZU	*Reserve*	8794	BS	Kaisersaugst
8771	RS	Landquart	8795	BS	Möhlin
8772	WT	*Reserve*	8796	ZU	Regensdorf-Watt
8773	BS	Frenkendorf-Füllinsd	8797 *	RS	Landquart
8774	OL	*Reserve*			

CLASS Tm^{III}   B

These tractors are fitted with a hydraulic platform for overhead line maintenance work.

Built: 1981–6.
Builder: RACO.
Engine: Saurer D2K 165 kW.
Transmission: Hydraulic.
Maximum Tractive Effort: kN.
Driving Wheel Dia.: 950 mm.
Weight: 28 tonnes.
Overall Length: 8.74 m.
Max. Speed: 60 km/h.
New Class No.: 231.1.

Number	Depot	Station	Number	Depot	Station
9451	LS	Puidoux-Chexbres	9458	GE	Genève
9452	ER	Erstfeld	9459	BS	Muttenz
9453	ZU	Zürich	9460	OL	Dulliken
9454	ZU	Brugg	9461	LZ	Emmenbrücke
9455	WT	Winterthur Grüze	9462	BE	Airolo
9456	ZU	Rapperswil	9463	BE	Giubiasco
9457	BI	Delémont			

CLASS Tm^{III}   B

Similar to the previous class, but fitted with a 3 tonne hydraulic crane and an open platform for use on permanent way work.

Built: 1976–88.
Builder: RACO.
Engine: Saurer D2K 165 kW.
Transmission: Hydraulic.
Maximum Tractive Effort: kN.
Driving Wheel Dia.: 950 mm.

Weight: 24 tonnes.
Overall Length: 8.74 m.
Max. Speed: 60 km/h.
New Class No.: 231.2.

* Fitted for snowplough use.

Number	Depot	Station	Number	Depot	Station
9501	BI	Biel	9553	LZ	Luzern
9502	BR	Brig	9554	OL	*Reserve*
9503	LS	St Maurice	9555	ZU	Wallisellen
9504	BS	Laufen	9556	ZU	Pfäffikon
9505	LS	Yverdon	9557	WT	Bülach
9506	BS	Basel	9558	ZU	Dietikon
9507	BE	Airolo	9559	RS	Buchs
9508	OL	Solothurn	9560	WT	Wetzikon
9509	LZ	Arth-Goldau	9561	ZU	Zürich Altstetten
9510	BS	Liestal	9562	BE	Airolo
9511	ZU	Brugg	9563	OL	Olten
9512	WT	Schaffhausen	9564	OL	Langenthal
9513	WT	Winterthur	9565	LZ	Zug
9514	WT	Wil	9566	CH	Chiasso
9515	ZU	Rapperswil	9567	GE	Nyon
9516	LS	Lausanne	9568	BR	Sion
9517	OL	Dullikon	9569	BI	Payerne
9518	ZU	Zürich	9570	BN	Bern
9519	OL	Dullikon	9571	BN	Thun
9520	ZU	Zürich	9572	GE	Genève
9521	WT	Frauenfeld	9573	BI	Delémont
9522	BS	Stein Säckingen	9574	LS	Lausanne
9523	ZU	Zürich	9575	BR	Brig
9524	LZ	Sursee	9576	BN	Fribourg
9525	BE	Bellinzona	9577	ER	Erstfeld
9526	OL	Langenthal	9578	OL	Lenzburg
9527	LZ	Sursee	9579	BE	Rivera
9528	BS	Muttenz	9580	LZ	Luzern
9529	OL	Aarau	9581	BS	Muttenz
9530	LS	Puidoux-Chexbres	9582	ZU	Dietikon
9531	LS	St Maurice	9583	WT	Frauenfeld
9532 *	BI	Neuchâtel	9584	RS	Romanshorn
9533 *	BI	Neuchâtel	9585	ZU	Pfäffikon
9534 *	BI	St Imier	9586	ZU	Zürich
9535 *	LS	Cossonay	9587	ZU	Stein Säckingen
9536 *	ZU	Ziegelbrücke	9588	RS	St Gallen
9537 *	RS	St Gallen	9589	RS	Chur
9538 *	RS	Buchs	9590	OL	*Reserve*
9539 *	WT	Wetzikon	9591	BE	Bellinzona
9540 *	BS	Liestal	9592	LZ	Arth Goldau
9541 *	LZ	Luzern	9593	OL	Aarau
9542 *	BI	Neuchâtel	9594	LZ	Konolfingen
9543 *	ZU	Chur	9595	LS	Nyon
9551	GE	Genève	9596	BN	Bern
9552	BI	Biel	9597	LS	Fribourg

CLASS Tm^{IV}   B

Identical with the 8751 series, these tractors are in departmental use.

Built: 1971–7.
Builder: SLM.
Engine: MAN R8V 16/18 280 kN.
Transmission: Hydraulic.
Maximum Tractive Effort: kN.
Driving Wheel Dia.: 1040 mm.
Weight: 30 tonnes.
Overall Length: 7.67 m.

Max. Speed: 60 km/h.
New Class No.: 232.2.

* Purchased 1987 from SLM (was their works pilot).

Number	Depot	Station	Number	Depot	Station
9651	WT	Wil	9669	ZU	Zürich
9652	ZU	Zürich	9670	BI	Neuchâtel
9653	WT	Schaffhausen	9671	LS	Lausanne
9654	BI	Reserve	9672	BR	Sion
9655	BE	Airolo	9673	LS	Reserve
9656	LZ	Arth-Goldau	9674	BI	Delémont
9657	OL	Reserve	9675	BN	Bern
9658	LS	Lausanne	9676	BS	Muttenz
9659	BR	Reserve	9677	OL	Reserve
9660	BN	Reserve	9678	OL	Reserve
9661	BI	Reserve	9679	BE	Rivera
9662	BE	Bellinzona	9680	OL	Reserve
9663	OL	Solothurn	9681	WT	Winterthur
9664	BE	Bellinzona	9682	ZU	Rapperswil
9665	RS	St Gallen	9683	ZU	Wallisellen
9666	ZU	Brugg	9684	ZU	Stein-Säckingen
9667	ZU	Rapperswil	9685	*	Olten Works
9668	ZU	Zürich			

CLASS Tm 230 B

A unique design of tractor for shunting the traverser at Biel/Bienne Works, previously numbered Tm 900.

Built: 1963.
Builder: SBB Biel/Bienne.
Engine: VW 22 kW.
Transmission: Mechanical.
Maximum Tractive Effort: kN.
Driving Wheel Dia.: 600 mm.
Weight: 2.3 tonnes.
Overall Length: 2.00 m.
Max. Speed: 20 km/h.

Number	Depot	Station
230 000-2		Biel/Bienne Works

CLASS Tm 235 B

A new design of tractor for permanent way work with a much lower platform than its predecessors.

Built: 1991-2.
Builder: Robel.
Engine: Deutz 368 kW.
Transmission: Hydraulic.
Maximum Tractive Effort: kN.
Driving Wheel Dia.: mm.
Weight: 19 tonnes.
Overall Length: 10.04 m.
Max. Speed: 80 km/h.

This class is to be renumbered Tm 233.000-14.
* These tractors are used by permanent way contractors and are not allocated to an SBB depot.

Number	Depot	Station	Number	Depot	Station
235 000-7	*	Rapperswil	235 005-6	*	Zürich Altstetten
235 001-5	LZ	Rotkreuz	235 006-4	*	Brugg
235 002-3	BR	Brig	235 007-2	*	Bülach
235 003-1	*	Winterthur	235 008-0	OL	Olten
235 004-9	*	Winterthur	235 009-8	ER	Erstfeld

235 010-6	*	Wallisellen	235 013-0	*	Schaffhausen
235 011-4	*	Romanshorn	235 014-8	BN	Bern
235 012-2	LS	Lausanne			

CLASS Ta 251   Bo

A modern design of battery tractor for use as works pilots.

Built: 1990.
Builder-Mech. Parts: Stadler.
Builder-Elec. Parts: Bosch.
Traction Motors:
One Hour Rating: 9 kW.
Transmission: Electric.
Maximum Tractive Effort: kN.
Driving Wheel Dia.:   mm.
Weight: 7 tonnes.
Overall Length: 3.36 m.
Max. Speed: 10 km/h.

This class is to be renumbered Ta 200.002-5.

Number	Depot	Station	Number	Depot	Station
251 002-2		Olten Works	251 004-8		Olten Works
251 003-0		Olten Works	251 005-5		Olten Works

CLASS Tm 283   Bo

A second hand tractor purchased in 1989.

Built: 1973.
Builder: Gmeinder.
Engine: MAN 650 kW.
Transmission: Electric.
Maximum Tractive Effort: kN.
Driving Wheel Dia.:   mm.
Weight: 23 tonnes.
Overall Length: 7.63 m.
Max. Speed: 60 km/h.

Number	Depot	Station	
283 000-8	OL	Solothurn	

1.2. ELECTRIC RAILCARS

Railcars are either made up of fixed formations, or are single motor coaches which may be coupled to randomly formed driving and intermediate trailer cars to make up push-pull trains. Apart from class RABe 560, they are double ended. Trailers are numbered in the carriage series.

Under 'accommodation' are shown the number of 1st and 2nd class seats, followed by the number of toilets, e.g. 60/– 1T indicates 60 first class seats, no second class seats and one toilet.

CLASS RAe2/4

The last survivor of a number of lightweight, single units built during the 1930s, known as 'Red Arrows' because of their livery. This car is normally used on charter work.

Built: 1935.
Builder-Mech. Parts: SLM.
Builder-Elec. Parts: BBC/MFO/SAAS.
Traction Motors: 2 single phase commutator type, fully suspended with BBC spring drive.
One Hour Rating: 400 kW.
Maximum Tractive Effort: 25 kN.
Driving Wheel Dia.: 900 mm.
Weight: 41 tonnes.
Overall Length: 25.20 m.
Max. Speed: 125 km/h.
Wheel Arrangement: 2–Bo.
Accommodation: 60/– 1T.
New Class No.:

1001 **R**   BN |

CLASS RABe EC

These 4-voltage six-car units were built for use on International TEE trains, and at one time could be seen as far afield as Brussels, Paris and Genova. All were refurbished for use on Eurocity services from Zürich, Genève & Lausanne to Milano. This resulted in the installation of 2nd class seats in these once 1st class only units which are unusual in having separate toilet facilities for ladies and gentlemen. However, following problems with axle failures, they have been withdrawn from the Milano sevices, and now only operate the Bern-Frasne TGV connections. Two sets have been withdrawn and the future of the remainder is uncertain.

Sets 1051–4 were built as 5-car units, and lengthened to 6 cars in 1967 when the 5th unit was delivered.

All are mw fitted (for up to 2 sets in multiple).

Built: 1961–7.
Builder-Mech. Parts: SIG.
Builder-Elec. Parts: MFO.
Traction Motors: 4 single phase commutator type, fully suspended with BBC spring drive.
One Hour Rating: 2345 kW.
Maximum Tractive Effort: 157 kN.
Driving Wheel Dia.: 1110 mm.
Wheel Arrangement: 2–2 + 2–2 + A1A–A1A + 2–2 + 2–2 + 2–2.
Accommodation: 42/– 2T + 42/– 2T + baggage/kitchen + –/39 15R + –/54 2T + –/54 2T.
Weight: 296 tonnes.
Overall Length: 14.97 m.
Max. Speed: 160 km/h.
System: 1500 V d.c./3000 V d.c., 15 kV $16^2/_3$ Hz/25 kV 50 Hz.
New Class No.: 506.

1051 **E**   ZU |1053 **E** ZU | 1055 **E**   ZU |

CLASS RABDe12/12

Three-car units built for Zürich suburban services. Originally there were 20 sets, but 6 coaches were written off in accidents in 1971, and others renumbered to fill the gaps. Used mainly on the Zürich–Hinwil and Winterthur–Bülach services.

Although the single pantograph is mounted on the centre coach, the control gear and two transformers are on the outer coaches. Automatic speed and acceleration control and regenerative braking are fitted.

mw fitted for up to 4 sets in multiple.

Built: 1965–7.
Builder-Mech. Parts: SWP/FFA.
Builder-Elec. Parts: SAAS/BBC.
Traction Motors: 12 single phase commutator type, fully suspended with BBC spring drive.
One Hour Rating: 2475 kW.
Maximum Tractive Effort: 239 kN.
Driving Wheel Dia.: 850 mm.
Weight: 170 tonnes.
Overall Length: 73.30 m.
Max. Speed: 125 km/h.
Wheel Arrangement: Bo–Bo + Bo–Bo + Bo–Bo.
Accommodation: –/72 1T + 56/– 1T + –/72 1T.
New Class No.: 510.

Refurbishment and renumbering of these railcars has commenced; the driving cars will become 510.000–033 and the intermediate cars 510.200–217.

1101 **D**	ZU		1106 **D**	ZU		1111 **D**	ZU		1115 **D**	ZU
1102 **D**	ZU		1107 **D**	ZU		1112 **D**	ZU		1116 **D**	ZU
1103 **D**	ZU		1108 **D**	ZU		1113 **D**	ZU		1117 **D**	ZU
1104 **D**	ZU		1109 **D**	ZU		1114 **D**	ZU		1118 **D**	ZU
1105 **D**	ZU		1110 **D**	ZU						

CLASS RBe4/4

Originally built for longer distance push-pull workings, these motor coaches are now mainly used on the Zürich S-Bahn, and most have been formed into 4-coach push-pull sets. 1419/54 were written off in accidents. Most vehicles have been rebuilt and renumbered in the RBe 540 series. 1401–6 will not be rebuilt, and are expected to be transferred to staff train duties.

Built: 1959–60.
Builder-Mech. Parts: SIG/SWS.
Builder-Elec. Parts: BBC/MFO.
Traction Motors: 4 single phase, commutator type, fully suspended with BBC spring drive.
One Hour Rating: 2030 kW.
Maximum Tractive Effort: 188 kN.
Driving Wheel Dia.: 1040 mm.
Weight: 64 tonnes.
Overall Length: 22.90 m.
Overall Length: 23.70 m.
Max. Speed: 125 km/h.
Wheel Arrangement: Bo–Bo.
Accommodation: –/64 1T.

All are push-pull & mw fitted (can mw with Re4/4II, Re4/4III, Re4/4IV & Re6/6 classes).

1401 **L**	*	LZ		1403 **L**	*	LZ		1405 **L**	*	LZ
1402 **L**	*	LZ		1404 **L**	*	LZ		1406 **L**	*	LZ

CLASS BDe4/4

These railcars, bearing a distinct resemblance to the Re4/4I, are used on local and branch line services in the north and west of the country. Some have had the gangway at the luggage end removed. Now being withdrawn, some are to be retained to work staff trains.

Built: 1952–5.
Builder-Mech. Parts: SLM/SWP.
Builder-Elec. Parts: BBC/MFO/SAAS.
Traction Motors: 4 single phase commutator type, axle suspended.
One Hour Rating: 1195 kW.
Maximum Tractive Effort: 98 kN.
Driving Wheel Dia.: 940 mm.

Weight: 57 tonnes.
Overall Length: 22.70 m.
Max. Speed: 110 km/h.
Wheel Arrangement: Bo–Bo.
Accommodation: –/40 1T.
New Class No.: 536.

Rheostatic brake and push-pull fitted.
* Fitted for one person operation.
† Historic railcar.

1623 **G** * OL	1631 **G** OL	1641 **G** WT	1649 **G** WT
1629 **G** * OL	1632 **G** OL	1643 **G** † WT	1651 **G** * LS
1630 **G** OL	1639 **G** WT	1646 **G** LS	

CLASS De4/4

Once a class of 25 motor luggage vans originally built for use on local services. Eleven (1661–71) were rebuilt with new bodies in 1966–71 and used for many years on the Seetalbahn and Pont Brassus line, but have now been withdrawn. The last survivor, in unrebuilt condition, is now a museum car.

Built: 1928.
Builder-Mech. Parts: SIG/SWS.
Builder-Elec. Parts: MFO.
Traction Motors: 4 single phase commutator type, axle suspended.
One Hour Rating: 820 kW.
Maximum Tractive Effort: 86 kN.
Driving Wheel Dia.: 1040 mm.
Weight: 59 tonnes.
Overall Length: 15.20 m.
Max. Speed: 85 km/h.
Wheel Arrangement: Bo–Bo.
New Class No.: 546.

1679 **G** RS |

CLASS RABDe8/16

Four-car, lightweight, thyristor controlled units built for Zürich suburban services. However, this design has not proved to be very successful, and no further examples have been built since the 4 prototypes. They are now stored, and will probably be sold or scrapped. They are gangwayed within set and nicknamed 'Chiquitas'.

Built: 1976.
Builder-Mech. Parts: SIG/SWS/SWP.
Builder-Elec. Parts: SAAS.
Traction Motors: 8 single phase, fully suspended with BBC spring drive.
One Hour Rating: 2280 kW.
Maximum Tractive Effort: 187 kN.
Driving Wheel Dia.: 850 mm.
Weight: (per set) 149 tonnes.
Overall Length: 100.00 m.
Max. Speed: 125 km/h.
Wheel Arrangement: Bo–Bo+2–2+2–2+Bo–Bo.
Accommodation: –/72 1T + 54/– 1T + –/80 1T + –/72S.
New Class No.: 512.

mw fitted (for up to 2 sets in multiple).

2001 **R** ZU (Z)	2002 **V** ZU (Z)	2003 **R** ZU (Z)	2004 **V** ZU (Z)

CLASS RABDe 500

New tilting train sets on order. Full details as to the relationship between the numbers and sets is not known.

Built: On order (due 1998).
Builder-Mech. Parts:

Builder-Elec. Parts:
Traction Motors:
One Hour Rating:
Maximum Tractive Effort:
Driving Wheel Dia.:
Weight:
Overall Length:
Max. Speed:
Wheel Arrangement:
Accommodation:

500 000-5	500 008-8	500 016-1
500 001-3	500 009-6	500 017-9
500 002-1	500 010-4	500 018-7
500 003-9	500 011-2	500 019-5
500 004-7	500 012-0	500 020-3
500 005-4	500 013-8	500 021-1
500 006-2	500 014-6	500 022-9
500 007-0	500 015-3	500 023-7

CLASS RBe 540

Originally built for longer distance push-pull workings, these motor coaches are now mainly used on the Zürich S-Bahn, and most have been formed into 4-coach push-pull sets. 1419/54 were written off in accidents. Rebuilt with thyristor control and renumbered from RBe4/4 in 1990–97 with new doors and capability for one person operation.

Built: 1963–66.
Builder-Mech. Parts: SIG/SWS.
Builder-Elec. Parts: BBC/MFO.
Traction Motors: 4 single phase, commutator type, fully suspended with BBC spring drive.
One Hour Rating: 2030 kW.
Maximum Tractive Effort: 188 kN.
Driving Wheel Dia.: 1040 mm.
Weight: 68 tonnes.
Overall Length: 22.90 m.
Overall Length: 23.70 m.
Max. Speed: 125 km/h.
Wheel Arrangement: Bo–Bo.
Accommodation: –/60 1T.

All are push-pull & mw fitted (can mw with Re4/4ᴵᴵ, Re4/4ᴵᴵᴵ, Re4/4ᴵⱽ & Re6/6 classes).

540 006-4 (1407)	**N**	LZ	540 030-4 (1432)	**N**	WT	540 054-4 (1457)	**N**	WT
540 007-2 (1408)	**N**	LZ	540 031-2 (1433)	**N**	WT	540 055-1 (1458)	**N**	WT
540 008-0 (1409)	**N**	WT	540 032-0 (1434)	**N**	WT	540 056-9 (1459)	**N**	WT
540 009-8 (1410)	**N**	LZ	540 033-8 (1435)	**N**	WT	540 057-7 (1460)	**N**	WT
540 010-6 (1411)	**N**	WT	540 034-6 (1436)	**N**	WT	540 058-5 (1461)	**N**	WT
540 011-4 (1412)	**N**	LZ	540 035-3 (1437)	**N**	WT	540 059-3 (1462)	**N**	WT
540 012-2 (1413)	**N**	WT	540 036-1 (1438)	**N**	WT	540 060-1 (1463)	**N**	WT
540 013-0 (1414)	**N**	WT	540 037-9 (1439)	**N**	WT	540 061-9 (1464)	**N**	WT
540 014-8 (1415)	**N**	WT	540 038-7 (1440)	**N**	WT	540 062-7 (1465)	**N**	WT
540 015-5 (1416)	**N**	WT	540 039-5 (1441)	**N**	WT	540 063-5 (1466)	**N**	WT
540 016-3 (1417)	**N**	WT	540 040-3 (1442)	**N**	WT	540 064-3 (1467)	**N**	WT
540 017-1 (1418)	**N**	LZ	540 041-1 (1443)	**N**	WT	540 065-0 (1468)	**N**	WT
540 018-9 (1420)	**N**	WT	540 042-9 (1444)	**N**	WT	540 066-8 (1469)	**N**	WT
540 019-7 (1421)	**N**	WT	540 043-7 (1445)	**N**	WT	540 067-6 (1470)	**N**	WT
540 020-5 (1422)	**N**	WT	540 044-5 (1446)	**N**	WT	540 068-4 (1471)	**N**	WT
540 021-3 (1423)	**N**	WT	540 045-2 (1447)	**N**	WT	540 069-2 (1472)	**N**	WT
540 022-1 (1424)	**N**	WT	540 046-0 (1448)	**N**	WT	540 070-0 (1473)	**N**	WT
540 023-9 (1425)	**N**	WT	540 047-8 (1449)	**N**	WT	540 071-8 (1474)	**N**	WT
540 024-7 (1426)	**N**	WT	540 048-6 (1450)	**N**	WT	540 072-6 (1475)	**N**	WT
540 025-4 (1427)	**N**	WT	540 049-4 (1451)	**N**	WT	540 073-4 (1476)	**N**	WT
540 026-2 (1428)	**N**	WT	540 050-2 (1452)	**N**	WT	540 074-2 (1477)	**N**	WT
540 027-0 (1429)	**N**	WT	540 051-0 (1453)	**N**	WT	540 075-9 (1478)	**N**	WT
540 028-8 (1430)	**N**	WT	540 052-8 (1455)	**N**	WT	540 076-7 (1479)	**N**	WT
540 029-6 (1431)	**N**	LZ	540 053-6 (1456)	**N**	WT	540 077-5 (1480)	**N**	WT

540 078-3 (1481) **N** WT | 540 079-1 (1482) **N** WT |

CLASS Bem 550

These are lightweight articulated railcars for operating on the Genève to La Plaine line which is electrified at 1500 V d.c. They have a diesel engine to allow access under their own power to the depot.

Built: 1994.
Builder-Mech. Parts: ACMV.
Builder-Elec. Parts: ABB.
Traction Motors:
One Hour Rating:
Maximum Tractive Effort: 71 kN.
Driving Wheel Dia.: mm.
Weight: 42.5 tonnes.
Overall Length: 31.00 m.
Max. Speed: 100 km/h.
Wheel Arrangement: Bo–2–Bo.
Accommodation: –/79.

550 000-4	N	GE		550 002-0	N	GE	550 004-6	N	GE
550 001-2	N	GE		550 003-8	N	GE		

CLASS RBDe 560

This new design for local services is formally known as the 'NPZ' – Neue Pendel Zug or 'new shuttle train' – and informally, though officially, as the 'Kolibri' or 'humming bird'. Four prototypes were delivered in 1984 with series production beginning in 1987. They are equipped with solid state control. Operating in sets of varying length, with control and intermediate trailers, they can also multiple with other members of the class. Gangwayed at the non-driving end only. They are found everywhere.

Built: 1984* 1987–90 1993–6§.
Builder-Mech. Parts: FFA/SIG/SWP/ABB (SWG-A/SWG-P/SIG §).
Builder-Elec. Parts: BBC (ABB).
One Hour Rating: 1650 kW.
Maximum Tractive Effort: 166 kN.
Driving Wheel Dia.: 950 mm.
Weight: 70 tonnes. ·
Overall Length: 25.00 m.
Max. Speed: 140 km/h.
Wheel Arrangement: Bo–Bo.
Accommodation: –/65 1T.

560 000–83 renumbered from 2100–83 respectively.

560 000-2	N	* LS	Altstätten SG	560 020-0	N	BI	Birsfelden
560 001-0	N	* LS	Münsingen	560 021-8	N	BI	Entlebuch
560 002-8	N	* LS	Sempach-Neuenkirch	560 022-6	N	BI	Rothenburg
560 003-6	N	* LS	Frenkendorf-Füllinsdorf	560 023-4	N	BI	Ebikon
560 004-4	N	LS	Grandvaux	560 024-2	N	BI	Bauma
560 005-1	N	LS	Untersiggenthal	560 025-9	N	BI	Düdigen
560 006-9	N	LS	Wünnewil-Flammatt	560 026-7	N	BI	Versoix
560 007-7	N	LS	Rekingen AG	560 027-5	N	BI	Tenero-Contra
560 008-5	N	LS	Buttes	560 028-3	N	BI	Saint Ursanne
560 009-3	N	LS	Lachen	560 029-1	N	LZ	Saint Imier
560 010-1	N	LS	Jona	560 030-9	N	LZ	Amriswil
560 011-9	N	LS	Aesch	560 031-7	N	LZ	Rolle
560 012-7	N	LS	Zwingen	560 032-5	N	LZ	Birr-Lupfig
560 013-5	N	LS	Oberbuchsiten	560 033-3	N	LZ	Avenches
560 014-3	N	LS	Näfels-Mollis	560 034-1	N	LZ	Cressier NE
560 015-0	N	LS	Lausen	560 035-8	N	LZ	Niederbipp
560 016-8	N	LS	Dottikon-Dintikon-Villmergen	560 036-6	N	LZ	Andelfingen
560 017-6	N	LS	Bad Ragaz	560 037-4	N	LZ	Brügg BE
560 018-4	N	LS	Les Hauts Geneveys	560 038-2	N	LZ	Müchenbuchsee
560 019-2	N	BI	Rivera-Bironico	560 039-0	N	LZ	Steinhausen

560 040-8	N	LZ	Tecknau	560 080-4	N		BI	Palézieux
560 041-6	N	LZ	Wassen	560 081-2	N		BI	Busswil
560 042-4	N	LZ	Saint Gingolph	560 082-0	N		BI	Schüpfen
560 043-2	N	LZ	Pully	560 083-8	N		BI	Courtelary
560 044-0	N	BI	Twann	560 100-0	N	§	BE	
560 045-7	N	BI	Glovelier	560 101-8	N	§	BE	
560 046-5	N	BI	Muralto	560 102-6	N	§	BE	
560 047-3	N	BI	Les Eplatures	560 103-4	N	§	BE	
560 048-1	N	BI	Frick	560 104-2	N	§	BE	
560 049-9	N	BI	Reinach	560 105-9	N	§	BE	
560 050-7	N	BI	La Neuveville	560 106-7	N	§	BE	
560 051-5	N	BI	Egerkingen	560 107-5	N	§	LZ	Hunzenschwil
560 052-3	N	BI	Dagmersellen	560 108-3	N	§	LS	
560 053-1	N	BI	Boncourt-Delle	560 109-1	N	§	LS	Bazenheid
560 054-9	N	BI	Küssnacht a/R	560 110-9	N	§	LS	Lichtensteig
560 055-6	N	BI	Saint Blaise	560 111-7	N	§	LS	Triengen
560 056-4	N	BI	Sins	560 112-5	N	§	LS	Hasle
560 057-2	N	BI	Reconvilier	560 113-3	N	§	LS	Riehen
560 058-0	N	BI	Saxon	560 114-1	N	§	LS	Ouchy
560 059-8	N	BI	Gurtnellen	560 115-8	N	§	LS	Thal-Staad-Altenrhein
560 060-6	N	BI	Kaiseraugst	560 116-6	N	§	LS	Matt/Mâche-Bözingen/Boujean
560 061-4	N	BI	Sins	560 117-4	N	§	LS	Lucenz
560 062-2	N	BI	Deitingen	560 118-2	N	§	LS	Ittigen
560 063-0	N	BI	Giornico	560 119-0	N	§	LS	
560 064-8	N	BI	Koblenz	560 120-8	N	§	WT	
560 065-5	N	BI	Laufenberg	560 121-6	N	§	WT	
560 066-3	N	WT	Schüpfheim	560 122-4	N	§	WT	
560 067-1	N	BI	Moudon	560 123-2	N	§	WT	
560 068-9	N	BI	Gisikon Root	560 124-0	N	§	WT	
560 069-7	N	WT	Sirnach	560 125-7	N	§	WT	
560 070-5	N	WT	Trubschachen	560 126-5	N	§	WT	
560 071-3	N	WT	Leuk	560 127-3	N	§	WT	
560 072-1	N	BI	Vernayaz	560 128-1	N	§	WT	
560 073-9	N	BI	Gland	560 129-9	N	§	WT	
560 074-7	N	BI	Gorgier-St. Aubin	560 130-7	N	§	WT	
560 075-4	N	BI	Grellingen	560 131-5	C	§	LS	Saint-Saphorin
560 076-2	N	BI	Orbe	560 132-3	N	§	LS	
560 077-0	N	BI	Puidoux-Chexbres	560 133-1	N	§	WT	
560 078-8	N	BI	Grand Saconnex Genève Aéroport	560 134-9	N	§	WT	
560 079-6	N	BI	Moudon	560 135-6	N	§	WT	

CLASS RBDe 562

Six of the RBDe 560 class have been rebuilt for dual voltage operation for use on through local services to Mulhouse in France. They can operate on 15 kV $16^2/_3$ Hz and 25 kV 50 Hz.

Built: 1996 (rebuilt 1997).
Builder-Mech. Parts: SWG-A/SWG-P/SIG.
Builder-Elec. Parts: ABB.
One Hour Rating:
Maximum Tractive Effort:
Driving Wheel Dia.: 950 mm.
Weight:
Overall Length: 25.00 m.
Max. Speed:
Wheel Arrangement: Bo–Bo.
Accommodation:

Rebuilt from RBDe 560 136–141 respectively.

562 000-0	N	BS		562 003-4	N	BS
562 001-8	N	BS	Basel St. Johann	562 004-2	N	BS
562 002-6	N	BS	Mulhouse	562 005-9	N	BS

1.3. MAIN LINE ELECTRIC LOCOMOTIVES
CLASS Re4/4^I   Bo–Bo

A development of the RFe4/4 motor luggage vans (later De4/4 of the SOB and SZU), the Re4/4^I was introduced to work lightweight expresses. It was the first production design to omit carrying wheels and to have a maximum speed of over 110 km/h. Various liveries have been carried, the most significant variation being TEE red and cream applied to 10033/34/46/50 in 1972; all those remaining are now in standard livery. After many year's service on local trains, they are now being displaced by new railcars. Some are being withdrawn, and others redeployed mainly on postal trains. The BS locos are used for carriage pilot work.

Built: 1946–48 p (1950–51 remainder).
Builder-Mech. Parts: SLM.
Builder-Elec. Parts: BBC/MFO/SAAS.
Traction Motors: 4 single phase commutator type, fully suspended with BBC spring drive.
One Hour Rating: 1854 (1830 p) kW.
Maximum Tractive Effort: 137 kN.
Driving Wheel Dia.: 1040 mm.
Weight: 57 tonnes.
Overall Length: 14.90 m (14.70 m p).
Max. Speed: 125 km/h.
New Class No.: 410.

p Fitted for push-pull working with regenerative braking and corridor connections.

10001 **R** p*OL	10013 **G** p LS	10026 **G** p LS	10038 **R** RS
10002 **G** p OL	10014 **R** p LS	10028 **R** RS	10039 **G** RS
10004 **R** p OL	10015 **G** p LS	10030 **R** BS	10040 **G** RS
10005 **R** p OL	10016 **R** p LS	10031 **R** RS	10041 **G** RS
10006 **R** p OL	10017 **R** p LS	10032 **R** BS	10044 **R** LS
10007 **G** p OL	10018 **R** p LS	10033 **R** BS	10045 **R** LS
10008 **R** p OL	10019 **R** p LS	10034 **R** BS	10046 **G** LS
10009 **R** p OL	10020 **G** p LS	10035 **R** LS	10048 **R** LS
10011 **R** p OL	10022 **R** p LS	10037 **R** LS	10049 **R** LS
10012 **R** p LS	10023 **R** p LS		

CLASS Ae3/5   1Co1

A museum loco, the last survivor of a class once totalling 26.

Built: 1924.
Builder-Mech. Parts: SLM.
Builder-Elec. Parts: SAAS.
Traction Motors: 6 single phase commutator type, body mounted with hollow axle drive.
One Hour Rating: 1340 kW.
Maximum Tractive Effort: 137 kN.
Driving Wheel Dia.: 1610 mm.
Pony Wheel Dia.: 950 mm.
Weight: 81 tonnes.
Overall Length: 12.32 m.
Max. Speed: 90 km/h.

10217 **G**   BN

CLASS Ae3/6^{III}   2Co1

Another museum loco, this class being a lengthened version of the previous one, with a bogie at one end instead of a pony truck.

Built: 1926.
Builder-Mech. Parts: SLM.
Builder-Elec. Parts: SAAS.
Traction Motors: 6 single phase commutator type, body mounted with hollow axle drive.
One Hour Rating: 1340 kW.
Maximum Tractive Effort: 137 kN.

Driving Wheel Dia.: 1610 mm.
Pony Wheel Dia.: 950 mm.
Weight: 89 tonnes.
Overall Length: 13.76 m.
Max. Speed: 90 km/h.

10264 **B**   LS |

CLASS Ae3/6ᴵᴵ   2C1

Yet another museum loco, this class differs from the other Ae3/6 series in having rod drive. Once a class of 60 locos, several others survive as heating units.

Built: 1925.
Builder-Mech. Parts: SLM.
Builder-Elec. Parts: MFO.
Traction Motors: 2 single phase commutator type, body mounted with jackshaft/side rod drive.
One Hour Rating: 1490 kW.
Maximum Tractive Effort: 147 kN.
Driving Wheel Dia.: 1610 mm.
Pony Wheel Dia.: 950 mm.
Weight: 98 tonnes.
Overall Length: 14.15 m.
Max. Speed: 100 km/h.

10439 **B**   OL |

CLASS Ae3/6ᴵ   2Co1

Once a class of 114 units, this was the most successful of several general purpose types introduced in the early years of electrification. The powered wheels are rigid with the frame and are each driven by a motor mounted above in the locomotive body through a 'Büchli' drive. This is carried in a circular casing outside the wheels on one side only, completely obscuring them on that side. The class was finally withdrawn from regular service in 1994, the two survivors being museum locos.

Built: 1926–8
Builder-Mech. Parts: SLM.
Builder-Elec. Parts: BBC 10664, MFO 10700.
Traction Motors: 3 single phase commutator type, frame mounted with BBC Büchli flexible drive.
One Hour Rating: 1560 kW.
Maximum Tractive Effort: 147 kN.
Driving Wheel Dia.: 1610 mm.
Pony Wheel Dia.: 950 mm.
Weight: 95.5 tonnes 10664, 93.8 tonnes 10700.
Overall Length: 14.70 m.
Maximum Speed: 110 km/h.

10664 **G**   ZU | 10700 **B**   BN |

CLASS Ae4/7   2Do1

An enlargement of the Ae3/6ᴵ class, this was for many years the most numerous type in Switzerland until exceeded by the Re4/4ᴵᴵ, and formed the mainstay of SBB mainline passenger power well into the 1960s. The class was finally withdrawn from regular service in 1996, the survivors being retained as museum locos.

Built: 1927–31.
Builder-Mech. Parts: SLM.
Builder-Elec. Parts: BBC 10908, MFO 10976.
Traction Motors: 4 single phase commutator type, frame mounted with BBC Büchli flexible drive.
One Hour Rating: 2300 kW.
Maximum Tractive Effort: 196 kN.
Driving Wheel Dia.: 1610 mm.
Pony Wheel Dia.: 950 mm.
Weight: 118 tonnes 10908, 123 tonnes 10976.
Overall Length: 16.76 m.
Max. Speed: 100 km/h.

10905 **G**   RS | 10976 **G**   LS |

CLASSES Re4/4^{II} & Re4/4^{III} Bo–Bo

With 273 examples in service, this was the standard SBB electric loco for some 20 years and is to be found throughout the system. The first six appeared in 1964 with series production beginning in 1967. The different lengths arise from variations in the body below the cabs. Those which have carried "Swiss Express" livery were fitted with automatic couplers, but have now reverted to standard. 11172, 11282 and 11312 were withdrawn following accidents.

Class Re4/4^{III} is a variation with a lower gear ratio for use on the Gotthard line. Three locos of this class (11351–3) were sold to the Südostbahn but have since been returned to the SBB together with an identical locomotive built new for the SOB in exchange for the Re4/4^{IV} class.

Built: 1964–85.
Builder-Mech. Parts: SLM.
Builder-Elec. Parts: BBC/MFO/SAAS.
Traction Motors: 4 single phase commutator type, fully suspended with BBC spring drive.
One Hour Rating: 4700 (4650*) kW.
Maximum Tractive Effort: 255 (280*) kN.
Driving Wheel Dia.: 1260 mm.
Weight: 80 tonnes.
Overall Length: 14.80 –15.58 m.
Max. Speed: 140 (125*) km/h.
New Class No.: 420/430*.
Pantographs:

11101–11155: One, double arm Swiss.
11195–11200: Two, single arm, one Swiss and one DB/ÖBB-type for through working to Lindau. There are many variations in length.

11101–11106 (Prototypes)	14.80 m	(15.58 m a)
11107–11155 (1st production series)	14.90 m	(15.52 m f)
11156–11219, 11236–11238 (2nd production series)	15.41 m	(15.465 m e, 15.52 m f)
11220–11235, 11239–11254 (2nd production series, mod.)	15.51 m	
11255–11349, 11350–11397 (Final production series)	15.52 m	

All locos are push-pull and mw fitted and can multiple work with Classes Re4/4^{III}, Re4/4^{IV}, Re6/6 and RBe4.4.

§ Ex SOB 41/4/2/3 respectively.

11101 **R**		RS	11128 **R**		LZ	11155 **R**		LZ	11183 **R**		BN
11102 **G**		RS	11129 **R**		LZ	11156 **R**		LZ	11184 **R**		BN
11103 **O**	a	RS	11130 **R**		LZ	11157 **R**	e	LZ	11185 **R**		BN
11104 **R**		RS	11131 **R**		LZ	11158 **G**		LZ	11186 **R**		BN
11105 **G**		RS	11132 **R**		LZ	11159 **G**		LZ	11187 **R**		BN
11106 **O**	a	RS	11133 **R**		LZ	11160 **G**		LZ	11188 **R**		BN
11107 **R**		RS	11134 **R**		LZ	11161 **G**		LZ	11189 **R**		BN
11108 **O**	f	RS	11135 **R**		LZ	11162 **R**		LZ	11190 **R**		BN
11109 **O**	f	RS	11136 **R**		LZ	11163 **R**		BS	11191 **R**		BN
11110 **G**		RS	11137 **G**		LZ	11164 **R**		BS	11192 **R**		BN
11111 **R**		RS	11138 **R**		LZ	11165 **R**		BS	11193 **R**		BN
11112 **R**	f	RS	11139 **R**		LZ	11166 **R**	f	BS	11194 **R**		BN
11113 **R**	f	RS	11140 **R**		LZ	11167 **R**		BS	11195 **R**		RS
11114 **R**		RS	11141 **O**	f	LZ	11168 **R**		BS	11196 **R**		RS
11115 **R**		RS	11142 **G**		LZ	11169 **R**	f	BS	11197 **R**		RS
11116 **R**		RS	11143 **R**		LZ	11170 **R**		BS	11198 **R**		RS
11117 **G**		RS	11144 **R**		LZ	11171 **R**		BS	11199 **R**		RS
11118 **R**		LZ	11145 **R**		LZ	11173 **R**		BS	11200 **G**		RS
11119 **G**		LZ	11146 **R**		LZ	11174 **R**		BS	11201 **R**		RS
11120 **R**		LZ	11147 **R**		LZ	11175 **R**		BS	11202 **G**		RS
11121 **R**		LZ	11148 **R**		LZ	11176 **R**		BN	11203 **R**		RS
11122 **R**		LZ	11149 **R**		LZ	11177 **R**		BN	11204 **R**		RS
11123 **G**		LZ	11150 **R**		LZ	11178 **R**		BN	11205 **G**		RS
11124 **R**		LZ	11151 **R**		LZ	11179 **R**		BN	11206 **R**		RS
11125 **R**		LZ	11152 **R**		LZ	11180 **R**		BN	11207 **G**		RS
11126 **R**		LZ	11153 **R**		LZ	11181 **R**		BN	11208 **G**		RS
11127 **R**		LZ	11154 **R**		LZ	11182 **R**		BN	11209 **R**		RS

No.				No.				No.				No.			
11210	G	RS		11257	G	BN		11305	G	LS		11352	R	*§	ER
11211	G	RS		11258	G	BN		11306	G	LS		11353	R	*§	ER
11212	G	RS		11259	R	BN		11307	G	LS		11354	R	*	ER
11213	G	RS		11260	G	BN		11308	G	LS		11355	R	*	ER
11214	R	RS		11261	G	BN		11309	G	LS		11356	R	*	ER
11215	G	RS		11262	G	BN		11310	G	LS		11357	R	*	ER
11216	G	RS		11263	G	BN		11311	G	LS		11358	R	*	ER
11217	G	RS		11264	G	BN		11313	G	LS		11359	R	*	ER
11218	G	RS		11265	R	BN		11314	G	LS		11360	R	*	ER
11219	G	BN		11266	R	BN		11315	R	LS		11361	R	*	ER
11220	G	BN		11267	G	BN		11316	G	LS		11362	R	*	ER
11221	G	BN		11268	G	BN		11317	G	LS		11363	R	*	ER
11222	G	BN		11269	G	BN		11318	G	LS		11364	G	*	ER
11223	R	BN		11270	G	BN		11319	G	LS		11365	R	*	ER
11224	G	BN		11271	G	BN		11320	G	LS		11366	R	*	ER
11225	R	BN		11272	G	BN		11321	G	LS		11367	R	*	ER
11226	R	BN		11273	G	BN		11322	G	LS		11368	G	*	ER
11227	G	BN		11274	R	BN		11323	G	LS		11369	R	*	ER
11228	G	BN		11275	R	BN		11324	G	LS		11370	R	*	ER
11229	R	BN		11276	G	RS		11325	G	LS		11371	G		RS
11230	R	BN		11277	R	RS		11326	G	LS		11372	G		RS
11231	G	BN		11278	R	RS		11327	G	LS		11373	G		RS
11232	G	BN		11279	R	RS		11328	G	LS		11374	G		RS
11233	R	BN		11280	R	RS		11329	R	LS		11375	G		RS
11234	G	BN		11281	R	RS		11330	G	LS		11376	G		RS
11235	G	BN		11283	R	RS		11331	G	LS		11377	R		RS
11236	R	BN		11284	R	RS		11332	G	LS		11378	R		RS
11237	R	BN		11285	R	RS		11333	G	LS		11379	R		RS
11238	R	BN		11286	R	RS		11334	G	LS		11380	R		RS
11239	R	BN		11287	R	RS		11335	G	LS		11381	R		RS
11240	R	BN		11288	R	RS		11336	G	LS		11382	R		RS
11241	R	BN		11289	R	RS		11337	G	LS		11383	R		RS
11242	R	BN		11290	R	RS		11338	G	LS		11384	R		RS
11243	G	BN		11291	R	RS		11339	G	LS		11385	R		RS
11244	R	BN		11292	R	RS		11340	G	LS		11386	R		RS
11245	R	BN		11293	R	RS		11341	G	LS		11387	R		RS
11246	R	BN		11294	R	RS		11342	G	LS		11388	R		RS
11247	R	BN		11295	R	RS		11343	R	LS		11389	R		RS
11248	G	BN		11296	G	RS		11344	G	LS		11390	R		RS
11249	R	BN		11297	G	RS		11345	G	LS		11391	R		RS
11250	R	BN		11298	R	RS		11346	G	LS		11392	R		RS
11251	R	BN		11299	R	BN		11347	G	LS		11393	R		RS
11252	R	BN		11300	R	BN		11348	G	LS		11394	R		RS
11253	R	BN		11301	R	BN		11349	G	LS		11395	R		RS
11254	G	BN		11302	R	BN		11350	R	*§	ER	11396	R		RS
11255	R	BN		11303	R	BN		11351	R	*§	ER	11397	R		RS
11256	R	BN		11304	R	BN									

Name: 11239 PORRENTRUY

CLASS Ae6/6 Co–Co

Built for general use on the Gotthard and Simplon lines, this class has been displaced to other routes. The locos are used mainly on frieght work, only a handful of passenger turns now remaining. It was the first SBB type to receive names and emblems and to carry the White Cross on the ends. 11401–25 carry chrome decorations.

Built: 1952–3*, 1955–66.
Builder-Mech. Parts: SLM.
Builder-Elec. Parts: BBC/MFO.
Traction Motors: 6 single phase commutator type, fully suspended with BBC spring drive.
One Hour Rating: 4300 kW.
Maximum Tractive Effort: 392 kN (324 kN*).
Driving Wheel Dia.: 1260 mm.
Weight: 128 tonnes (124 tonnes*).
Overall Length: 18.40 m.

Max. Speed: 125 km/h.
New Class No.: 610.

Some locos carry names in different languages on opposite sides.

11401	R	* ZU	TICINO	11461	G	ZU	LOCARNO
11402	R	* ZU	URI	11462	G	ZU	BIASCA
11403	G	OL	SCHWYZ	11463	R	ZU	GÖSCHENEN
11404	G	OL	LUZERN	11464	R	ZU	ERSTFELD
11405	G	OL	NIDWALDEN	11465	G	BI	OERLIKON
11406	G	OL	OBWALDEN	11466	R	BI	SURSEE
11407	G	OL	AARAU	11467	G	BI	ZOFINGEN
11408	G	OL	SOLOTHURN	11468	G	BI	LENZBURG
11409	G	OL	BASELLAND	11469	G	BI	THALWIL
11410	R	OL	BASEL-STADT	11470	R	BI	BRUGG
11411	G	OL	ZUG	11471	G	BI	PRATTELN
11412	G	OL	ZÜRICH	11472	R	BI	BRIG
11413	G	OL	SCHAFFHAUSEN	11473	G	BI	ST MAURICE
11414	R	OL	BERN/BERNE	11474	G	BI	VEVEY
11415	G	OL	THURGAU	11475	G	BI	VALLORBE
11416	R	OL	GLARUS	11476	G	BI	LES VERRIÈRES
11417	R	OL	FRIBOURG/FREIBURG	11477	R	BI	MARTIGNY
11418	R	OL	LT GALLEN	11478	G	BI	SIERRE
11419	R	OL	APPENZELL I.RH	11479	G	BI	VISP
11420	R	OL	APPENZELL A.RH	11480	G	BI	MONTREUX
11421	G	OL	GRISCHUN/GRAUBÜNDEN	11481	G	BI	LA CHAUX DE FONDS
11422	R	OL	VAUD	11482	G	BI	DELÉMONT
11423	R	OL	VALAIS/WALLIS	11483	G	BI	JURA
11424	R	OL	NEUCHÂTEL	11484	G	BI	ROMONT
11425	R	ZU	GENÈVE	11485	G	BI	THUN
11426	R	ZU	STADT ZÜRICH	11486	G	BI	BURGDORF
11427	G	ZU	STADT BERN	11487	G	BI	LANGENTHAL
11428	R	ZU	STADT LUZERN	11488	G	BI	MENDRISIO
11429	R	ZU	ALTDORF	11489	G	OL	AIROLO
11430	R	ZU	GEMEINDE SCHWYZ	11490	R	OL	ROTKREUZ
11431	R	ZU	SARNEN	11491	G	OL	WOHLEN AG
11432	R	ZU	STANS	11492	G	OL	EMMEN
11433	G	ZU	GLARUS	11493	G	BS	SISSACH
11434	R	ZU	STADT ZUG	11494	G	BS	SCHLIEREN
11435	G	ZU	FRIBOURG	11495	G	BS	BÜLACH
11436	G	ZU	STADT SOLOTHURN	11496	G	BS	STADT WIL
11437	R	ZU	STADT BASEL	11497	G	BS	ST MARGRETHEN
11438	G	ZU	LIESTAL	11498	G	BS	BUCHS SG
11439	R	ZU	SCHAFFHAUSEN	11499	G	BS	SARGANS
11440	R	ZU	HERISAU	11500	G	BS	LANDQUART
11441	R	ZU	APPENZELL	11501	G	BS	RENENS
11442	R	ZU	ST GALLEN	11502	G	BS	NYON
11443	R	ZU	CHUR	11503	G	BS	PAYERNE
11444	G	ZU	AARAU	11504	G	BS	LE LOCLE
11445	R	ZU	FRAUENFELD	11505	G	BS	LYSS
11446	R	ZU	BELLINZONA	11506	G	BS	GRENCHEN
11447	G	ZU	LAUSANNE	11507	G	BS	WILDEGG
11448	R	ZU	SION	11508	G	BS	WETTINGEN
11449	G	ZU	NEUCHÂTEL	11509	G	BS	GOSSAU SG
11450	R	ZU	VILLE DE GENÈVE	11510	G	BS	RHEINFELDEN
11451	G	ZU	WINTERTHUR	11511	G	BS	DIETIKON
11452	G	ZU	BADEN	11512	R	BS	HORGEN
11453	G	ZU	ARTH-GOLDAU	11513	G	BS	WALLISELLEN
11454	R	ZU	YVERDON	11514	G	BS	WEINFELDEN
11455	R	ZU	BIEL/BIENNE	11515	G	BS	KREUZLINGEN
11456	R	ZU	OLTEN	11516	G	BS	BAAR
11457	R	ZU	ROMANSHORN	11517	G	BS	BRUNNEN
11458	G	ZU	RORSCHACH	11518	G	BS	FLÜELEN
11459	G	ZU	CHIASSO	11519	R	BS	GIUBIASCO
11460	G	ZU	LUGANO	11520	R	BS	LANGNAU I.E

CLASS Re6/6   Bo–Bo–Bo

Effectively an enlarged and uprated version of the Re4/4^{II}, this class was built to work on the mountain routes, but also appears elsewhere. The wheel arrangement was selected to provide a total adhesion weight similar to the Ae6/6, but with a better ability to run through curves, and to reduce weight transfer. Four prototypes were built, the first two having a hinged body with the axis of the hinge horizontal; the rigid body design was adopted for the production version. The entry into service of the Re 460 class has seen a reduction of turns on the Gottard route, and the class now appears over a much wider area than previously. 11638 was withdrawn following an accident.

Built: 1972*, 1975–80.
Builder-Mech. Parts: SLM.
Builder-Elec. Parts: BBC/SAAS (BBC*).
Traction Motors: 6 single phase commutator type, fully suspended with BBC spring drive.
One Hour Rating: 7850 kW.
Maximum Tractive Effort: 398 kN (394 kN*).
Driving Wheel Dia.: 1260 mm.
Weight: 120 tonnes.
Overall Length: 19.31 m.
Max. Speed: 140 km/h.
New Class No.: 620.

All locos are mw fitted (can mw with Re4/4^{II}, Re4/4^{III}, Re4/4^{IV}, RBe4/4 classes).

11601	R	* ER	WOLHUSEN	11643	G	LS	LAUFEN
11602	R	* ER	MORGES	11644	G	LS	CORNAUX
11603	R	* ER	WÄDENSWIL	11645	G	LS	COLOMBIER
11604	R	* ER	FAIDO	11646	G	LS	BUSSIGNY
11605	R	ER	USTER	11647	G	LS	BEX
11606	R	ER	TURGI	11648	G	LS	AIGLE
11607	G	ER	WATTWIL	11649	G	LS	AARBERG
11608	G	ER	WETZIKON	11650	G	LS	SCHÖNENWERD
11609	G	ER	UZWIL	11651	G	LS	DORNACH-ARLESHEIM
11610	R	ER	SPREITENBACH	11652	G	ER	KERZERS
11611	R	ER	RÜTI ZH	11653	G	ER	GÜMLINGEN
11612	G	ER	REGENSDORF	11654	G	ER	VILLENEUVE
11613	R	ER	RAPPERSWIL	11655	G	ER	COSSONAY
11614	G	ER	MEILEN	11656	G	ER	TRAVERS
11615	R	ER	KLOTEN	11657	G	ER	ESTAVAYER-LE-LAC
11616	G	ER	ILLNAU-EFFRETIKON	11658	G	ER	AUVERNIER
11617	G	ER	HEERBRUGG	11659	G	ER	CHAVORNAY
11618	R	ER	DÜBENDORF	11660	G	ER	TAVANNES
11619	R	ER	ARBON	11661	G	ER	GAMPEL-STEG
11620	G	ER	WANGEN BEI OLTEN	11662	G	ER	REUCHENETTE-PÉRY
11621	G	ER	TAVERNE-TORRICELLA	11663	G	ER	EGLISAU
11622	R	ER	SUHR	11664	G	ER	KÖNIZ
11623	G	ER	RUPPERSWIL	11665	G	ER	ZIEGELBRÜCKE
11624	G	ER	ROTHRIST	11666	G	ER	STEIN AM RHEIN
11625	G	ER	OENSINGEN	11667	G	ER	BODIO
11626	G	ER	ZOLLIKOFEN	11668	G	ER	STEIN-SÄCKINGEN
11627	G	ER	LUTERBACH-ATTISHOLZ	11669	G	ER	HÄGENDORF
11628	G	ER	KONOLFINGEN	11670	G	BE	AFFOLTERN AM ALBIS
11629	G	ER	INTERLAKEN	11671	G	BE	OTHMARSINGEN
11630	R	LS	HERZOGENBUCHSEE	11672	R	BE	BALERNA
11631	G	LS	DULLIKEN	11673	G	BE	CHAM
11632	G	LS	DÄNIKEN	11674	R	BE	MURGENTHAL
11633	G	LS	MURI AG	11675	G	BE	GELTERKINDEN
11634	G	LS	AARBURG-OFTRINGEN	11676	G	BE	ZURZACH
11635	R	LS	MUTTENZ	11677	G	BE	NEUHAUSEN AM RHEINFA
11636	R	LS	VERNIER-MEYRIN	11678	G	BE	BASSERSDORF
11637	R	LS	SONCEBOZ-SOMBEVAL	11679	G	BE	CADENAZZO
11639	G	LS	MURTEN	11680	G	BE	MÖHLIN
11640	G	ER	MÜNCHENSTEIN	11681	G	BE	IMMENSEE
11641	G	LS	MOUTIER	11682	G	BE	PFÄFFIKON SZ
11642	G	LS	MONTHEY	11683	G	BE	AMSTEG-SILENEN

11684 **G**	BE	UZNACH		11687 **G**	BE	BISCHOFSZELL
11685 **G**	BE	SULGEN		11688 **G**	BE	LINTHAL
11686 **G**	BE	HOCHDORF		11689 **G**	BE	GERRA-GAMBAROGNO

CLASS Ae8/14 1AA1AA1 + 1AA1AA1

This museum loco is effectively two Ae4/7s permanently coupled with the wheels and electrical equipment rearranged. Regenerative braking is fitted. It was the first of three high power, twin units built for the Gotthard route between 1931 and 1940; experience showed smaller, single units to be more practical.

Built: 1931.
Builder-Mech. Parts: SLM.
Builder-Elec. Parts: BBC.
Traction Motors: 8 single phase commutator type, frame mounted with BBC Büchli flexible drive.
One Hour Rating: 4650 kW.
Maximum Tractive Effort: 490 kN.
Driving Wheel Dia.: 1610 mm.
Pony Wheel Dia.: 950 mm.
Weight: 240 tonnes.
Overall Length: 34.00 m.
Max. Speed: 100 km/h.

11801 **G**   ER |

CLASS Be4/6 1B–B1

Another museum loco, the last survivor of a class of 40 built for passenger use when the Gotthard line was electrified. Each bogie carries two motors geared to a single layshaft connected to the driving wheels by coupling rods.

Built: 1921.
Builder-Mech. Parts: SLM.
Builder-Elec. Parts: BBC.
Traction Motors: 4 single phase commutator type, frame mounted with jackshaft/side rod drive.
One Hour Rating: 1520 kW.
Maximum Tractive Effort: 177 kN.
Driving Wheel Dia.: 1530 mm.
Pony Wheel Dia.: 950 mm.
Weight: 110 tonnes.
Overall Length: 16.56 m.
Max. Speed: 75 km/h.

12320 **B**   WT |

CLASS Be4/7 1Bo1Bo1

The survivor of a class of 6 locos, a design from the early years of electrification which never went into series production. It is now a museum loco.

Built: 1922.
Builder-Mech. Parts: SLM.
Builder-Elec. Parts: SAAS.
Traction Motors: 8 single phase commutator type, body mounted with hollow axle drive.
One Hour Rating: 1790 kW.
Maximum Tractive Effort: 196 kN.
Driving Wheel Dia.: 1610 mm.
Pony Wheel Dia.: 950 mm.
Weight: 111 tonnes.
Overall Length: 16.30 m.
Max. Speed: 80 km/h.

12504 **B**   BI |

CLASS Ce6/8^{II} 1C–C1

The 'Crocodile' configuration arose from the need to build a locomotive with high power, adequate adhesion weight and the ability to negotiate tight curves. Two motors in each frame are geared to a single shaft connected to the driving wheels by coupling rods. This loco was modernised and uprated in 1947, being reclassified Be6/8^{II} and renumbered 13253. It reverted to its original classification and number on becoming a museum loco. The specification is from rebuilding.

Built: 1920.
Builder-Mech. Parts: SLM.
Builder-Elec. Parts: MFO.
Traction Motors: 4 single phase commutator type, bogie mounted with jackshaft/side rod drive.
One Hour Rating: 2688 kW.
Maximum Tractive Effort: 294 kN.
Driving Wheel Dia.: 1350 mm.
Pony Wheel Dia.: 950 mm.
Weight: 126 tonnes.
Overall Length: 19.46 m.
Max. Speed: 65 km/h.

14253 **B**   ER |

CLASS Ce6/8^{III} 1C–C1

This loco represents the 2nd series of 18 'Crocodiles'. Renumbered 13305 in 1956, it also reverted to its original number on becoming a museum loco.

Built: 1926.
Builder-Mech. Parts: SLM.
Builder-Elec. Parts: MFO.
Traction Motors: 4 single phase commutator type, bogie mounted with jackshaft/side rod drive.
One Hour Rating: 1820 kW.
Maximum Tractive Effort: 294 kN.
Driving Wheel Dia.: 1350 mm.
Pony Wheel Dia.: 950 mm.
Weight: 131 tonnes.
Overall Length: 20.06 m.
Max. Speed: 65 km/h.

14305 **G**   BS |

CLASS Re 450   Bo–Bo

These are single-ended locos to work push-pull trains on the Zürich S-Bahn, which commenced operation in May 1990. They have 3-phase traction motors, SLM 'shifting axle drive', which allows radial adjustment of the axles within the bogies, and regeneration braking. The class was to have been numbered in the 10500 series.

Built: 1989–97.
Builder-Mech. Parts: SLM.
Builder-Elec. Parts: ABB.
Traction Motors: 4 3-phase axle-hung, nose suspended.
One Hour Rating: 3200 kW.
Maximum Tractive Effort: 240 kN.
Driving Wheel Dia.: 1100 mm.
Weight: 74 tonnes.
Overall Length: 18.40 m.
Max. Speed: 130 km/h.

450 000-5 **S**	ZU		450 008-8 **S**	ZU	Riesbach
450 001-3 **S**	ZU		450 009-6 **S**	ZU	Hedingen
450 002-1 **S**	ZU	Oberwinterthur	450 010-4 **S**	ZU	
450 003-9 **S**	ZU	Zollikon	450 011-2 **S**	ZU	Oberrieden
450 004-7 **S**	ZU	Stettbach	450 012-0 **S**	ZU	Schwamendingen
450 005-4 **S**	ZU	Kilchberg	450 013-8 **S**	ZU	Niederglatt
450 006-2 **S**	ZU	Rafz	450 014-6 **S**	ZU	Seuzach
450 007-0 **S**	ZU		450 015-3 **S**	ZU	Erlenbach

Number			Name
450016-1	S	ZU	Altstetten
450017-9	S	ZU	Bubikon
450018-7	S	ZU	Hirslanden–Hottingen
450019-5	S	ZU	Stäfä
450020-3	S	ZU	Pfäffikon
450021-1	S	ZU	Seusach
450022-9	S	ZU	Richterswil
450023-7	S	ZU	
450024-5	S	ZU	Pfungen
450025-2	S	ZU	Winterthurseen
450026-0	S	ZU	
450027-8	S	ZU	Zürich Enge
450028-6	S	ZU	
450029-4	S	ZU	Altikon
450030-2	S	ZU	Rumlang
450031-0	S	ZU	
450032-8	S	ZU	Mettmenstetten
450033-6	S	ZU	Thalheim
450034-4	S	ZU	
450035-1	S	ZU	Schöfflisdorf
450036-9	S	ZU	Dietikon
450037-7	S	ZU	Niederweningen
450038-5	S	ZU	
450039-3	S	ZU	
450040-1	S	ZU	
450041-9	S	ZU	
450042-7	S	ZU	Hettluigen
450043-5	S	ZU	
450044-3	S	ZU	Henggart
450045-0	S	ZU	Feldbach
450046-8	S	ZU	Zürich Affoltern
450047-6	S	ZU	
450048-4	S	ZU	
450049-2	S	ZU	
450050-0	S	ZU	Wien
450051-8	S	ZU	
450052-6	S	ZU	Lotstetten
450053-4	S	ZU	Witikon
450054-2	S	ZU	
450055-9	S	ZU	
450056-7	S	ZU	Otelfingen
450057-5	S	ZU	
450058-3	S	ZU	
450059-1	S	ZU	Cronau
450060-9	S	ZU	Glattfelden
450061-7	S	ZU	Mönchaltorf
450062-5	S	ZU	Gossau ZH
450063-3	S	ZU	
450064-1	S	ZU	City of Osaka
450065-8	S	ZU	
450066-6	S	ZU	
450067-4	S	ZU	
450068-2	S	ZU	
450069-0	S	ZU	Wiesendangen
450070-8	S	ZU	Winterthur Wulfingen
450071-6	S	ZU	
450072-4	S	ZU	
450073-2	S	ZU	
450074-0	S	ZU	
450075-7	S	ZU	Ossingen
450076-5	S	ZU	
450077-3	S	ZU	Oberstammheim
450078-1	S	ZU	
450079-9	S	ZU	
450080-7	S	ZU	
450081-5	S	ZU	Weiningen
450082-3	S	ZU	
450083-1	S	ZU	
450084-9	S	ZU	
450085-6	S	ZU	
450086-4	S	ZU	
450087-2	S	ZU	Zell ZH
450088-0	S	ZU	Wangen SZ
450089-8	S	ZU	Bäretswil
450090-6	S	ZU	
450091-4	S	ZU	
450092-2	S	ZU	
450093-0	S	ZU	Wil ZH
450094-8	S	ZU	
450095-5	S	ZU	
450096-3	S	ZU	
450097-1	S	ZU	Maur
450098-9	S	ZU	
450099-7	S	ZU	
450100-3	S	ZU	
450101-1	S	ZU	Obfelden
450102-9	S	ZU	Wangen-Brütisellen
450103-7	S	ZU	
450104-5	S	ZU	
450105-2	S	ZU	
450106-0	S	ZU	
450107-8	S	ZU	
450108-6	S	ZU	
450109-4	S	ZU	
450110-2	S	ZU	
450111-0	S	ZU	
450112-8	S	ZU	
450113-6	S	ZU	
450114-4	S	ZU	

CLASS Re 460   Bo–Bo

A new class of high speed locos for the 'Bahn 2000' project. They see use on Intercity services Zürich–Genève, and on both passenger and freight (often in multiple) on the mountain routes. They were originally to have been numbered in the 10700 series.

Built: 1991-6.
Builder-Mech. Parts: SLM/Krauss Maffei.
Builder-Elec. Parts: ABB.
Traction Motors: 4 3-phase fully suspended.
One Hour Rating: 6100 kW.
Maximum Tractive Effort: 275 kN.

Driving Wheel Dia.: 1100 mm.
Weight: 84 tonnes.
Overall Length: 18.50 m.
Max. Speed: 230 km/h.

Number			Name	Number			Name
460 000-3	R	LS	Grauholz	460 060-7	R	BE	
460 001-1	R	LS	Lötschberg	460 061-5	R	BE	Wiggental
460 002-9	R	LS	Seeland	460 062-3	R	BE	
460 003-7	R	LS	Milieu de Monde	460 063-1	R	BE	Brunegg
460 004-5	R	LS	Uetliberg	460 064-9	R	BE	Mythen
460 005-2	R	LS	Val d'Anniviers	460 065-6	R	BE	Rotsee
460 006-0	R	LS	Lavaux	460 066-4	R	BE	Finse
460 007-8	R	LS	Junior	460 067-2	R	BE	
460 008-6	R	LS		460 068-0	R	BE	
460 009-4	R	LS	Le Jet d'Eau	460 069-8	R	BE	
460 010-2	R	LS	Löwenberg	460 070-6	R	BE	
460 011-0	R	LS	Léman	460 071-4	R	BE	
460 012-8	R	LS	Erguël	460 072-2	R	BE	
460 013-6	R	LS	Nord Vaudris	460 073-0	R	BE	
460 014-4	A	LS		460 074-8	A	BE	
460 015-1	A	LS	Dübendorf II	460 075-5	R	BE	
460 016-9	A	LS	TRAMONT	460 076-3	R	BE	
460 017-7	A	LS	Märklin	460 077-1	R	BE	
460 018-5	A	LS	Louis Danzas	460 078-9	R	BE	
460 019-3	R	LS	Miele	460 079-7	R	BE	
460 020-1	A	LS	Tilsiter	460 080-5	R	BE	
460 021-9	A	LS	Milch	460 081-3	R	BE	
460 022-7	A	LS		460 082-1	R	BE	
460 023-5	A	LS		460 083-9	R	BE	
460 024-3	R	LS	Rheintal	460 084-7	A	BE	
460 025-0	R	LS	Striegel	460 085-4	R	BE	
460 026-8	R	LS	Fricktal	460 086-2	R	BE	
460 027-6	R	LS	Joggeli	460 087-0	R	BE	Säuliamt
460 028-4	R	LS	Seetal	460 088-8	R	BE	Helvetia
460 029-2	R	LS	Eulach	460 089-6	R	BE	Freiamt
460 030-0	R	LS	Säntis	460 090-4	R	BE	Goffersberg
460 031-8	R	LS	Chaumont	460 091-2	R	BE	
460 032-6	A	LS	Leutschenbach II	460 092-0	R	BE	
460 033-4	A	LS	Ascolino	460 093-8	R	BE	
460 034-2	A	LS		460 094-6	R	BE	Rätia
460 035-9	R	LS		460 095-3	R	BE	
460 036-7	R	LS		460 096-1	R	BE	Furttal
460 037-5	A	LS		460 097-9	R	BE	Studenland
460 038-3	R	BE	Hauenstein	460 098-7	R	BE	Balsberg
460 039-1	R	BE		460 099-5	R	ZU	Bodensee
460 040-9	R	BE	Napf	460 100-1	R	ZU	Tösstal
460 041-7	R	BE	Mendrisiotto	460 101-9	R	ZU	Bözberg
460 042-5	R	BE	Albis	460 102-7	R	ZU	Lägern
460 043-3	R	BE	Dreispitz	460 103-5	R	ZU	Heitersberg
460 044-1	R	BE	Zugerland	460 104-3	R	ZU	Toggenburg
460 045-8	R	BE	Rigi	460 105-0	R	ZU	Fürstenland
460 046-6	R	BE	Polmengo	460 106-8	R	ZU	Munot
460 047-4	R	BE	Maderanertal	460 107-6	R	ZU	Glärnisch
460 048-2	R	BE	Züri Wyland	460 108-4	R	ZU	Engiadina
460 049-0	R	BE	Pfaffensteil	460 109-2	R	ZU	Alpstein
460 050-8	R	BE	Züspa	460 110-0	R	ZU	Mariaberg
460 051-6	R	BE	Staffelegg	460 111-8	R	ZU	Kempt
460 052-4	R	BE	Eigenamt	460 112-6	R	ZU	Thurtal
460 053-2	R	BE	Suhrental	460 113-4	R	ZU	Irchel
460 054-0	R	BE		460 114-2	R	ZU	Landuf Landab
460 055-7	R	BE	Lillehammer	460 115-9	R	ZU	Heidiland
460 056-5	R	BE		460 116-7	R	ZU	Ostschweiz
460 057-3	R	BE		460 117-5	R	ZU	Zürichsee
460 058-1	R	BE		460 118-3	R	ZU	
460 059-9	R	BE					

1.4. ELECTRIC SHUNTING LOCOMOTIVES

CLASS Ee3/3   C

The first production electric shunters of the SBB, developed from the Ee3/4 of 1923 (now withdrawn). As with the subsequent variations, they have a single motor geared to a layshaft and driving through a jackshaft and coupling rods. However, unlike later Ee3/3, these locomotives have a cab at one end, and a shunter's platform at the other.

Built: 1928.
Builder-Mech. Parts: SLM.
Builder-Elec. Parts: BBC.
Traction Motors: 1 single phase frame mounted with jackshaft/side rod drive.
One Hour Rating: 428 kW.
Maximum Tractive Effort: 88 kN.
Driving Wheel Dia.: 1040 mm.
Weight: 45 tonnes.
Overall Length: 9.06 m.
Max. Speed: 40 km/h.
New Class No.: 930.

16313	**P**	GE	16315	**P**	BN	16319	**P**	LZ
16314	**P**	LS	16316	**P**	BN	16324	**P**	BE

16325	**P**	RS
16326	**P**	RS

CLASS Ee3/3   C

A development of the previous class, with a centre cab and a shunter's platform at one end.

Built: 1930–1.
Builder-Mech. Parts: SLM.
Builder-Elec. Parts: BBC.
Traction Motors: 1 single phase frame mounted with jackshaft/side rod drive.
One Hour Rating: 428 kW.
Maximum Tractive Effort: 88 kN.
Driving Wheel Dia.: 1040 mm.
Weight: 45 tonnes.
Overall Length: 9.15 m (9.894 m *).
Max. Speed: 40 km/h.
New Class No.: 930.
* Rebuilt with extended buffer beams for fitting of auto couplers.

16331	**R**	LS	16337	**R**	BI	16342	**P**	BE	16347	**P**	ZU
16332	**P**	LS	16338	**P**	BI	16343	**P**	BE	16348	**R**	ZU
16333	**P**	LS	16339	**R**	BI	16344	**P**	ER	16349	**P**	BR
16334	**R**	LS	16340	**R**	* BI	16345	**P**	ER	16350	**P**	BR
16335	**R**	BI	16341	**P**	BI	16346	**P**	ER			

CLASS Ee3/3   C

This development of the standard electric shunter has a centre cab, and shunter's platforms at both ends.

Built: 1932–47.
Builder-Mech. Parts: SLM.
Builder-Elec. Parts: BBC (BBC/MFO/SAAS*).
Traction Motors: 1 single phase frame mounted with jackshaft/side rod drive.
One Hour Rating: 428 kW (502 kW*).
Maximum Tractive Effort: 88 kN (98 kN).
Driving Wheel Dia.: 1040 mm.
Weight: 45 tonnes (39 tonnes*).
Overall Length: 9.75 m (9.51 m *).
Max. Speed: 40 km/h (50 km/h*).
New Class No.: 930.

16351	**R**	ER	16353	**R**	BE	16355	**R**	WT	16357	**R**	WT
16352	**R**	OL	16354	**R**	ZU	16356	**P**	ZU	16358	**P**	WT

16359	R	RS	16372	R	LS	16390	R	BN	16403	R	LZ
16360	R	RS	16373	R	LS	16391	R	BS	16404	P	LZ
16361	P	RS	16374	R	LS	16392	R	BS	16405	P	LZ
16362	P	WT	16375	R	LS	16393	R	BS	16406	P	LZ
16363	P	WT	16376	R	LS	16394	P	OL	16407	P	LZ
16364	P	WT	16381	R	BS	16395	R	OL	16408	P	LZ
16365	P	WT	16382	R	BI	16396	R	OL	16409	R	LZ
16366	R	BI	16383	P	BI	16397	R	OL	16410	P	LZ
16367	P	BR	16385	R	BI	16398	P	OL	16411	P	LZ
16368	P	BR	16386	P	LS	16399	P	OL	16412	P	LZ
16369	R	BR	16387	R	BN	16400	P	OL	16413	R	LZ
16370	R	LS	16388	R	BN	16401	P	OL	16414	P	LZ
16371	R	LS	16389	R	BN	16402	R	OL			

CLASS Ee3/3   C

The final development of the Ee3/3.

Built: 1951–66.
Builder-Mech. Parts: SLM.
Builder-Elec. Parts: BBC/MFO/SAAS.
Traction Motors: 1 single phase frame mounted with jackshaft/side rod drive.
One Hour Rating: 502 kW.
Maximum Tractive Effort: 118 kN.
Driving Wheel Dia.: 1040 mm.
Weight: 45 tonnes (44 tonnes*).
Overall Length: 9.51 m.
Max. Speed: 45 km/h.
New Class No.: 930.

16421	R		LS	16431	R		ZU	16441	R	*	BE	16451	R	*	BN
16422	P		LS	16432	R		ZU	16442	P	*	OL	16452	R	*	BN
16423	R		LS	16433	R		ZU	16443	R	*	OL	16453	R	*	BI
16424	R		BN	16434	R		ZU	16444	R	*	OL	16454	P	*	BI
16425	R		BN	16435	R		ZU	16445	P	*	OL	16455	R	*	BI
16426	P		RS	16436	R		ZU	16446	P	*	OL	16456	P	*	BI
16427	R		RS	16437	R		ZU	16447	R	*	OL	16457	P	*	BR
16428	R		RS	16438	R		ZU	16448	P	*	OL	16458	P	*	BR
16429	P		RS	16439	R		ZU	16449	P	*	LZ	16459	P	*	BR
16430	P		RS	16440	R		ZU	16450	R	*	LZ	16460	P	*	BR

CLASS Ee3/3^{II}   C

The dual-voltage version of the Ee3/3, which can be used under the 25 kV 50 Hz wires of the SNCF. 16501–6 are used around Basel where the SNCF a.c. electrification extends into the SBB station. 16511–9 were built for the SNCF (C 20151–9) for use around Basel, but were sold to the SBB in 1971. Their dual-voltage capability sees little use at present but the mw facility is put to use for yard shunting. There are detail differences within the class.

Built: 1957–63
Builder-Mech. Parts: SLM.
Builder-Elec. Parts: BBC*, MFO†, SAAS (remainder).
Traction Motors: 1 single phase (AC†) frame mounted with jackshaft/side rod drive.
One Hour Rating: 506 kW (525 kW†).
Maximum Tractive Effort: 132 kN (128 kN†).
Driving Wheel Dia.: 1040 mm.
Weight: 46 tonnes (52 tonnes m).
Overall Length: 9.510 m (9.42 m m).
Max. Speed: 45 km/h.
System: 15 kV, $16^2/_3$ Hz/25kV 50Hz.
New Class No.: 932.

m mw fitted.   † a.c. traction motors.

16501	P	*	BS	16505	P		BS	16512	R	m	BI	16515	R	m	BN
16503	P	†	BS	16506	P		BS	16513	P	m	BI	16516	R	m	BR
16504	P	†	BS	16511	P	m	BN	16514	R	m	BI	16517	R	m	BR

16518 **R** m LS | 16519 **R** m LS |

CLASS Ee3/3^{IV} & Ee 934 C

The four-voltage version of the Ee3/3, for use at border stations. It differs from the others in having two d.c. motors, one geared directly to the centre and one to the end axle, there being no intermediate jackshaft. They are to be found at Genève where the SNCF 1500 V d.c. system extends into the station, and at Chiasso for use under the FS 3000 V d.c. wires. The 25 kV facility is not used at present. This class is in the process of being modernised and renumbered.

Built: 1962–3.
Builder-Mech. Parts: SLM.
Builder-Elec. Parts: SAAS.
Traction Motors: 2 d.c. series wound, axle suspended with side rod drive.
One Hour Rating: 390 kW.
Maximum Tractive Effort: 118 kN.
Driving Wheel Dia.: 1040 mm.
Weight: 48 tonnes.
Overall Length: 10.02 m.
Max. Speed: 60 km/h.
System: 1500 V d.c./3000 V d.c./15 kV $16^2/_3$ Hz/25 kV 50 Hz.
New Class No.: 934.

	(16551) **P**	GE	934 555-5	(16555) **R**	GE	934 558-8	(16558) **R**	BE
934 552-1	(16552) **R**	GE	934 556-2	(16556) **R**	GE		(16559) **P**	BE
934 553-9	(16553) **R**	GE	934 557-0	(16557) **R**	BE		(16560) **P**	BE
934 554-7	(16554) **R**	GE						

CLASS Ee6/6 C–C

A design for heavy yard shunting, effectively a pair of Ee3/3 combined as one loco. Both locos are used in Muttenz Yard near Basel.

Built: 1952.
Builder-Mech. Parts: SLM.
Builder-Elec. Parts: BBC/SAAS.
Traction Motors: 2 single phase bogie mounted with jackshaft/side rod drive.
One Hour Rating: 1008 kW.
Maximum Tractive Effort: 235 kN.
Driving Wheel Dia.: 1040 mm.
Weight: 90 tonnes.
Overall Length: 14.84 m.
Max. Speed: 45 km/h.
New Class No.: 961.

16801 **R**   BS | 16802 **P**   BS |

CLASS Ee6/6^{II} C–C

A modern design of heavy yard loco which replaced some converted 'Crocodiles' previously used for such work; fitted with 3-phase traction motors supplied through an inverter. They can be radio controlled and are to be found in the yards at Limmattal (Zürich), Buchs, Muttenz (Basel), Denges (Lausanne) and Bern.

Built: 1980.
Builder-Mech. Parts: SLM.
Builder-Elec. Parts: BBC.
Traction Motors: 6 3-phase axle hung, nose suspended.
One Hour Rating: 730 kW.
Maximum Tractive Effort: 360 kN.
Driving Wheel Dia.: 1260 mm.
Weight: 111 tonnes.
Overall Length: 17.40 m.
Max. Speed: 85 km/h.
New Class No.: 962.

16811 **P**	ZU		16813 **P**	ZU		16815 **P**	ZU		16817 **P**	LS
16812 **P**	RS		16814 **P**	RS		16816 **P**	BS		16818 **P**	LS

▲ Te III No. 138 shunts a short train at Weinfelden on 15th April 1992. These are now the oldest SBB tractors in service.   **Chris Booth**

▼ Tem III No. 277 at Biasca in March 1992. The Tem series have a diesel engine to facilitate shunting non-electrified sidings.   **David A. Haydock**

▲ Tm ¹ No. 431 stabled at Mullheim Wigoltingen on 15th April 1992. Small diesel tractors are now being withdrawn. **Chris Booth**

▼ Em No. 831.002 on Bern Depot on 24th December 1994 is one of three prototypes for a new generation of diesel shunters. **C.R. Appleby**

▲ RBe 4/4 No. 1402 arriving at Luzern on 2nd August 1994. The reflective stripes are to improve visibility on the roadside Seetalbahn. **T.M. Wallis**

▼ Bem No. 550.001 at Genève on a La Plaine train on 24th December 1994. These light railcars operate the service under the 1500V d.c. **C.R. Appleby**

▲ RBDe No. 560.114 at Cossonay on a Lausanne to Vallorbe service on 28th April 1995 is a 'Kolibri' unit, the latest design for local services. **John C. Baker**

▼ Ae 6/6 No. 11472 'BRIG' at Montreux in July 1992. Built for the mountain lines, this class has now been demoted to secondary work. **Eric Sawford**

▲ Re 6/6 No. 11625 'OENSINGEN' at Arth Goldau on 12th September 1995. A class built for mountain lines.   **T.N. Hall**

▼ Ee 6/6 ᴵᴵ No. 16818 shunting in Renens Yard in August 1994 is a design for heavy yard work.
David A. Haydock

▲ Re No. 450.079 at Rapperswil on 16th September 1995. These locomotives work push-pull with double deck stock on the Zürich S-Bahn.   **T.N. Hall**

▼ Re No. 460.019 at St Saphorin on the Genève Aéroport to Milano 'Cisalpin' IC Train is an an example of the latest generation of SBB elecrics.   **John C. Baker**

▲ Bm 6/6 No. 18502 on Basel Wolf depot in September 1996. These locomotives are used on shunting and trip work.   **David A. Haydock**

▼ HGe 101 967-8 at Luzern on an Interlaken train on 10th September 1995 is the normal power for through trains on the metre gauge Brünig line.   **T.N. Hall**

▲ De 110 005-0 at Interlaken Ost on 19th February 1993. Formerly rack fitted, the electric baggage
vans have been rebuilt for push-pull work on the adhesion sections of the metre gauge Buünig line.
Pete Moody

▼ SBB Brünig line Deh 120 012-0 at Luzern metre gauge depot on 23rd February 1996. An unrebuilt
survivor from the Brünig electrification now in reserve.   **Ray Smith**

▲ Re 4/4 No. 183 'KANDERSTEG' waits to leave Interlaken Ost on an express in July 1990. This is the most numerous BLS type.   **Eric Sawford**

▼ Ae 4/4 No. 251 arrives at Interlaken Ost on 19th February 1993. This was the first Swiss main line electric loco with all axles powered, and is now an historic locomotive.   **Pete Moody**

▲ BLS Ae 8/8 No. 271 between duties on Brig depot on 17th April 1992. These twin unit locomotives are now in reserve.   **Chris Booth**

▼ BN RBDe 4/4 No. 742 propels a train into Spiez with driving trailer ABt 996 leading. These modern units work most BLS local services.   **T.N. Hall**

▲ BLS ABDe 4/8 No. 746 arrives at Interlaken Ost on19th February 1993. These units are due for replacement with new low-floor railcars.   **Pete Moody**

▼ BLS Tm 72 stands at Interlaken West on 23rd July 1991. These tractors are normally used by the permanent way department.   **Bob Sweet**

▲ RhB Gem 2/4 No. 211 at Disentis 17th February 1993. This shunter is rebuilt from an early electric locomotive, and has been fitted with an auxiliary diesel engine.   **Pete Moody**

▼ RhB Gm 4/4 No. 243 at Chur Sand depot on 6th April 1996. These locomotives were purchased to operate ballast trains.   **C.R. Appleby**

▲ RhB Ge 6/6 No. 411 at Bergun 7/94 on a freight. These 'Baby Crocodiles' are now in reserve and see little use. **Eric Sawford**

▼ RhB Ge 4/4 III No. 648 'SUSCH' at Filisur on 6th April 1996. These modern 3-phase locomotives now work most Chur–St Moritz expresses. **C.R. Appleby**

RhB Ge 4/4 ¹ No. 607 'SURSELVA' at Filisur on 6th April 1996 on a Davos train. These locomotives have been rebuilt with new cabs and push-pull equipment for working local trains.

C.R. Appleby

▲ RhB ABe 4/4 Nos. 504 + 501 at Samedan on 6th April 1996. These elderly railcars all work in this area. **C.R. Appleby**

▼ RhB ABe 4/4 Nos. 30 + 34 at Chur on 16th February 1993. These railcars date from the opening of the Berninabahn, and are now reserve power on that line and the Chur–Arosa. **Pete Moody**

▲ RhB ABe 4/4 No. 42 on Poschiaro Depot on 6th April 1996. These railcars, together with the 51 series, operate most Berninabahn services.   **C.R. Appleby**

▼ RhB No. 56 on Tirano train. Bernina Diavalozza July 1994. These are the newest Berninabahn railcars.   **Eric Sawford**

16819 **P** LS | 16820 **P** BN |

CLASS Eem6/6 (Em6/6*) C+C

An unusual design of electro-diesel shunter, comprising two close coupled Ee3/3[IV] chassis, with the cab and electrical gear mounted on one and a diesel engine on the other. However, starting with 17006 in 1984, the class is being converted to diesel electric. They are used for yard shunting in Basel and Chiasso.

Built: 1970–1.
Builder-Mech. Parts: SLM.
Builder-Elec. Parts: SAAS.
Traction Motors: 4 d.c. series wound, axle suspended with side rod drive.
One Hour Rating: 393 kW (diesel) 780 kW (electric).
Maximum Tractive Effort: 235 kN.
Driving Wheel Dia.: 1040 mm.
Weight: 104 tonnes.
Overall Length: 17.875 m.
Max. Speed: 65 km/h.
Engine: SLM 12YD20 TrTH of 895 kW.
New Class No.: .

17001 **P** * BE	17003 **P** BE	17005 **P** * BS	17006 **P** * BS
17002 **P** * BE	17004 **P** * BS		

1.5. DIESEL LOCOMOTIVES

Bm4/4 CLASS   Bo–Bo

Locos for shunting and trip working on non-electrified tracks.

Built: 1960-70.
Builder-Mech. Parts: SLM.
Builder-Elec. Parts: SAAS.
Engine: SLM 12YD20TrTH of 895 kW.
Transmission: Electric.
Maximum Tractive Effort: 216 kN.
Driving Wheel Dia.: 1040 mm.
Weight: 72 tonnes.
Overall Length: 12.65 m. (13.21 m*, 13.15 m†).
New Class No.: 840.

* Rebuilt with extended buffer beams for additional shunter protection.

18401	P	*	BE	18410	P	LS	18420	P	RS	18429	R	†	ZU	18438	R	†	BS
18402	P		BE	18411	P	BI	18421	P	ZU	18430	R	†	BE	18439	R	†	BS
18403	P		BE	18412	P	GE	18422	R	ZU	18431	P	†	BE	18440	R	†	BS
18404	P		BE	18413	P	BI	18423	P	ZU	18432	R	†	OL	18441	R	†	BS
18405	P		BE	18414	P	BN	18424	R	ZU	18433	R	†	BS	18442	R	†	BS
18406	P		BE	18415	P	BN	18425	P	WT	18434	R	†	BS	18443	P	†	BS
18407	P		GE	18416	P	BI	18426	R	WT	18435	P	†	BS	18444	R	†	BS
18408	P		GE	18418	P	RS	18427	P	† ZU	18436	P	†	BS	18445	P	†	BS
18409	P		LS	18419	P	WT	18428	P	† ZU	18437	P	†	BS	18446	R	†	BS

Bm4/4ᴵᴵ CLASS   Bo–Bo

The survivor of pair of elderly diesels which have had a varied life, being moved around as electrification progressed. Nowadays it sees little use, being retained as a museum loco.

Built: 1939.
Builder-Mech. Parts: SLM.
Builder-Elec. Parts: BBC.
Engine: Sulzer of 820 kW.
Transmission: Electric.
Maximum Tractive Effort: 112 kN.
Driving Wheel Dia.: 1040 mm.
Weight: 66 tonnes.
Overall Length: 14.90 m.
Max. Speed: 75 km/h.
New Class No.: 841 & 842.

18451 **G**   OL

Bm6/6 CLASS   Co–Co

Centre cab diesels used for yard shunting and trip working. Each bonnet contains its own engine and generator set.

Built: 1954-61.
Builder-Mech. Parts: SLM.
Builder-Elec. Parts: BBC/SAAS.
Engine: Two Sulzer 6LDA25 of 635 kW each.
Transmission: Electric.
Maximum Tractive Effort: 334 kN.
Driving Wheel Dia.: 1040 mm.
Weight: 106 tonnes.
Overall Length: 17.00 m. (17.56 m*).
Max. Speed: 75 km/h.
New Class No.: 861.

18501	P	BS	18502	R	BS	18503	R	BS	18504	R	BS	18505	R	BE

18506 **P**	BE	18508 **R**	BE	18510 **P**	BR	18512 **P**	BN	18514 **P**	WT
18507 **R**	BE	18509 **P**	LS	18511 **P**	RS	18513 **R** * WT			

Am6/6 CLASS   Co–Co

Heavy shunting locos, built specifically for use in the new Limmattal Yard near Zürich. They have three phase traction motors supplied from a fixed frequency alternator via frequency conversion equipment.

Built: 1976.
Builder-Mech. Parts: Thyssen Henschel.
Builder-Elec. Parts: BBC.
Engine: SEMT.
Transmission: Electric.
Maximum Tractive Effort: 393 kN.
Driving Wheel Dia.: 1260 mm.
Weight: 111 tonnes.
Overall Length: 17.40 m.
Max. Speed: 85 km/h.
New Class No.: 863.

18521 **P**	ZU	18523 **P**	ZU	18524 **P**	ZU	18525 **P**	ZU	18526 **P**	ZU
18522 **P**	ZU								

Em3/3 CLASS   C

General purpose shunting locos found throughout the system.

Built: 1959* 1962-3.
Builder-Mech. Parts: SLM.
Builder-Elec. Parts: BBC/SAAS.
Engine: SLM 6VD20TrTH of 450 kW. (SLM 8YD20TrD of 450 kW*).
Transmission: Electric.
Maximum Tractive Effort: 124 kN (118 kN*).
Driving Wheel Dia.: 1040 mm.
Weight: 49 tonnes.
Overall Length: 10.02 m.
Max. Speed: 65 km/h.
New Class No.: 830.

18801 **P** * ZU	18810 **P**	BS	18818 **P**	BE	18826 **P**	OL	18834 **P**	RS
18802 **P** * ZU	18811 **P**	BS	18819 **P**	BE	18827 **P**	OL	18835 **P**	RS
18804 **P** * ZU	18812 **P**	BS	18820 **P**	BE	18828 **P**	ZU	18836 **P**	RS
18805 **P** * ZU	18813 **P**	BS	18821 **R**	LZ	18829 **P**	WT	18837 **P**	BN
18806 **P** * ZU	18814 **P**	BS	18822 **P**	LZ	18830 **P**	WT	18838 **P**	BN
18807 **R** BS	18815 **P**	BS	18823 **P**	OL	18831 **P**	WT	18839 **P**	GE
18808 **P** BS	18816 **P**	BS	18824 **P**	OL	18832 **P**	WT	18840 **P**	GE
18809 **P** BS	18817 **P**	BS	18825 **P**	OL	18833 **P**	RS	18841 **P**	LS

Em 831 CLASS C   o

These are the prototypes of a new generation of diesel shunters.

Built: 1992.
Builder-Mech. Parts: RACO.
Builder-Elec. Parts: ABB.
Engine: Cummins of 900 kW.
Transmission: Electric.
Maximum Tractive Effort: kN.
Driving Wheel Dia.:   mm.
Weight: 54 tonnes.
Overall Length: 9.0 m.
Max. Speed: 80 km/h.

831 000-5	**R**	OL	831 001-3	**R**	BE	831 002-1	**R**	OL

Am 841 CLASS   Bo–Bo

A new design of diesel locomotive for use on shunting and trip work. Similar to RENFE 311 Class.

Built: 1996-97.
Builder-Mech. Parts: SLM/GECAE.
Builder-Elec. Parts: GECA.
Engine: One MTU V8 of 920 kW.
Transmission: Electric.
Maximum Tractive Effort: .
Driving Wheel Dia.: .
Weight: 72 tonnes.
Overall Length: 14.16 m.
Max. Speed: 80 km/h.

841 000-3	R	GE	841 010-2	R	RS	841 020-1	R	BS	841 030-0	R
841 001-1	R	GE	841 011-0	R	OL	841 021-9	R	ZU	841 031-8	R
841 002-9	R	GE	841 012-8	R	RS	841 022-7	R	ZU	841 032-6	R
841 003-7	R	GE	841 013-6	R	BE	841 023-5	R	BE	841 033-4	R
841 004-5	R	OL	841 014-4	R	RS	841 024-3	R	LZ	841 034-2	R
841 005-2	R	BS	841 015-1	R	LS	841 025-0	R	LS	841 035-9	R
841 006-0	R	BS	841 016-9	R	LS	841 026-8	R	LS	841 036-7	R
841 007-8	R	LS	841 017-7	R	OL	841 027-6	R	WT	841 037-5	R
841 008-6	R	LS	841 018-5	R	LZ	841 028-4	R	ZU	841 038-3	R
841 009-4	R	LS	841 019-3	R	RS	841 029-2	R	LZ	841 039-1	R

Am 842 CLASS   B–B

A pair of diesel locomotives purchased in 1993/4 from permanent way contractor Sersa AG. They continue to be used on ballast trains.

Built: 1992-93.
Builder: MaK.
Engine:
Transmission: Hydraulic.
Maximum Tractive Effort: .
Driving Wheel Dia.: .
Weight: 60 tonnes.
Overall Length: 12.50 m.
Max. Speed: 80 km/h.

842 000-2	R	ZU	842 001-0	R	ZU	

1.6. DEPARTMENTAL LOCOMOTIVES

Several former electric locos remain in use as heating units for carriage preheating and other purposes.

HEATING UNITS

Class Ae4/7

10977   Basel Wolf
10983   Genève
10989   Basel Wolf

SNOWPLOUGHS

Xrote	50	SLM/MFO	1944	MR	Meiringen
Xrotm	51	Beil	1986	MR	Meiringen
Xrotm	95	Beilhack	1982		
Xrotm	96	Beilhack	1982		
Xrotm	97	SLM/SAAS/Beilhack	1967	ER	Erstfeld
Xrotm	98	SLM/SAAS/Beilhack	1967	ER	Biasca
Xrote	99	SLM/MFO	1946	LS	Lausanne
Xtm	101	RACO/Beilhack/Deutz	1969	MR	Meiringen
Xtm	102	RACO/Beilhack/Deutz	1972	ER	Airolo
Xtm	103	RACO/Beilhack/Deutz	1972	LZ	Konolfingen
Xtm	104	RACO/Beilhack/Deutz	1971	ZU	Ziegelbrücke
Xtm	105	RACO/Beilhack/Deutz	1972	WT	Wetzikon
Xtm	106	RACO/Beilhack/Deutz	1972	BR	Brig/Brigue
Xtm	107	RACO/Beilhack/Deutz	1972	BI	Neuchâtel
Xtm	108	RACO/Beilhack/Deutz	1972	LS	Cossonay
Xtm	109	RACO/Beilhack/Deutz	1972	BI	Neuchâtel
Xtm	116	RACO/Beilhack/Deutz	1979	LS	

All the above are rotaries, the Xtm & Xrotm being self propelled, and the others requiring propulsion by a loco. The MR based snowploughs are metre gauge

1.7. BRÜNIG LINE

Although Switzerland possesses a considerable mileage of narrow gauge, only one such line is operated by the SBB. This is the metre gauge Brünig Line running from Interlaken to Luzern. The section between Meiringen and Giswil over the Brünig Pass has stretches of Riggenbach rack. Hence most electric locos, and two of the tractors, are fitted for rack and adhesion operation.

1.7.1. ELECTRIC LOCOMOTIVES
CLASS HGe 101   Bo–Bo

These eight locos are based on prototypes 1951–2 (now sold to the FO) to enable all through trains to be worked by this type of loco.

Built: 1989–90.
Builder-Mech. Parts: SLM.
Builder-Elec. Parts: ABB.
Traction Motors:
One Hour Rating: kW.
Maximum Tractive Effort: kN.
Driving Wheel Dia.:   mm.
Weight: tonnes.
Overall Length: .   m.
Max. Speed: km/h.

101961-1 **R**	MR	HORW	101965-2 **R**	MR	LUNGERN
101962-9 **R**	MR	HERGISWIL	101966-0 **R**	MR	HASLIBERG-BRÜNIG
101963-7 **R**	MR	ALPNACH	101967-8 **R**	MR	BRIENZ
101964-5 **R**	MR	SACHSEN	101968-6 **R**	MR	RINEGENBERG

1.7.2. ELECTRIC RAILCARS
CLASS De 110   Bo–Bo

These motor luggage vans are rebuilt from those dating from the electrification of the line (see class Deh 120). The rack equipmenet has been removed, and push-pull equipment fitted. They are used on local trains on the adhesion sections (Luzern to Giswil and Interlaken to Meiringen).

Built: 1941–2, rebuilt 1987–93.
Builder-Mech. Parts: SLM.
Builder-Elec. Parts: MFO†, SAAS*.
One Hour Rating: 930 kW.
Maximum Tractive Effort: 102 kN.
Driving Wheel Dia.: 900 mm.
Weight: 40 tonnes.
Overall Length: 14.60 m.
Max. Speed: 75 km/h.
Former Class: Deh 4/4.

110000-7 **R**	* MR	110002-3 **R**	† MR	110004-9 **R**	† MR
110001-5 **R**	* MR	110003-1 **R**	† MR	110005-6 **R**	* MR

CLASS De 120   Bo–2–Bo

These motor luggage vans were built for the electrification of the line. On the rack sections heavy trains needed to be double, or even triple headed. The outer bogies are used during adhesion working, while on the rack sections the centr rack fitted bogie provides most of the power. Of the sixteen examples built, 6 have been rebuilt for adhesion only operation (sse class De 110), 2 have been sold to the LSE (also rebuilt to adhesion only) and 3 have been withdrawn. The survivors are in reserve for use at times of heavy traffic.

Built: 1941–2.
Builder-Mech. Parts: SLM.
Builder-Elec. Parts: BBC (MFO†, SAAS*).
One Hour Rating: 930 kW.

Maximum Tractive Effort: 102 kN (adhesion), 216 kN (rack).
Driving Wheel Dia.: 900 mm. **Pony Wheel Dia.:** 710 mm.
Weight: 54 tonnes.
Overall Length: 14.60 m.
Max. Speed: 75 km/h (adhesion), 33km/h (rack).
Former Class: Deh 4/4.

120006-2	**R**		MR		120010-4	**R**	† MR		
120008-8	**R**		MR		120011-2	**R**	MR		

120012-0 **G** * MR

1.7.3. SHUNTING TRACTORS

CLASS Te^I   B

The narrow gauge equivalent of the 1–60 series.

Built: 1941.
Builder-Mech. Parts: SLM.
Builder-Elec. Parts: MFO.
Traction Motors: .
One Hour Rating: 95 kW.
Maximum Tractive Effort: kN.
Driving Wheel Dia.:   mm.
Weight: 13 tonnes.
Overall Length: 5.8 m.
Max. Speed: 60 km/h.
New Class No.:

Number	Depot	Station		Number	Depot	Station
198	LZ	Hergiswil		199	LZ	Sarnen

CLASS Te^{III}   Bo

The narrow gauge equivalent of the 139–179 series.

Built: 1962.
Builder-Mech. Parts: SLM.
Builder-Elec. Parts: MFO.
Traction Motors: .
One Hour Rating: 260 kW.
Maximum Tractive Effort: kN.
Driving Wheel Dia.: mm.
Weight: 26 tonnes.
Overall Length: 6.05 m.
Max. Speed: 60 km/h.
New Class No.:

Number	Depot	Station		Number	Depot	Station
201	LZ	Luzern		203	MR	Meiringen
202	LZ	Giswil				

CLASS Tm^{II}   B

The narrow gauge equivalent of the 601–853 series; in fact 980/4 are rebuilds from 709 & 828 in 1987 & 1983 respectively.

Built: 1959–66.
Builder/Constructeur: RACO.
Engine/Moteur: Saurer C615D of 70 kW.
Transmission: Mechanical/Mécanique.
Maximum Tractive Effort: kN.
Driving Wheel Dia.: 600 mm.
New Class No.:
Weight: 10 tonnes.
Overall Length: 5.15 m.
Max. Speed: 45 km/h.

* Fitted for snowplough use.

Number	Depot	Station
596	LZ	*Reserve*
597	MR	Brienz
598	MR	*Reserve*
980	MR	Meiringen

Number	Depot	Station
981 *	MR	Meiringen
982 *	MR	Meiringen
983	MR	Meiringen
984	LZ	Luzern

CLASS Tm^{III} B

Purchased second hand from SWEG (Germany) in 1982.

Built: 1957.
Builder/Constructeur: Gmeinder.
Engine/Moteur: Saurer of 165 kW.
Transmission: Hydraulic.
Maximum Tractive Effort: kN.
Driving Wheel Dia.:   mm.
New Class No.:
Weight: 24 tonnes.
Overall Length: 7.23 m.
Max. Speed: 60 km/h.

Number	Depot	Station
599	LZ	Alpnach Dorf

CLASS Tmh   B

The rack and adhesion version of the Tm^{II} class for use on works trains in the Brünig Pass.

Built: 1965.
Builder/Constructeur: RACO/VON ROLL.
Engine/Moteur: Saurer.
Transmission: Hydraulic.
Maximum Tractive Effort: kN.
Driving Wheel Dia.:   mm.
New Class No.:
Weight: 12 tonnes.
Overall Length: 5.35 m.
Max. Speed: 40 km/h (adhesion), 27 km/h (rack).

Number	Depot	Station
985	LZ	Luzern

Number	Depot	Station
986	MR	Meiringen

2. BLS GROUP OF RAILWAYS

Bern Lötschberg Simplon (230, 300, 310)	**BLS**
Bern Neuenberg (220, 296)	**BN**
Gürbetal Bern Schwarzenburg (297, 298)	**GBS**
Moutier–Lengnau Bahn (230)	**MLB**
Spiez Erlenbach Zweisimmen (320)	**SEZ**

The BLS Group of railways is second only in route mileage to the RhB among the Swiss Private Railways, and the only one with through express and international services. The Lötschberg Pass forms part of the Bern to Milano main line, and extensive joint through working occurs with the SBB. The railway also provides the principal services to Interlaken, operates frequent suburban services from Bern, and the branch to Zweisimmen connects with the MOB. The MLB is isolated from the rest of the BLS system, and is operated by the SBB. It is expected that the subsidiary companies will be absorbed into the BLS proper in the near future.

Electrical system: 15 kV 16$^2/_3$ Hz.
Depots: Spiez, Bern Holligen, Brig, Schwarzenberg, Erlenbach, Zweisimmen.
Gauge: 1435 mm.

Note: Unless shown as belonging to one of the three subsidiary companies (BN, GBS, SEZ), all motive power is owned by the BLS proper. In fact, much of the stock is in common usage throughout the system.
All motive power is allocated to Spiez, the works and principal depot.

Liveries:

B	Blue & cream
G	Green
N	Brown

2.1. ELECTRIC LOCOMOTIVES

CLASS Re4/4   Bo–Bo

The standard BLS electric loco, found everywhere on all types of work.

Built: 1964–83.
Builder-Mech. Parts: SLM.
Builder-Elec. Parts: BBC.
Traction Motors: 4 d.c. type, fully suspended with BBC spring drive.
One Hour Rating: 4990 kW.
Maximum Tractive Effort: 314 kN.
Driving Wheel Dia.: 1250 mm.
Weight: 80 tonnes.
Overall Length: 15.47 (15.10 m *).
Max. Speed: 140 km/h.
New Numbers: Re 425.161–195.

All locos mw and push-pull fitted.

Nr.	Liv.	Co.	Name	Nr.	Liv.	Co.	Name
161	N	*	DOMODOSSOLA	178	N	GBS	SCHWARZENBURG
162	N	*	COURT	179	N	BN	BERN
163	N	*	GRENCHEN	180	N	BN	VILLE DE NEUCHÂTEL
164	N	*	LENGNAU	181	N		INTERLAKEN
165	N	*	MOUTIER	182	N		KANDERGRUND
166	N	*	AESCHI	183	N		KANDERSTEG
167	N	*	AUSSERBERG	184	N		KRATTIGEN
168	N	*	BALTSCHIEDER	185	N		LALDEN
169	N	*	BÖNIGEN	186	N		LEISSIGEN
170	N	*	BRIG-GLIS	187	N		MUND
171	N	*	DÄRLIGEN	188	N		NATERS
172	N	*	EGGERBERG	189	N		NIEDERGESTELN
173	N	*	LÖTSCHENTAL	190	N		RARON
174	N		FRUTIGEN	191	N		REICHENBACH
175	N		GAMPEL	192	N		SPIEZ
176	N		HOHTENN	193	N		STEG
177	N	SEZ	ZWEISIMMEN	194	N		THUN

195 **N**   UNTERSEEN |

CLASS Ae6/8   1Co–Co1

This elderly loco was one of a class of eight built for main line work on the Lötschberg route. It is retained as an historic loco.

Built: 1939.
Builder-Mech. Parts: SLM.
Builder-Elec. Parts: SAAS.
Traction Motors: 12 single phase, fully suspended with SAAS spring drive.
One Hour Rating: 4416 kW.
Maximum Tractive Effort: 353 kN.
Driving Wheel Dia.: 1350 mm.
Pony Wheel Dia.: 950 mm.
Weight: 140 tonnes.
Overall Length: 20.26 m.
Max. Speed: 100 km/h.
New Numbers: Ae 015.205.

Rheostatic brake fitted.

205 **N** |

CLASS Ae4/4   Bo–Bo

A very advanced design at the time of its introduction, this was the first electric type to achieve 1000 h.p. per axle. Now in reserve and due for early withdrawal. Nos. 253–6 have been rebuilt to the Ae8/8 class, detailed next. 251 is now an historic locomotive.

Built: 1944–55.
Builder-Mech. Parts: SLM.
Builder-Elec. Parts: BBC.
Traction Motors: 4 single phase fully suspended with BBC flexible disc drive.
One Hour Rating: 3238 kW.
Maximum Tractive Effort: 235 kN.
Driving Wheel Dia.: 1250 mm.
Weight: 80 tonnes.
Overall Length: 15.60 m.
Max. Speed: 125 km/h.
New Numbers: Ae 415.251–8.

All locos mw and push-pull fitted, rheostatic brake fitted.

251 **N** | 257 **N** | 258 **N** |

CLASS Ae8/8   Bo–Bo+Bo–Bo

These are double locos, in effect a pair of Ae4/4 class permanently coupled, with the cabs at the inner ends removed. 275 is a rebuild of 255–6. Now in reserve and due for early withdrawal.

Built: 1959–63, 1948–52 *.
Builder-Mech. Parts: SLM.
Builder-Elec. Parts: BBC.
Traction Motors: 8 single phase fully suspended with BBC flexible disc drive.
One Hour Rating: 6476 kW.
Maximum Tractive Effort: 471 kN.
Driving Wheel Dia.: 1250 mm.
Weight: 160 tonnes.
Overall Length: 30.23 m.
Max. Speed: 125 km/h.
New Numbers: Ae 485.271–5.

All locos are mw & rheostatic brake fitted.
* Rebuilt 1966 from Ae4/4.

271 **N** | 272 **N** | 273 **N** | 275 **N**

CLASS Ce4/4 B–B

A class built for mixed traffic duties at the time of electrification. The survivors are used on local freight work around Bern & Thun. They were built as 1BB1, rebuilt to BB in the 1950s. An unrebuilt example of the class (307) is an operational preserved loco.

Built: 1920–4, rebuilt 1954–6.
Builder-Mech. Parts: SLM.
Builder-Elec. Parts: BBC.
Traction Motors: 4 single phase bogie mounted with jackshaft/side rod drive.
One Hour Rating: 736 kW.
Maximum Tractive Effort: 108 kN.
Driving Wheel Dia.: 1230 mm.
Weight: 64 tonnes.
Overall Length: 12.34 m.
Max. Speed: 65 km/h.
New Numbers: Ce 015.311–6.

| 311 | N | GBS | | 313 | N | GBS | | 316 | N | | |

CLASS Ee3/3 C

A classic centre-cab jackshaft drive shunter, similar to the SBB locos. Used as station pilot at Spiez.

Built: 1943.
Builder-Mech. Parts: SLM.
Builder-Elec. Parts: SAAS.
Traction Motors: 1 single phase frame mounted with jackshaft/side rod drive.
One Hour Rating: 452 kW.
Maximum Tractive Effort: 88 kN.
Driving Wheel Dia.: 1040 mm.
Weight: 38 tonnes.
Overall Length: 9.2 m.
Max. Speed: 40 km/h.
New Number: Ee 935.401.

| 401 | N | LISI | |

CLASS Eea3/3 C

A new design of electric shunter fitted with auxiliary batteries for use on non-electrified sidings, based on the latest Ee3/3 for the PTT. It operates around Ütendorf.

Built: 1991.
Builder-Mech. Parts: SLM.
Builder-Elec. Parts: ABB.
Traction Motors:
One Hour Rating: kW.
Maximum Tractive Effort: kN.
Driving Wheel Dia.: mm.
Weight: tonnes.
Overall Length: 11.20 m.
Max. Speed: km/h.
New Number: Ee 935.402.

| 402 | N | GBS | |

CLASS Re 465 Bo–Bo

A new class of general purpose locos based on the SBB 460 class. They operate principally on main line services on the Bern–Brig–Domodossola route. 465 009–18 are actually owned by the SBB, but are lettered for and maintained by the BLS.

Built: 1994–7.
Builder-Mech. Parts: SLM.
Builder-Elec. Parts: ABB (001-8), ADtranz (009-18).
Traction Motors: 4 3-phase fully suspended.

One Hour Rating: 7000 kW.
Maximum Tractive Effort: 320 kN.
Driving Wheel Dia.: 1100 mm.
Weight: 82 tonnes.
Overall Length: 18.50 m.
Max. Speed: 230 km/h.

All locos are push-pull & mw fitted (can work with BLS Re4/4, plus SBB Re 460, Re 4/4 II, Re 4/4 III, Re 6/6).

465 001-6	B	Simplon/Sempione	465 010-7	B	Stadt Kanawa	
465 002-4	B	Gornergrat	465 011-5	B		
465 003-2	B	Jungfraujoch-TopofEurope	465 012-3	B	Eurotunnel	
465 004-0	B	Mittelallalin	465 013-1	B		
465 005-7	B	Niesen	465 014-9	B		
465 006-5	B	Lauchernalp-Lötschental	465 015-6	B		
465 007-3	B	Schilthorn-Piz Gloria	465 016-4	B		
465 008-1	B	Niederhorn-Beatenberg	465 017-2	B		
465 009-9	B		465 018-0	B		

2.2. ELECTRIC RAILCARS
RBDe4/4 CLASS

Modern railcars, found on local services throughout the system, particularly in the Bern area. They operate with matching driving and intermediate trailers as 2- and 3-car sets. Fitted with thyristor control.

Built: 1982–92.
Builder-Mech. Parts: SIG/SWS.
Builder-Elec. Parts: BBC (721–738) ABB (739–742).
Traction Motors:
One Hour Rating: 1700 kW.
Maximum Tractive Effort: 186 kN.
Driving Wheel Dia.: 940 mm.
Weight: 69.7 tonnes.
Overall Length: 25.0 m.
Max. Speed: 125 km/h.
Wheel Arrangement: BoBo.
Accommodation: –/55 1T.
New Numbers: RBDe 565.721–42.

721	B		727	B	GBS	733	B	SEZ	738	B	BN			
722	B		728	B	GBS	734	B	GBS	739	B	SEZ			
723	B	SEZ	729	B	GBS	735	B	GBS	740	B	GBS			
724	B	SEZ	730	B	BN	736	B	GBS	741	B	BN			
725	B	GBS	731	B		737	B	BN	742	B	BN			
726	B	GBS	732	B	SEZ									

ABDe4/8 CLASS

Twin units for local services. They normally work with driving trailers as 3-car sets (746–50 have only one driving cab, and thus cannot work as 2-car sets).

Built: 1954, 1957 †, 1964 *.
Builder-Mech. Parts: SIG/BBC/BLS.
Builder-Elec. Parts: SAAS.
Traction Motors:
One Hour Rating: 1176 kW.
Maximum Tractive Effort: 98 kN.
Weight: 85, 90†, 96* tonnes.
Overall Length: 47.465 m, 47.30 m†, 47.80 m*.
Max. Speed: 125 km/h.
Wheel Arrangement: 2–Bo+Bo–2.
Accommodation: 24/40 1T+–/64 1T (24/32 1T+–/56 1T*).
New Numbers: ABDe 535.746–55.

746	B		749	B		752	B	*	BN		754	B	*	BN
747	B		750	B		753	B	*	GBS		755	B	*	BN
748	B		751	B										

Be4/4 CLASS

Motor coaches, made up into sets as required with driving and intermediate trailers.

Built: 1953–6.
Builder-Mech. Parts: SIG.
Builder-Elec. Parts: SAAS.
Traction Motors
One Hour Rating: 1472 kW.
Maximum Tractive Effort: 128 kN.
Driving Wheel Dia.: 1040 mm.
Weight: 68 tonnes.
Overall Length: 23.70 m.
Max. Speed: 120 km/h.
Wheel Arrangement: Bo–Bo.
Accommodation: 60S 1L.
New Numbers: Be 545.761–3.

| 761 | G | BN | | 762 | G | BN | | 763 | G | GBS | |

RABe 525 CLASS

A new design of low-floor railcar for use on the Bern suburban services.

Built: On Order.
Builder-Mech. Parts: Vevey/Talbot.
Builder-Elec. Parts: Holec.
Traction Motors
One Hour Rating:
Maximum Tractive Effort:
Driving Wheel Dia.:
Weight:
Overall Length:
Max. Speed:
Wheel Arrangement:
Accommodation:

| 525 001-4 | | 525 003-0 | | 525 005-5 | | 525 007-1 |
| 525 002-2 | | 525 004-8 | | 525 006-3 | | 525 008-9 |

2.3. TRACTORS

A varied selection of tractors are in use for light shunting and departmental operation.
Livery: Orange, except Ta 1–2 which are yellow.

Number		Rly	Builder	km/h	Tonnes	kW	Built
Ta	1		BLS	15	4.5	6	1941
Ta	2		BLS	6.5	8.6	5.5	1975
Te	215 011-8		SLM/MFO	45	15	96	1950
Te	215 012-6		SLM/MFO	45	15	96	1950
Te	215 013-4		SLM/MFO	45	15	96	1950
Te	215 014-2		SLM/MFO	45	15	96	1950
Te	215 015-9	BN	SLM/MFO	45	15	96	1954
Te	215 016-7	BN	SLM/MFO	45	15	96	1954
Te	215 017-5	BN	SLM/MFO	45	15	96	1954
Te	215 031-6		SLM/MFO/BLS	45	36	360	1925
Te	215 033-2		BLS/SAAS	45	21	294	1960
Tem	225 041-3		SLM/MFO/BBC/SAAS	65	30	258/146	1960
Tem	225 042-1		SLM/MFO/BBC/SAAS	65	30	258/146	1960
Tem	225 043-9		BLS/MFO/BBC/SAAS	65	30	258/146	1965
Tem	225 045-4		BLS/SLM/MFO/SAAS/DZ	65	30	258/180	1960

Tem	225 046-2	BLS/SLM/MFO/SAAS/DZ	65	30	258/180	1960
Tem	225 055-3	BLS/MFO/BBC/SAAS/DZ	65	30	258/180	1967
Tem	225 056-1	BLS/MFO/BBC/SAAS	65	30	258/146	1967
Tem	225 057-9	BLS/MFO/BBC/SAAS	65	30	258/146	1967
Tem	225 058-7	BLS/MFO/BBC/SAAS	65	30	258/146	1967
Tm	235 061-9	BLS/SLM/DZ	45	9	74	1974
Tm	235 062-7	BLS/SLM/DZ	45	9	74	1968
Tm	235 063-5	BLS	45	8.4	74	1960
Tm	235 064-3	BLS/SLM/DZ	45	9	74	1962
Tm	235 065-0	BLS/SLM/DZ	45	9	74	1963
Tm	235 066-8	BLS/SLM/DZ	45	9	74	1965
Tm	235 067-6BN	BLS/SLM/DZ	45	9	74	1965
Tm	235 068-4BN	BLS/SLM/DZ	45	9	74	1965
Tm	235 069-2SEZ	BLS/SLM/DZ	45	9	74	1968
Tm	235 070-0	BLS/SLM/DZ	45	9	74	1972
Tm	235 071-8	BLS/SLM/DZ	45	9	74	1975
Tm	235 072-6	BLS/SLM/DZ	45	9	74	1974
Tm	235 075-9SEZ	STAD/MERC	30	15	57	1952
Tm	235 079-1	RACO/DZ	75	19	176	1993
Tm	235 080-9	RACO/DZ	75	19	176	1993
Tm	235 081-7	RACO/DZ	75	19	176	1991
Tm	235 082-5	RACO/DZ	75	19	176	1977
Tm	235 083-3SEZ	RACO/DZ	75	19	176	1980
Tm	235 084-1GBS	RACO/DZ	75	19	176	1980
Tm	235 085-8BN	RACO/DZ	75	19	176	1980
Tm	235 086-6	RACO/DZ	75	19	176	1983
Tm	235 087-4	RACO/DZ	75	19	176	1983
Tm	235 088-2	RACO/DZ	75	19	176	1983
Tm	235 089-0	RACO/DZ	75	19	176	1991
Tm	235 091-6	STAD/VM/BBC	80	38	618	1980
Tm	235 092-4	STAD/VM/BBC	80	38	618	1980
Tm	235 093-2	STAD/VM/BBC	80	38	618	1980
Tm	235 094-0	STAD/VM/BBC	80	38	618	1981
Tm	235 095-7GBS	STAD/MB/BBC	80	29	350	1984
Tm	235 096-5GBS	STAD/MB/BBC	80	29	350	1984
Tm	235 097-3BN	STAD/MB/BBC	80	29	350	1984
Tm	235 098-1BN	STAD/MB/BBC	80	29	350	1985
Tm	235 099-9BN	STAD/MB/BBC	80	29	350	1995
Tm	235 100-5BN	STAD/MB/BBC	80	29	350	1995
Tm	235 101-3	RACO/DZ/BEIL	60	25	166/191	1971
Tea	245 021-1SEZ	STAD/ABB	80	34	440	1993
Tea	245 022-9GBS	STAD/ABB	80	34	440	1993
Tea	245 023-7BN	STAD/ABB	80	34	440	1993
Tea	245 024-5GBS	STAD/ABB	80	34	440	1993

BLS Tem 225 045-4 at Kandersteg on 30th July 1994. **T.M.Wallis**

3. RHÄTISCHE BAHN

In terms of route mileage the RhB is the largest of the Swiss Private Railways. It operates all the lines in south east Switzerland, connecting with the SBB at Chur and Landquart, and serving the major tourist centre of St. Moritz. Branches also serve Disentis, Arosa, Scuol–Tarasp and Tirano (the latter being in Italy). Although the main system is electrified at 11 kV $16^2/_3$ Hz a.c, several of the branches, all at one time being separate companies, are electrified on d.c. These are:

Berninabahn (BB) (St. Moritz–Tirano). (1000 V d.c.).
Chur Arosa (ChA). (2000 V d.c., planned for conversion to 11 kV a.c.).
Bellinzona–Mesocco (BM) (an isolated 1500 V d.c. line, now freight only with just the section Castione Arbedo–Cama still in use. Tourist trains have run on this line since 1996).

All the lines of the RhB are very scenic, particularly the Berninabahn and the Albula pass.
Gauge: 1000 mm.
Depots: Lanquart, Chur, Davos Platz, Samedan (main system), Chur Sand (ChA), Pontresina (BB), Poschiavo (BB), Grono (BM).

3.1. LOCOS (MAIN SYSTEM)

CLASS Ge2/4 (Gem2/4*)   1B1

Built as mixed traffic locos at the time of electrification, these two locos were rebuilt in 1943 as shunters, with new off-centre-cab superstructure. They are used around Chur, Landquart and Samedan. One loco (211) was rebuilt with auxiliary batteries; it was further rebuilt with an auxiliary diesel engine in 1967.

Built: 1913, rebuilt 1943 ex 202/6 (* further rebuilt 1967).
Builder-Mech. Parts: SLM.
Builder-Elec. Parts: BBC/SAAS.
Engine: Deutz F12L714 172 kW *.
Traction Motor: 1 single phase frame mounted with side rod drive.
One Hour Rating: 228 kW (170 kW on diesel power*).
Maximum Tractive Effort: 60 kN.
Driving Wheel Dia.: 1070 mm.
Pony Wheel Dia.: 710 mm.
Weight: 33 tonnes.
Overall Length: 8.7 m.
Max. Speed: 55 km/h.

211   * | 212 |

CLASS Ge3/3   C

Modern shunting locos, a single motor drives all wheels through cardan shafts. Used at Landquart & Chur.

Built: 1984.
Builder-Mech. Parts: RACO.
Builder-Elec. Parts: BBC.
Traction Motor: 1 single phase frame mounted with cardan shift drive.
One Hour Rating: 425 kW.
Maximum Tractive Effort: 102 kN.
Driving Wheel Dia.: 920 mm.
Weight: 33 tonnes.
Overall Length: 8.64 m.
Max. Speed: 40 km/h.

214 | 215 |

CLASS Ge2/4   1B1

Originally part of the same class as 211–2, but when rebuilt for shunting in 1945/6 retained the original box cab. Since the delivery of 214/5, they are mainly held in reserve for use at Samedan and Landquart.

Built: 1913, rebuilt 1945–6 ex 203–4.
Builder-Mech. Parts: SLM.
Builder-Elec. Parts: BBC.
Traction Motor: 1 single phase frame mounted with side rod drive.
One Hour Rating: 428 kW.
Maximum Tractive Effort: 59 kN.
Driving Wheel Dia.: 1070 mm.
Pony Wheel Dia.: 710 mm.
Weight: 31.8 tonnes.
Overall Length: 8.7 m.
Max. Speed: 55 km/h.

221 | 222 |

CLASS Gm3/3   C

Diesel shunters used at Landquart and Chur, they have a 2-speed transmission giving different characteristics for shunting & line operation.

Built: 1975–6.
Builder: Moyse.
Engine: MTU of 396 kW.
Transmission: Hydraulic.
Maximum Tractive Effort: 153 kN.
Driving Wheel Dia.: 920 mm.
Weight: 34 tonnes.
Overall Length: 7.96 m.
Max. Speed: 55 km/h.

231 | 232 | 233 |

CLASS Gm4/4   B–B

A diesel purchased in 1988 from the Brohltalbahn in Germany for use on construction work on the new Vereina Tunnel. Now used on ballast trains throughout the system.

Built: 1964.
Builder: Mak.
Engines: 2 x 150 kW.
Transmission: Hydraulic.
Maximum Tractive Effort: kN.
Driving Wheel Dia.:   mm.
Weight: 39 tonnes.
Overall Length: 9.65 m.
Max. Speed: 45 km/h.

241 |

CLASS Gmf4/4   B–B

Two diesel locos, also for use on construction work on the Vereina Tunnel and now used on general ballast work.

Built: 1991.
Builder: Gmeinder/Kaelble/RhB.
Engine: Caterpillar 560 kW.
Transmission: Hydraulic.
Maximum Tractive Effort: 165 kN.
Driving Wheel Dia.:   mm.
Weight: 50 tonnes.
Overall Length: 11.70 m.
Max. Speed: 60 km/h.

242 | 243 |

CLASS Ge4/6   1D1

The last survivor of an assortment of locos of this wheel arrangement dating from the time of electrification. It has been retained as a historic loco. The body contains two traction motors geared to a single layshaft driving through an additional layshaft and coupling rods.

Built: 1914.
Builder-Mech. Parts: SLM.
Builder-Elec. Parts: MFO.
Traction Motors: 2 single phase frame mounted with side rod drive.
One Hour Rating: 588 kW.
Maximum Tractive Effort: 106 kN.
Driving Wheel Dia.: 1070 mm.
Pony Wheel Dia.: 710 mm.
Weight: 56.3 tonnes.
Overall Length: 11.10 m.
Max. Speed: 55 km/h.

353

CLASS Ge6/6   C–C

The survivors of 15 'Baby Crocodiles' built in the 1920s to the same configuration as their SBB counterparts. They no longer have any regular work, being retained as reserve locos and for specials.

Built: 1925–9.
Builder-Mech. Parts: SLM.
Builder-Elec. Parts: BBC/MFO.
Traction Motors: 2 single phase frame mounted with jackshaft/side rod drive.
One Hour Rating: 794 kW.
Maximum Tractive Effort: 172 kN.
Driving Wheel Dia.: 1070 mm.
Weight: 66 tonnes.
Overall Length: 13.30 m.
Max. Speed: 55 km/h.

411   412   414   415

CLASS Ge4/4^I Bo–Bo

Mixed traffic locos, recently extensively refurbished. They see use on push-pull local trains and will be used on the Arosa line when this is converted to a.c.

Built: 1947 (601–604), 1953 (605–610); rebuilt 1986–92.
Builder-Mech. Parts: SLM.
Builder-Elec. Parts: BBC/MFO.
Traction Motors: 4 single phase fully suspended with BBC spring drive.
One Hour Rating: 1176 kW.
Maximum Tractive Effort: 142 kN.
Driving Wheel Dia.: 1070 mm.
Weight: 47 tonnes.
Overall Length: 12.10 m.
Max. Speed: 80 km/h.

All fitted with regenerative brakes and rebuilt with new cabs and fitted for push-pull & mw operation.

601	ALBULA	606	KESCH
602	BERNINA	607	SURSELVA
603	BADUS	608	MADRISA
604	CALANDA	609	LINARD
605	SILVRETTA	610	VIAMALA

CLASS Ge4/4^{II} Bo–Bo

The standard RhB electric, used throughout the a.c. system, fitted with thyristor control & d.c. motors.

Built: 1973 (* 1984–5).
Builder-Mech. Parts: SLM.
Builder-Elec. Parts: BBC.
Traction Motors: 4 pulsating current fully suspended with BBC spring drive.

▲ RhB Class Ge 6/6 No. 707 at Samedan 5th August 1994. These articulated electrics have now been displaced from the principal expresses to lesser duties. **T.M. Wallis**

▼ RhB Gem 4/4 No. 801 'STEINBOCK' at Campocologno on 15th June 1995. The Gem 4/4 were purchased to operate on diesel traction under the 11 kV overhead. **Ray Smith**

One Hour Rating: 1648 kW.
Maximum Tractive Effort: 179 kN.
Driving Wheel Dia.: 1070 mm.
Weight: 50 tonnes.
Overall Length: 12.96 m.
Max. Speed: 90 km/h.

All fitted with regenerative brakes.

611		LANDQUART	623	*	BONADUZ
612		THUSIS	624	*	CELERINA/SCHLARIGNA
613		DOMAT/EMS	625	*	KÜBLIS
614		SCHIERS	626	*	MALANS
615		KLOSTERS	627	*	REICHENAU–TAMINS
616		FILISUR	628	*	S-CHANF
617		ILANZ	629	*	TIEFENCASTEL
618		BERGÜN/BRAVUOGN	630	*	TRUN
619		SAMEDAN	631	*	UNTERVAZ
620		ZERNEZ	632	*	ZIZERS
621	*	FELSBERG	633	*	ZUOZ
622	*	AROSA			

CLASS Ge4/4^{III}   Bo–Bo

A new design of general purpose locomotive used mainly on the Chur to St Moritz fast trains. It is planned to purchase 2–4 more locomotives of this type to operate car-carrying trains through the new Vereina tunnel.

Built: 1993–4.
Builder-Mech. Parts: SLM.
Builder-Elec. Parts: ABB.
Traction Motors: 4 three phase.
One Hour Rating: 2500 kW.
Maximum Tractive Effort: 200 kN.
Driving Wheel Dia.: 1070 mm.
Weight: 61 tonnes.
Overall Length: 16.00 m.
Max. Speed: 100 km/h.

641	MAIENFELD	646		STA. MARIA/VAL MÜSTAIR
642	BREIL/BRIGELS	647		GRÜTSCH
643	VALS	648		SUSCH
644	SAVOGNIN	649		LAVIN
645	TUJETSCH			

CLASS Ge6/6   Bo–Bo–Bo

Articulated locos, mainly used on heavy trains between Chur and St. Moritz. The two halves of the body are joined by a hinge with its axis horizontal; the centre bogie has some sideplay.

Built: 1958 *, 1965 †.
Builder-Mech. Parts: SLM.
Builder-Elec. Parts: MFO/BBC.
Traction Motors: 6 single phase fully suspended with BBC spring drive.
One Hour Rating: 1764 kW.
Maximum Tractive Effort: 214 kN.
Driving Wheel Dia.: 1070 mm.
Weight: 65 tonnes.
Overall Length: 14.50 m.
Max. Speed: 80 km/h.

701	*	RAETIA	705	†	PONTRESINA/PUNTRASCH
702	*	CURIA	706	†	DISENTIS/MUSTER
703	†	ST. MORITZ	707	†	SCUOL
704	†	DAVOS			

CLASS Gem4/4   Bo–Bo

These electro-diesels are the only main-line locos that can be used throughout the system. They operate as electrics on the Berninabahn and as diesel elsewhere. Used on the Bernina Express between Samedan and Tirano, on snowplough duties, and on works trains.

Built: 1968.
Builder-Mech. Parts: SLM.
Builder-Elec. Parts: BBC/MFO/SAAS/Cummins.
Diesel Engines: 2 Cummins VT12-825B1 463 kW.
Traction Motors: 4 single phase axle hung nose suspended.
One Hour Rating: 680 kW (electric), 926 kW (diesel).
Maximum Tractive Effort: 192 kN.
Driving Wheel Dia.: 920 mm.
Weight: 50 tonnes.
Overall Length: 13.54 m.
Max. Speed: 65 km/h.

Fitted for mw operation; can also mw with ABe4/4 41–9 under electric traction only.

| 801 | STEINBOCK | | 802 | MURMELTIER |

3.2. ELECTRIC RAILCARS (MAIN SYSTEM)
CLASS ABe4/4

Used on local services in the Samedan area, operating with driving trailers BDt 1721–3.

Built: 1939–40; rebuilt 1982–4.
Builder-Mech. Parts: SWS.
Builder-Elec. Parts: BBC/MFO.
Traction Motors:
One Hour Rating: 440 kW.
Maximum Tractive Effort: 78 kN.
Driving Wheel Dia.: 850 mm.
Weight: 39 tonnes.
Overall Length: 18.00 m.
Max. Speed: 70 km/h.
Wheel Arrangement: Bo–Bo.
Accommodation: 12/28 1T.

| 501 | | 502 | | 503 | | 504 |

CLASS Be4/4

Single ended motor coaches (gangwayed at the non-driving end), used on local services around Chur, operating as 3-car sets with driving trailers ABD 1711–6 and intermediate trailers B2411–6. They are fitted with thyristor control, d.c. motors & electropneumatic brakes.

Built: 1971 (* 1979).
Builder-Mech. Parts: FFA/SIG.
Builder-Elec. Parts: SAAS.
Traction Motors:
One Hour Rating: 776 kW.
Maximum Tractive Effort: 112 kN.
Driving Wheel Dia.: 750 mm.
Weight: 44.6 tonnes.
Overall Length: 18.70 m.
Max. Speed: 90 km/h.
Wheel Arrangement: Bo–Bo.
Accommodation: –/40 1T.

| 511 | | 513 | | 515 | * | | 516 | * |
| 512 | | 514 | | | | | |

3.3. STOCK OF DC BRANCHES
CLASS ABe4/4

The survivors, all much rebuilt, of the original Berninabahn stock. Used on works duties and as reserve power, on the BB and ChA. Fitted with track brakes for street running in Chur and Tirano.

Built: 1908–11; rebuilt.
Builder-Mech. Parts: SIG.
Builder-Elec. Parts: SAAS (SAAS/MFO §).
Traction Motors:
One Hour Rating: 382 kW (426 kW §).
Maximum Tractive Effort: 55 kN (57 kN §).
Driving Wheel Dia.: 850 mm.
Weight: 30 tonnes (31 tonnes †).
Overall Length: 13.93 m (14.66 m †).
Max. Speed: 55 km/h.
Wheel Arrangement: Bo–Bo.
Accommodation: 12/27 (12/29 †, 12/31 §).

30	†	32		35	§	37	§
31		34		36	§		

CLASS ABe4/4

These railcars together with 51-6, operate most trains on the Berninabahn.

Built: 1964–5 (* 1972).
Builder-Mech. Parts: SWS.
Builder-Elec. Parts: BBC/MFO/SAAS (*BBC/SAAS).
Traction Motors:
One Hour Rating: 680 kW.
Maximum Tractive Effort: 156 kN.
Driving Wheel Dia.: 920 mm.
Weight: 41 tonnes (43 tonnes *).
Overall Length: 16.54 m (16.89 m *).
Max. Speed: 65 km/h.
Wheel Arrangement: Bo–Bo.
Accommodation: 12/24.

mw & track brake fitted.

41		44		46		48	*
42		45		47	*	49	*
43							

CLASS ABe4/4[II]

New railcars built to supplement 41–9.

Built: 1987 (51–3), 1990 (54–6).
Builder-Mech. Parts: SWA.
Builder-Elec. Parts: ABB.
Traction Motors: 4 three phase.
One Hour Rating: 1016 kW.
Maximum Tractive Effort: 178 kN.
Driving Wheel Dia.: 920 mm.
Weight: 47 tonnes.
Overall Length: 16.90 m.
Max. Speed: 65 km/h.
Wheel Arrangement: Bo–Bo.
Accommodation: 12/16.

mw & track brake fitted.

51	POSCHIAVO	54	HAKONE
52	BRUSIO	55	DIAVOLEZZA
53	TIRANO	56	CORVIGLIA

▲ RhB De 2/2 No. 151 at Ospizio-Bernina on 5th August 1994. An unusual, much rebuilt, survivor from the opening of the Berninabahn. **T.M. Wallis**

▼ RhB Ge 2/2 No. 162 at Campocologno on 5th August 1994. These small electrics date from the opening of the Berninabahn. **T.M. Wallis**

CLASS De2/2

An ex-BB motor luggage van, much rebuilt and now used for shunting at Campocologno.

Built: 1909, rebuilt 1980.
Builder-Mech. Parts: SIG.
Builder-Elec. Parts: Alioth.
Traction Motors:
One Hour Rating: 147 kW.
Maximum Tractive Effort: kN.
Driving Wheel Dia.: 850 mm.
Weight: 14 tonnes.
Overall Length: 7.15 m.
Max. Speed: 45 km/h.
Wheel Arrangement: Bo.

151 |

CLASS Ge2/2

A pair of ex-BB electric locos, normally used for shunting around Poschiavo.

Built: 1911.
Builder-Mech. Parts: SIG.
Builder-Elec. Parts: Alioth.
Traction Motors:
One Hour Rating: 242 kW.
Maximum Tractive Effort: kN.
Driving Wheel Dia.: 975 mm.
Weight: 16 tonnes (18 tonnes*).
Overall Length: 7.72 m.
Max. Speed: 45 km/h.
Wheel Arrangement: Bo.

161 | 162   * |

CLASS ABDe4/4 (ABe4/4*, BDe4/4†)

481–8 are the normal motive power on the Chur–Arosa line, while 491 is the last remaining RhB car on the Bellinzona–Mesocco line (the reserve car here is a hired AB car). When the Chur–Arosa line is converted to a.c. 481–6 will be withdrawn and 487–8 rebuilt to driving trailers.

Built: 1957–8 (* 1973).
Builder-Mech. Parts: SWS.
Builder-Elec. Parts: BBC (BBC/SAAS *).
Traction Motors:
One Hour Rating: 500 kW (676 kW †).
Maximum Tractive Effort: 113 kN.
Driving Wheel Dia.: 920 mm.
Weight: 43 tonnes (45 tonnes*, 41 tonnes†).
Overall Length: 17.70 m. (16.70 m *).
Max. Speed: 65 km/h.

Fitted with track brakes (except 491).

481	484	486		488	*
482	485	487	*	491	†
483					

3.4. TRACTORS/SNOWPLOUGHS, ETC

As with other Swiss railways, the RhB owns a selection of tractors and snowploughs, plus an assortment of other departmental motive power. 9213 is a self-propelled steam rotary snowplough, still occasionally used at times of severe weather, but also used on specials!

Tm2/2	15§	RACO/SLM	30	9	37	1957
Tm2/2	16§	RACO/SLM	30	9	37	1957
Tm2/2	17§	RACO/SLM	30	9	37	1957
Tm2/2	18§	RACO/SLM	30	9	37	1957
Tm2/2	19§	RACO/SLM	30	9	41	1962
Tm2/2	20§	RACO/SLM	30	9	41	1962
Tm2/2	21§	RACO/SLM	30	9	41	1965
Tm2/2	22§	RACO/SLM	30	9	41	1965
Tm2/2	23§	RACO/SLM	30	9	41	1965
Tm2/2	24§	RACO/SLM	30	9	41	1965
Tm2/2	25§	RACO/SLM	30	9	41	1965
Tm2/2	26§	RACO/SLM	30	9	41	1969
Te2/2	71	SLM/SAAS	30	13	97	1946
Te2/2	72	SLM/SAAS	30	13	97	1946
Te2/2	73	SLM/SAAS	30	13	97	1946
Te2/2	74	SE/GSEG	50	24	216	1969
Te2/2	75	SE/GSEG	50	24	216	1969
Ta1/2	80	WIND	3.9	9.2	6	1980
Tm2/2	81	RACO/RhB	80	22	336	1987
Tm2/2	82	RACO/RhB	80	22	336	1987
Tm2/2	83	RACO/RhB	80	22	336	1987
Tm2/2	84	RACO/RhB	80	22	336	1987
Tm2/2	85	RACO/RhB	60	24	336	1990
Tm2/2	86	RACO/RhB	60	24	336	1990
Tm2/2	87	RACO/RhB	60	24	336	1990
Tm2/2	88	RACO/RhB	60	24	336	1990
Tm2/2	89	RACO/RhB	60	24	336	1990
Tm2/2	90	RACO/RhB	60	24	336	1994
Tm2/2	91	RACO/SAU	40	10.5	48	1959
Tm2/2	92	RACO/SAU	40	10.5	48	1959
Tm2/2	93	SCH/DZ	35	21	172	1971
Xrotd6/6	9213	SLM	36	63.5	–	1910
Xrote	9215	SIG/DMG/PUCH/RhB	36	21.5	74	1908
Xrotm	9216	RACO/BEIL	55	15	164	1958
Xrotmt	9217	BEIL/JMR/DZ	55	38	670	1981
Xrotet	9218	RACO/BEIL	55	24	522	1967
Xrotet	9219	RACO/BEIL	55	24	522	1967
Xm2/2	9912	RACO/SAU	30	10	41	1962
Xm2/2	9914	RhB/SAU/MFO	55	19	112	1950
Xm2/2	9915	PFING/SAU/MFO	55	20	112	1958
Xm2/2	9916	RACO/NEN/DZ	40	13	100	1963
Xm2/2	9917	STAD/RhB/DZ	55	27	224	1974
Xm4/4	9918	WIND/CUMM	90		485	1994
Xm4/4	9919	WIND/CUMM	90		485	1994
Xe4/4	9920	SIG/Alioth	45	31	298	1908
Xmf2/2	9921	RACO	50		283	1994
Xe4/4	9922*	SIG/SAAS		55	382	1911

* ex BDe4/4 38 in 1992.
§ 15–26 renumbered from, 64–7, 62/3, 57–61, 56 repectively.

4. OTHER PRIVATE RAILWAYS

Around 40% of the railway mileage in Switzerland does not belong to the SBB, but to one of the numerous so-called Private Railways. In fact, apart from some purely tourist lines, the basic difference is that these Private Railways are financed by local government as opposed to the SBB which is financed by central government. Most of these railways are purely local, often providing a branch line service connecting with the SBB, although some, notably the Bern–Lötschberg–Simplon (section 2) and the Rhätische Bahn (section 3), are main line railways in their own right. The railways provide a considerable contrast, ranging from those with some street or roadside running to those up to full main line standard, and of course mountain rack lines. Many of the railways are narrow gauge, and partly because of this, their operation is mostly self-contained. However, some joint through operation does exist, including some over SBB tracks Due to the large number of numerically small classes, a format has been adopted using one line for each item of motive power as follows:

1st Column: Classification: see'Classification of Swiss Motive Power' for details.
2nd Column: Running number.
3rd Column: Owner: only shown to indicate the actual owner where a group of railways have a common numbering scheme.
4th Column: Name (if any).
5th Column: Builder: see 'List of Builders' for abbreviations.
6th Column: Seats (if 1st & 2nd class, seating split shown in that order, e.g. 18/30 = 18 first 30 second.
7th Column: Max. speed in km/h (if rack & adhesion, adhesion speed shown first).
8th Column: Weight in tonnes.
9th Column: Hourly rating in kW (or engine rating for diesel locos).
10th Column: Date of construction (date in brackets indicates date of major rebuilding).

Certain of these columns are omitted for certain railways depending on individual circumstances. Also, new computer numbers are shown as the first column where applicable. When the second part of the computer number is the same as the original number for all stock of a particular railway, the original numbers are omitted. In this section, check digits are omitted because of space difficulties.

Some railways are under common management, and where these also share a common numbering scheme, they have been grouped together. To assist in locating the various railways, the numbers in brackets after the headings refer to the relevant table nos. in the Swiss Railway timetable.

All Swiss Railways have an official set of initials, and they have been put into alphabetical order of these, except where grouped together as noted above. Not included are the numerous cable and funicular railways. The urban tramways in Basel, Bern, Genève, Lausanne, Neuchâtel or Zürich, are shown in section 5.

INDEX TO PRIVATE RAILWAYS

FLP   Ferrovia Lugano Ponte Tresa
FO   Furka Oberalp
FW   Frauenfeld Wil
GBS   Gürbetal Bern Schwarzenburg (part of BLS Group)
GFM   Gruyère Fribourg Morat
GGB   Gornergratbahn
JB   Jungfraubahn
LEB   Lausanne Eschallens Bercher
LG   Lausanne Gare
LO   Lausanne Ouchy (included with LG)
LOKOOP   Lokoop AG
LSE   Luzern Stans Engelberg
MC   Martigny Châtelard
MG   Monte Generoso
MIB   Meiringen Innertkirchen Bahn
MO   Martigny Orsières
MOB   Montreux Oberland Bernois
MTGN   Montreux Territet Glion Naye
MThB   Mittel Thurgau Bahn
NStCM   Nyon St Cergue Morez
OC   Orbe Chavornay
OeBB   Oensingen Balsthal Bahn
OSST   Oberaargau Solothurn Seeland Transport
PB   Pilatus Bahn
PBr   Pont Brassus Bahn
PTT   Post Telephon Telegraph
RB   Rigi Bahnen
RBS   Regionalverkehr Bern Solthurn
RhB   Rhätische Bahn
RHB   Rorschach Heiden Bahn
RhW   Rheineck Walzenhausen
RVO   Regionalverkehr Oberaargau (part of OSST)
RVT   Chemin de Fer Régional du Val de Travers
SATEB   S.A. des Transports Emosson Barbarine
SEZ   Spiez Erlenbach Zweisimmen (part of BLS Group)
SMB   Solothurn Münster Bahn (part of EBT Group) (Münster = Moutier)
SNB   Solothurn Neiderbipp Bahn (now part of OSST)
SOB   Schweizerische Sudostbahn
SPB   Schynige Platte Bahn
SSIF   Società Subalpina di Imprese Ferroviarie (included with FART)
ST   Sursee Triengen
STB   Sensetalbahn
SZU   Sihltal Zürich Uetliberg
TB   Trogener Bahn
VHB   Vereinigte Huttwil Bahnen (part of EBT Group)
WAB   Wengernalpbahn
WB   Waldenburgerbahn
WM   Wohlen Meisterschwanden (included with BD)
WSB   Wynental und Suhrentalbahn
YSC   Yverdon St Croix

APPENZELLERBAHNEN (854, 855, 856) AB

After many years of common management, the Appenzellbahn (AB) and St. Gallen–Gais–Appenzell (SGA) merged in 1988 to form the Appenzellerbahnen. The former SGA is partly rack and some of the latest stock is intended for operation throughout the system.

Gauge: 1000 mm.
Electrical System: 1500 V d.c.
Depots: Gais, Herisau, Wasserauen, Appenzell.

Class	No.	Name	Builder	Seats	km/h	Tonnes	kW	Built
Ge4/4	1		STAD/SLM/ABB	-	75	50		1994
ABDeh4/4	5	*	SLM/SIG/BBC	6/39	40/24	40	450	1931
ABDeh4/4	6	ALTSTÄTTEN	SLM/BBC	6/32	55/25	35.6	480	1953
ABDeh4/4	7		SLM/BBC	6/32	55/25	35.6	480	1953
ABDeh4/4	8		SLM/BBC	6/32	55/25	35.6	480	1953
BDeh4/4	11	ST. GALLEN	FFA/SLM/BBC	40	65/40	44.5	830	1981
BDeh4/4	12	TEUFEN	FFA/SLM/BBC	40	65/40	44.5	830	1981
BDeh4/4	13	BÜHLER	FFA/SLM/BBC	40	65/40	44.5	830	1981
BDeh4/4	14	GAIS	FFA/SLM/BBC	40	65/40	44.5	830	1981
BDeh4/4	15	APPENZELL	FFA/SLM/BBC	40	65/40	44.5	830	1981
BDeh4/4	16		SWA/SIG/SLM/ABB	40	65/40	44.5	830	1993
BDeh4/4	17		SWA/SIG/SLM/ABB	40	65/40	44.5	830	1993
BDe4/4	31	GOSSAU	FFA/SIG/BBC	39	75	36	820	1985
BDe4/4	32	HERISAU	FFA/SIG/BBC	39	75	36	820	1985
BDe4/4	33	GONTEN	FFA/SIG/BBC	39	75	36	820	1985
BDe4/4	34		SWA/SIG/ABB	39	75	36	820	1993
BDe4/4	35		SWA/SIG/ABB	39	75	36	820	1993
ABe4/4	41		SIG/MFO	12/40	65	34.2	455	1933
ABe4/4	42	‡	SIG/MFO	12/40	65	34.2	455	1933
ABe4/4	43		SIG/MFO	12/40	65	34.2	455	1933
BDe4/4	46	WALDSTATT	FFA/SIG/BBC	32	65	37.8	565	1968
BDe4/4	47	URNÄSCH	FFA/SIG/BBC	32	65	37.8	565	1968
Te2/2	49		SWS/MFO/AB	-	45	12	95	1955
De4/4	50		FFA/MFO/AB	-	65	32.5	455	1966
Xm1/2	51		SWS/SIG/SAU/AB	-	45	15	75	1962
BCFm2/4	56	*	SIG/SZ/MFO	6/24	50	32	185	1929
ABDeh4/4	91	†	SLM/SIG/BBC	6/39	40/24	40	450	1931
Xrotm2/2	99		RACO/BEIL/DZ	-	30	18	150	1974
Tm2/2	501		OK/LMG	-	18	18.5	105	1957

* Historic cars.
† renumbered from ABDeh 4/4 1 in 1994.
‡ On loan to RhB for Misox line.

AB. Appenzellerbahnen Ge 4/4 No. 1 at Herisau depot on 17th June 1995 is the solitary example of its class.   **Ray Smith**

▲ **AB.** Ex SGA ABDeh 4/4 No. 4 at Alstetten shed on 28th August 1994. **J.D. Davis**

▲ **AB.** Another member of the same class, No. 5 in heritage livery at Gais depot on 17th June 1995.
Ray Smith

▼ **AB.** ABDeh 4/4 No. 7 on an engineers train at Altstetten on 28th August 1994. **J.D. Davis**

AIGLE–LEYSIN (125)   AL

This railway is under common management with the AOMC, ASD and BVB as the Transports Publics du Chablais (TPC). The differing electrical and rack systems prevent full integration. The AL has street running in Aigle and then climbs steeply with rack assistance. It is planned to extend the line from Leysin to La Berneuse, but this has been delayed for financial reasons.

Gauge: 1000 mm.
Electrical System: 1300 V d.c.
Depots: Aigle, Leysin Feydey.

Class	No.	Name	Builder	Seats	km/h	Tonnes	kW	Built
He2/2	12		SLM/MFO/SIG	-	7.5	20.3	264	1915
Te2/2	101		ACMV/AL/BBC	-	20	11.6	82	1949
ARSeh2/4	201		SLM/BBC	25	25/15	24.5	250	1946
BDeh2/4	202		SLM/BBC	48	25/15	24.5	250	1946
BDeh2/4	203		SLM/BBC	48	25/15	24.5	250	1946
BDeh4/4	301		SIG/SAAS	48	40/24	33	596	1966
BDeh4/4	302		SIG/SAAS	48	40/24	33	596	1966
BDeh4/4	303	YVORNE	ACMV/SLM/BBC	32	40/25	36	836	1987
BDeh4/4	304	OLLON	ACMV/SLM/BBC	32	40/25	36	836	1987
BDeh4/4	305		ACMV/SLM/ABB	32	40/25	36	836	1987

AIGLE–OLLON–MONTHEY–CHAMPÉRY (126)   AOMC

Really two separate lines radiating from Monthey, only the line to Champéry has rack sections. Hence the adhesion only cars are restricted to the Aigle line. The line has recently been extended slightly at the Champéry end.

Gauge: 1000 mm.
Electrical System: 850 V d.c.
Depot: Monthey (to be replaced by new depot at Aigle).

Class	No.	Name	Builder	Seats	km/h	Tonnes	kW	Built
BDeh4/4	1	VAUD	ACMV/SLM/BBC	32	65/30	40	656	1987
BDeh4/4	2	VALAIS	ACMV/SLM/BBC	32	65/30	40	656	1987
BDeh4/4	3		ACMV/SLM/ABB	32	65/30	40	656	1992
BDeh4/4	11		SWP/BBC	40	50/18	30.4	368	1954
BDeh4/4	12		SWP/BBC	40	50/18	30.4	368	1954
BDeh4/4	13		SWP/BBC	40	50/18	30.4	368	1954
BDeh4/4	14		SWP/BBC	40	50/18	30.4	368	1954
Be4/4	101*	YVORNE	SWP/BBC	44	65	27	382	1966
Be4/4	102*	CHABLAIS	SWP/BBC	44	65	27	382	1966
Be4/4	103*	COLLOMBEY-MURAZ	SWP/BBC	44	65	27	382	1966
Be4/4	104*	OLLON	SWP/BBC	44	65	27	382	1966
Be4/4	105*		SWP/BBC	44	65	27	382	1966

* ex BTB 14/2/3/6/1 respectively in 1985/6.

AIGLE–SÉPEY–DIABLERETS (124)   ASD

Recently under threat of closure, this line has now been modernised. The original 1913 stock operated all services until delivery of the new ACMV cars.

Gauge: 1000 mm.
Electrical System: 1350 V d.c.
Depots: Aigle, Les Diablerets.

Class	No.	Name	Builder	Seats	km/h	Tonnes	kW	Built
BCFe4/4	1	*	SWS/BBC	8/32	50	25	240	1913
BDe4/4	401	ORMONT DESSOUS	ACMV/SIG/SLM/BBC	32	65	32.5	820	1987
BDe4/4	402	ORMONT DESSUS	ACMV/SIG/SLM/BBC	32	65	32.5	820	1987
BDe4/4	403	OLLON	ACMV/SIG/SLM/BBC	32	65	32.5	820	1987
BDe4/4	404	AIGLE	ACMV/SIG/SLM/BBC	32	65	32.5	820	1987

* Historic car.

94

▲ **AL.** Aigle Leysin BDeh 4/4 302 at Aligle on 30th August 1994. J.D. Davis

▼ **AOMC.** BDeh 4/4 No. 13 shown at Monthey Ville is typical of the older cars on this line. J.D. Davis

ASD. Aigle Sépey Diablarets BDe 4/4 No. 403 outside Aigle depot on 31st August 1994. These cars operate all services on the line.　　　　　**J.D. Davis**

BIÈRE–APPLES–MORGES (156)　　　BAM

Unusually for Switzerland, this light railway is electrified on high voltage a.c. Once threatened with closure, new cars were delivered a few years ago. Car 14 was originally 13, renumbered for superstitious reasons!

Gauge: 1000 mm.
Electrical System: 15 kV $16^2/_3$ Hz a.c.
Depots: Bière, L'Isle.

Class	No.	Name	Builder	Seats	km/h	Tonnes	kW	Built
BDe4/4	1		SWS/SAAS	40	65	36	500	1943
BDe4/4	2		SWS/SAAS	40	65	36	500	1943
BDe4/4	3		SWS/SAAS	40	65	36	500	1943
BDe4/4	4		SWS/SAAS	40	65	36	500	1943
BDe4/4	5		SWS/SAAS	40	65	37	500	1949
Be4/4	11		ACMV/HESS/BBC	40		44.5	780	1981
Be4/4	12		ACMV/HESS/BBC	40		44.5	780	1981
Be4/4	14		ACMV/HESS/BBC	40		44.5	780	1981
Ge4/4	21	MORGES	SLM/ABB	–				1994
Ge4/4	22	VENOGE	SLM/ABB	–				1994
Tm2/2	41		RACO/Cumm	–			310	1988

BREMGARTEN–DIETIKON (654)　　　BD
WOHLEN–MEISTERSCHWANDEN (654)　WM

Two railways under common management but with totally different characteristics. The BD is a metre gauge light railway with mostly roadside running. The line continues from Bremgarten to Wohlen as mixed gauge, BD standard gauge diesels hauling freight on this section. The WM is a short standard gauge branch, and is expected to closed to passengers in June 1997. The Wohlen to Villmergen section remains open for freight traffic.

Gauge: 1000 mm (Bremgarten West–Dietikon), mixed 1000/1435 mm (Wohlen–Bremgarten West), 1435 mm (WM, Wohlen–Fahrwangen–Meisterschwanden).
Electrical System: 1200 V d.c. (BD), 15 kV, $16^2/_3$ Hz a.c. (WM).
Depots: Bremgarten (BD, 1000 mm), Bremgarten West (BD, 1435 mm), Fahrwangen, Meisterschwanden (WM).

Metre Gauge Stock: (all BD).

Class	No.	Name	Builder	Seats	km/h	Tonnes	kW	Built
BDe8/8	1	KANTON AARGAU	SWS/MFO	93	70	50.5	580	1969
BDe8/8	2	KANTON ZÜRICH	SWS/MFO	93	70	50.5	580	1969
BDe8/8	3	WOHLEN	SWS/MFO	93	70	50.5	580	1969
BDe8/8	4	BREMGARTEN	SWS/MFO	93	70	50.5	580	1969
BDe8/8	5	ZUFIKON	SWS/MFO	93	70	50.5	580	1969
BDe8/8	6	BERIKON	SWS/MFO	93	70	50.5	580	1969
BDe8/8	7	WIDEN	SWS/MFO	93	70	50.5	580	1969
BDe8/8	8	RUDOLFSTETTEN	SWS/MFO	93	70	50.5	580	1969
BDe8/8	9	DIETIKON	SWS/MFO	93	70	50.5	580	1969
BDre4/4	10		SWS/MFO		45	32	172	1928
Xe4/4	11		SWS/MFO	24	45	32	172	1932
Be4/8	21		SWA/SIG/ABB	120	80		600	1993
Be4/8	22		SWA/SIG/ABB	120	80		600	1993
Be4/8	23		SWA/SIG/ABB	120	80		600	1993
Be4/8	24		SWA/SIG/ABB	120	80		600	1993
Be4/8	25		SWA/SIG/ABB	120	80		600	1993
Tm2/2	51		STAD/BBC/SAU	–	50	13	88	1967
Tm2/2	52		STAD/BBC/SAU	–	50	13	88	1968

Standard Gauge Stock:

WM:

Number	Class	Old No.		Builder	Seats	km/h	Tonnes	kW	Built
BDe 578 401	BDe4/4	1		SIG/SWS/SAAS/BBC/MFO	48	100	63	1076	1966
BDe 578 402	BDe4/4	2		SIG/SWS/SAAS/BBC/MFO	48	100	63	1076	1966
BDe 578 403	BDe2/4	3	*	SWS/SAAS	60	75	39.5	330	1938
Em 828 421	Em2/2	101		SIG/BBC/SAU	–	55		243	1961
Em 828 451	Em4/4	151		CEM/POY	–	55	72	442	1968
	Ta2/2	–		BBC	–	15	9.9	9	1915

Name: 151 HANS REY.

BD

Number	Class	Old No.	Builder	Seats	km/h	Tonnes	kW	Built
Em 828 422	Em2/2	102	SIG/BBC/SAU	–	55	38	243	1966
Em 828 423	Em2/2	103	STAD/HESS/MB/GM/BBC	–	80	39.5	700	1984

* ex STB 101 in 1986.

BERGBAHN LAUTERBRUNNEN MÜRREN (313) BLM

Under common management with the BOB, JB, SPB & WAB, the BLM runs from Grütschalp (where there is a funicular connection from Lauterbrunnen) to Mürren. The line runs along a mountain ledge, serving an area with no road access.

Gauge: 1000 mm.
Electrical System: 550 V d.c.
Depot: Grütschalp.

Class	No.	Name	Builder	Seats	km/h	Tonnes	kW	Built
CFe2/4	11	*	SIG/MFO	40	25	17.5	100	1913
Be4/4	21		SIG/BBC/SAAS	48	30	25	200	1967
Be4/4	22		SIG/BBC/SAAS	48	30	25	200	1967
Be4/4	23		SIG/BBC/SAAS	48	30	25	200	1967
Xrotm	25		PETER/FORD	–	25	5	125	1956

* Historic car.

BERNER OBERLAND BAHNEN (311,312)   BOB

This line runs from Interlaken to Lauterbrunnen and Grindelwald, at both of which connections are made with the WAB. There are rack sections beyond Zweilütschinen on both routes.

Gauge: 1000 mm.
Electrical System: 1500 V d.c.
Depot: Zweilütschinen.

Class	No.	Name	Builder	Seats	km/h	Tonnes	kW	Built
Tm2/2	1	CHRIGEL	STAD/SAU/BBC/MFO	–	30	15	110	1946
HGe3/3	24		SLM/BBC/MFO	–	45/15	35.6	294	1914
HGe3/3	29		SLM/MFO	–	45/15	36.5	300	1926
HGm2/2	31		STECK/SLM/DZ	–	30	20	283	1985
ABDeh4/4	302		SLM/BBC	10/32	70/30	40	632	1949
BDeh4/4	303		SLM/BBC	42	70/30	40	632	1949
ABeh4/4	304		SLM/SIG/BBC	12/32	60/30	44	1000	1965
ABeh4/4	305		SLM/SIG/BBC	12/32	60/30	44	1000	1965
ABeh4/4	306		SLM/SIG/BBC	12/32	60/30	44	1000	1965
ABeh4/4	307		SLM/SIG/BBC	12/32	60/30	44	1000	1965
ABeh4/4	308		SLM/SIG/BBC	12/32	60/30	44	1000	1965
ABeh4/4	309		SLM/SIG/BBC	12/32	60/30	44	1000	1979
ABeh4/4	310		SLM/SIG/BBC	12/32	60/30	44	1000	1979
ABeh4/4"	311	GRINDELWALD	SLM/BBC	12/24	70/30	45	1256	1986
ABeh4/4"	312	INTERLAKEN	SLM/BBC	12/24	70/30	45	1256	1986
ABeh4/4"	313	LAUTERBRUNNEN	SLM/BBC	12/24	70/30	45	1256	1986

BRIENZ–ROTHORN BAHN (475)   BRB

One of the few non-electrified lines in Switzerland, the BRB was entirely steam operated until diesel locos were introduced to augment the fleet in the 1970s. However, most trains remain steam, and the railway has now purchased three new steam locos from SLM! The line is pure rack, and boasts the greatest height difference between lowest and highest stations of any Swiss railway.

Gauge: 800 mm.
Depot: Brienz.

Class	No.	Name	Builder	Seats	km/h	Tonnes	kW	Built
HII/3	1	*	SLM	–	9.5	17	175	1892
HII/3	2		SLM	–	9.5	17	175	1891
HII/3	3		SLM	–	9.5	17	175	1892
HII/3	4		SLM	–	9.5	17	175	1892
HII/3	5	†	SLM	–	9.5	17	175	1891
HII/3	6		SLM	–	9.5	20	225	1933
HII/3	7		SLM	–	9.5	20	225	1936
Hm2/2	9		STECK/MTU/BIBUS	–	14	13.5	485	1975
Hm2/2	10		STECK/MTU/BIBUS	–	14	13.5	485	1975
Hm2/2	11	OIGAWA	STECK/MTU/BIBUS	–	14	13.5	485	1987
HII/3	12	BERN	SLM	–	14	15.7	300	1992
HII/3	14		SLM	–	14	15.7	300	1996
HII/3	15		SLM	–	14	15.7	300	1996

* ex FMG 7, 1962.
† ex WAB 1, 1911.

BODENSEE TOGGENBURG (853, 870)   BT

This railway forms the eastern section of the Luzern to Romanshorn route, some services hence being jointly operated with the SBB and the SOB. A joint BT/SBB Wil to Nesslau service also operates.

Gauge: 1435 mm.
Electrical System: 15 kV 16^2/$_3$ Hz a.c.
Depots: Herisau, Nesslau-Neu St. Johann.

Number	Class	Name	Builder	Seats	km/h	Tonnes	kW	Built
Tm 236 001	Tm2/2		RACO/SAU	-	45	10	70	1962

▲ **BVB.** Bex Villars Bretaye BDeh 2/4 No. 23 at Bex on 31st August 1994. This rack line terminates in the street outside the SBB station. **J.D. Davis**

▼ **BVZ.** Brig Visp Zermatt HGe 4/4 No. 12 at Brig on 28th July 1994 dates from the electrification of the line. **T.M. Wallis**

Tm	236 002	Tm2/2		RACO/SAU	-	45	10	70	1964
Tm	236 004	Tm2/2	HERKULES	RACO/DZ	-	80	18	200	1977
Tm	236 005	Tm2/2		RACO/DZ	-	80	27	176	1992
Tm	236 006	Tm^{IV}	MAX	SLM/MAN	-	60	30	280	1971
Tm	236 007	Tm^{IV}	MORITZ	SLM/MAN	-	60	30	280	1973
Tm	236 008	Tm2/2	*	RACO/HÜR	-	45	7	22	1937
Tm	236 010	Tm2/2	ANTONIO	SIG/BBC/SAU	-	55	38	243	1960
Te	216 035	Te^{III}		SLM/MFO	-	65	28	239	1966
Be	416 011	Be4/4		SLM/SAAS	-	80	66	1180	1931
Be	416 012	Be4/4		SLM/SAAS	-	80	66	1180	1931
Re	456 091	Re4/4	ROMANSHORN	SLM/BBC	-	130	68	3200	1987
Re	456 092	Re4/4	WITTENBACH	SLM/BBC	-	130	68	3200	1987
Re	456 093	Re4/4	ST. GALLEN	SLM/BBC	-	130	68	3200	1987
Re	456 094	Re4/4	HERISAU	SLM/BBC	-	130	68	3200	1987
Re	456 095	Re4/4	DEGERSHEIM	SLM/BBC	-	130	68	3200	1988
Re	456 096	Re4/4	WATTWIL	SLM/BBC	-	130	68	3200	1988
Be	556 043	Be3/4	TINO	SIG/SAAS	46	80	68	885	1938
RBDe	566 071	RBDe4/4	MUOLEN	FFA/SIG/BBC	48	125	71	1700	1982
RBDe	566 072	RBDe4/4	HÄGGENSCHWIL	FFA/SIG/BBC	48	125	71	1700	1982
RBDe	566 073	RBDe4/4	ROGGWIL–BERG	FFA/SIG/BBC	48	125	71	1700	1982
RBDe	566 074	RBDe4/4	MOGELSBERG	FFA/SIG/BBC	48	125	71	1700	1982
RBDe	566 075	RBDe4/4	BRUNNADERN	FFA/SIG/BBC	48	125	71	1700	1982
RBDe	566 076	RBDe4/4	LICHTENSTEIG	FFA/SIG/BBC	48	125	71	1700	1982
BDe	576 050	BDe4/4	EGNACH	SIG/BBC	32	110	70	2100	1960
BDe	576 051	BDe4/4	EBNAT–KAPPEL	SIG/BBC	32	110	73	2100	1966
BDe	576 052	BDe4/4	KRUMENTAL	SIG/BBC	32	110	73	2100	1966
BDe	576 053	BDe4/4	NESSLAU	SIG/BBC	32	110	73	2100	1967
Eea	936 031	‡		HEN/AEG	-	50	60	530	1966
Eea	936 032	‡		HEN/AEG	-	50	60	530	1966

‡ Ex Ruhrköhle AG, Germany in 1995.
* ex SBB 533.

BEX–VILLARS–BRETAYE (127, 128, 129) BVB

This rack and adhesion line is normally run in two sections, Bex–Villars and Villars–Bretaye. In addition, there is a local tram service from Bex to Bévieux which meets most SBB trains at Bex.

Gauge: 1000 mm.
Electrical System: 700 V d.c.
Depots: Bévieux, Villars.

Class	No.	Name	Builder	Seats	km/h	Tonnes	kW	Built
He2/2	2		SLM/IEG	-	10	14.8	162	1900
Be2/2	8	*	SWS/MFO	18	35	12.7	108	1907
Be2/2	9	*†	SWS/MFO	20	37	15	108	1915
Be2/3	15		SWS/SLM/MFO	28	40	15	96	1948
Be2/3	16		SWS/SLM/MFO	28	40	15	96	1948
BDeh2/4	21		SLM/MFO	53	35/18	19	96	1940
BDeh2/4	22		SLM/MFO	53	35/18	19	96	1940
BDeh2/4	23		SLM/MFO	53	35/18	19	96	1941
BDeh2/4	24		SLM/MFO	53	35/18	19	96	1941
BDeh2/4	25		SLM/MFO	53	35/18	19	96	1944
BDeh2/4	26		SLM/MFO	53	35/18	19	96	1945
HGe4/4	31		SIG/MFO	-	35	24.4	368	1953
HGe4/4	32		SIG/MFO	-	35	24.4	368	1964
Te2/2	42		SIG/BVB/ACEC/MFO	-	35	8.5	108	1898
BDeh4/4	81		SLM/SWP/SAAS	24	40/16	36.5	720	1977
BDeh4/4	82		SLM/SWP/SAAS	24	40/16	36.5	720	1977
BDeh4/4	83		ACMV/SLM/BBC	24	40/25	37	736	1988
Xrote	313		Rolba/Oehler/BVB/MFO	-		5.5	60	1952
Xrotm	320		Rolba/FFA	-		16.5	220	1971
Xe4/4	1501	‡	SWS/BBC	-	35	15	148	1941

* ex VBZ 1148, 1225 in 1953/8.
‡ ex VBZ Be4/4 1501 in 1980.   † Historic car.

BRIG–VISP–ZERMATT (140, 141)   BVZ

This line provides the transport link to Zermatt to which road traffic is not permitted. Hence, in addition to the main service from Brig, there is a frequent shuttle service from Täsch (the end of the valley road) to Zermatt. Through coaches also operate to Chur & St. Moritz via the FO & RhB.

Gauge: 1000 mm.
Electrical System: 11 kV $16^2/_3$ Hz a.c.
Depots: Visp, Brig Glisergrund, Zermatt.

Class	No.	Name	Builder	Seats	km/h	Tonnes	kW	Built
HGe4/4ᴵᴵ	1	MATTERHORN	SLM/ABB	–	90/35	64	1932	1990
HGe4/4ᴵᴵ	2	MONTE ROSA	SLM/ABB	–	90/35	64	1932	1990
HGe4/4ᴵᴵ	3	DOM	SLM/ABB	–	90/35	64	1932	1990
HGe4/4ᴵᴵ	4	TÄSCHHORN	SLM/ABB	–	90/35	64	1932	1990
HGe4/4ᴵᴵ	5	MOUNT FUJI	SLM/ABB	–	90/35	64	1932	1990
HGe4/4	11		SLM/SWS/MFO	–	45/25	46.8	736	1929
HGe4/4	12		SLM/SWS/MFO	–	45/25	46.8	736	1929
HGe4/4	13		SLM/SWS/MFO	–	45/25	46.8	736	1929
HGe4/4	14		SLM/SWS/MFO	–	45/25	46.8	736	1929
HGe4/4	15		SLM/SWS/MFO	–	50/25	46.6	736	1930
HGe4/4	16		SLM/MFO	–	50/25	46.6	736	1939
Deh4/4	21	STALDEN	SIG/SLM/SAAS	–	65/35	49	1094	1975
Deh4/4	22	ST. NIKLAUS	SIG/SLM/SAAS	–	65/35	49	1094	1975
Deh4/4	23	RANDA	SIG/SLM/SAAS	–	65/35	49	1094	1976
Deh4/4	24	TÄSCH	SIG/SLM/SAAS	–	65/35	49	1094	1976
Gm3/3	71		MOY/DZ	–	49	26	191	1975
Gm3/3	72		MOY/DZ	–	49	26	191	1975
Tm2/2	73		SCH/DZ	–	40	21	158	1972
Tm2/2	74	*	RUHR/MWM	-	30	25	184	1958
ABDeh6/6	2031		SIG/SLM/SAAS	92	55/30	71	882	1960
ABDeh6/6	2032		SIG/SLM/SAAS	92	55/30	71	882	1960
ABDeh8/8	2041	BRIG	SIG/SLM/SAAS	108	55/30	88	1176	1964
ABDeh8/8	2042	VISP	SIG/SLM/SAAS	108	55/30	88	1176	1965
ABDeh8/8	2043	ZERMATT	SIG/SLM/SAAS	108	55/30	88	1176	1965
Tm2/2	2921		RACO/SLM	–	30	9.8	40	1957
Tm2/2	2922		RACO/DZ	–	30	10.2	40	1959
Xrotm	2931		BEIL	–			222	1987
Xm1/2	2962		STECK/DZ	–	50/21	4.2	66	1982

* ex Tanklager Rösrath, Germany in 1991; previously DB 333.901.

CEV. Chemins de Fer Electriques Veveysans BDe 4/4 No. 105 at Blonay on 31st August 1994 is an elderly car now in reserve.   **J.D. Davis**

CHEMINS DE FER ÉLECTRIQUES VEVEYSANS (112)   CEV

Once a much larger system, two sections remain in operation, the adhesion line from Vevey to Blonay and the rack continuation from Blonay to Les Pléiades. Only the modern railcars 71–5 can operate throughout. The Blonay–Chamby museum line was once part of the CEV, but it is planned to reinstate a regular service on this section. The CEV has been part of the MOB from 01/01/90.

Gauge: 1000 mm.
Electrical System: 900 V d.c.
Depots: Vevey, Blonay.

Class	No.	Name	Builder	Seats	km/h	Tonnes	kW	Built
He2/2	1		SLM/MFO/SIG	-	20	17.4	390	1911
He2/2	2		SLM/MFO/SIG	-	20	17.4	390	1911
Xe2/3	12		SWS/SLM/CEV/ACEC	-	45	15.5	114	1902
BDeh2/4	71		SWP/SAAS/BBC	60	50/16	33.8	428	1969
BDeh2/4	72		SWP/SAAS/BBC	60	50/16	33.8	428	1970
BDeh2/4	73		SWP/SAAS/BBC	60	50/16	33.8	428	1970
BDeh2/4	74		SWP/SAAS/BBC	60	50/16	33.8	428	1970
BDeh2/4	75		SWP/SAAS/BBC	60	50/16	33.8	428	1983
Te2/2	81		SWS/MFO/CEV	–	30	12	62	1921
Te2/2	82		CEV/MFO	–	25	9.9	60	1938
BDe4/4	103		SWS/MFO	38	45	22.3	208	1903
BDe4/4	105	ST. LEGIER	SWS/MFO	40	45	23.5	208	1913
Xrote	–							

On order - 4 x Be2/6 (Stad/SLM/AD).

CHEMINS DE FER DU JURA (236, 237, 238)   CJ

The CJ comprises two separate systems, a short standard gauge branch linking Porrentruy and Bonfol, and a lengthy metre gauge system meeting the SBB at Chaux de Fonds, Tavannes and Glovelier. Proposals exist to extend the metre gauge from Glovelier to Delémont by adding a third rail to the existing SBB line.

Gauge: 1435/1000 mm.
Electrical System: 15 kV 16²/₃ Hz a.c. (1435 mm), 1500 V d.c. (1000 mm).
Depots: Bonfol (1435 mm), Tramelan, Saignelégier, Noirmont (1000 mm).

Standard Gauge Stock:

Number	Class	Old No.	Name	Builder	Seats	km/h	Tonnes	kW	Built
Xm	077 491	Xm1/2	182		ROBEL/DZ	–	50	7.3	62	1961
Tm	237 481	Tmᴵⱽ	181		SLM/MAN	–	60	30	280	1971
BDe	577 401	BDe4/4	101 BONFOL	SWS/MFO/BBC	60	70	51	640	1968
BDe	577 402	BDe4/4	102 ALLE	SWS/MFO/BBC	48	70	51	640	1980
De	587 451	De4/4	111 VENDLINCOURT	SWS/BBC	–		40	620	1980

Metre Gauge Stock:

Class	No.		Builder	Seats	km/h	Tonnes	kW	Built
De4/4	401		SIG/SAAS	–	60	36	544	1952
De4/4	402		SIG/SAAS	–	60	36	544	1953
De4/4	411		SIG/SAAS	–	90	36	544	1953
Xe2/4	503	*	SWS/BBC	32	45	22	126	1913
Te	504		BBC	–	45	15	126	1913
Gm4/4	508		BL/REN	–	60	49	440	1950
Xm	509		BEIL	–				1985
BDe4/4	601		SIG/SAAS	34	70	26.5	332	1953
BDe4/4	602		SIG/SAAS	34	70	26.5	332	1953
ABDe4/4	603		SIG/SAAS	9/17	70	26.5	332	1953
BDe4/4	604		SIG/SAAS	34	70	26.5	332	1953
BDe4/4	605		SIG/SAAS	34	70	26.5	332	1953
BDe4/4	606		SIG/SAAS	34	70	26.5	332	1953
BDe4/4	607		SIG/SAAS	34	70	26.5	332	1953

CJ. Chemins de Fer du Jura BDe 4/4 No. 602 at Le Noirmont on 2nd September 1994.   **J.D. Davis**

BDe4/4	608		SIG/SAAS	34	70	26.5	332	1953
BDe4/4[II]	611		FFA/BBC	32				1985
BDe4/4[II]	612		FFA/BBC	32				1985
BDe4/4[II]	613		FFA/BBC	32				1985
BDe4/4[II]	614		FFA/BBC	32				1985
BDe4/4	621	‡	SWS/MFO	40	60	26		1947

* Restored as museum car BCe2/4 70.
‡ ex FW 207 in 1991.

CHEMINS DE FER DES MONTAGNES NEUCHÂTELOIS (214, 222) CMN

This railway comprises two separate lines, Chaux de Fonds to Les Ponts de Martel and Le Locle to Les Brenets. The future of both lines was uncertain for some time, but new stock has now been delivered. The Italian built cars are unusual for Switzerland.

Gauge: 1000 mm.
Electrical System: 1500 V d.c.
Depots: Les Brenets, Les Ponts de Martel.

Class	No.	Builder	Seats	km/h	Tonnes	kW	Built
BDe4/4	2	REG/BBC/SAAS	48	60	23.5	320	1950
BDe4/4	3	REG/BBC/SAAS	48	60	23.5	320	1950
BDe4/4	4	REG/BBC/SAAS	48	60	23.5	320	1950
BDe4/4	5	REG/BBC/SAAS	48	60	23.5	320	1950
BDe4/4	6	ACMV/ABB		80	34	800	1991
BDe4/4	7	ACMV/ABB		80	34	800	1991
BDe4/4	8	ACMV/ABB		80	34	800	1996
Tm2/2	11	RACO/DZ	–	75	19	177	1983

DOLDERBAHN (732)   Db

Converted from a funicular in 1973, this rack railway connects with the Zürich trams at its lower terminus of Romerhof.

Gauge: 1000 mm.
Electrical System: 600 V d.c.
Depot: Dolder. (the upper station is convertible to a depot!).

Class	No.	Name	Builder	Seats	km/h	Tonnes	kW	Built
Bhe1/2	1		SLM/GANG/BBC	26	25	14.4	150	1973
Bhe1/2	2		SLM/GANG/BBC	26	25	14.4	150	1973

EMMENTHAL–BURGDORF–THUN (440)　　EBT
SOLOTHURN–MÜNSTER BAHN (411)　　SMB
VEREINIGTE HUTTWIL BAHNEN (441, 442)　VHB

These three railways under common management operate an extensive standard gauge network to the east of Bern. Although two branches have closed, much of the fleet has been modernised during recent years. The three companies are expected to merge as a single entity in the near future; this will be known as the RM (Regionalverkehr Mittelland).

Gauge: 1435 mm.
Electrical System: 15 kV $16\frac{2}{3}$ Hz a.c.
Depots: Burgdorf, Huttwil, Oberburg.

Number		Class	OldNo.	Co.	Name	Builder	Seats	km/h	Tonnes	kW	Built
Te	216 121	Te^{III}	121	EBT		SLM/SAAS	–	60	29	257	1945
Te	216 122	Te^{III}	122	EBT	(ex SBB 137)	SLM/SAAS	–	60	29	257	1945
Te	216 123	Te^{III}	123	EBT		SLM/SAAS	–	60	29	257	1952
Te	216 124	Te^{III}	124	EBT		SLM/SAAS	–	60	29	257	1952
Te	216 161	Te^{III}	161	VHB		SLM/SAAS	–	60	29	257	1945
Te	216 321	Te^{I}	21	EBT		SLM/MFO	–	45	12.4	90	1944
Te	216 322	Te^{I}	22	EBT		SLM/MFO	–	45	12.4	90	1944
Te	216 323	Te^{I}	23	EBT		SLM/MFO	–	45	12.4	90	1944
Te	216 324	Te^{I}	24	EBT		SLM/MFO	–	45	12.4	90	1946
Te	216 325	Te^{I}	25	EBT		SLM/MFO	–	45	12.4	90	1946
Te	216 326	Te^{I}	26	EBT		SLM/MFO	–	45	12.4	90	1946
Te	216 327	Te^{I}	27	EBT		SLM/MFO	–	45	12.4	90	1946
Te	216 328	Te^{I}	28	EBT		SLM/MFO	–	45	13	90	1955
Te	216 329	Te^{I}	29	EBT		SLM/MFO	–	45	13	90	1955
Te	216 361	Te^{I}	61	VHB		SLM/MFO	–	45	13	90	1963
Tm	236 310	Tm	10	EBT	MAX	DIEMA/DZ	–	40	24	140	1978
Tm	236 312	Tm	12	EBT		RACO/SAU	–	45	10	74	1962
Tm	236 313	Tm	13	EBT		RACO/SAU	–	45	10	74	1972
Tm	236 314	Tm	14	EBT		RACO/SAU	–	45	10	74	1975
Tm	236 315	Tm	15	EBT		HEN/CAT	–	60	54		1958
Tm	236 352	Tm	52	VHB		RACO/SAU	–	45	10	74	1971
Tm	236 353	Tm	53	VHB		RACO/SAU	–	45	10	74	1971
Tm	236 354	Tm	54	VHB		RACO/SAU	–	45	10	74	1972
Tm	236 355	Tm	55	VHB		RACO/SAU	–	45	10	74	1972
Tm	236 356	Tm	56	VHB		RACO/DZ	–	75	19	177	1980
Tm	236 357	Tm	57	VHB		HEN/CAT	–	50	45		1965
Tm	236 371	Tm	71	SMB		RACO/SAU	–	45	10	74	1964
Tm	236 372	Tm	72	SMB		RACO/DZ	–	75	19	177	1983
Be	406 101	Be4/4	101	EBT		SLM/SAAS	–	80	64.7	1177	1932
Be	406 102	Be4/4	102	EBT		SLM/SAAS	–	80	64.7	1177	1932
Be	406 103	Be4/4	103	EBT		SLM/SAAS	–	80	64.7	1177	1933
Be	406 104	Be4/4	104	EBT		SLM/SAAS	–	80	64.7	1177	1933
Be	406 105	Be4/4	105	EBT		SLM/SAAS	–	80	64.7	1177	1933
Be	406 106	Be4/4	106	EBT		SLM/SAAS	–	80	64.7	1177	1933
Be	406 107	Be4/4	107	EBT		SLM/SAAS	–	80	64.7	1177	1944
Be	406 108	Be4/4	108	EBT		SLM/SAAS	–	80	64.7	1177	1953
Be	406 171	Be4/4	171	SMB		SLM/SAAS	–	80	64.7	1177	1932
Be	406 172	Be4/4	172	SMB		SLM/SAAS	–	80	64.7	1177	1932
Re	436 111	Re4/4	111	EBT		SLM/BBC/MFO/SAAS	–	120	80	4653	1969
Re	436 112	Re4/4	112	EBT		SLM/BBC/MFO/SAAS	–	120	80	4653	1969
Re	436 113	Re4/4	113	EBT		SLM/BBC/MFO/SAAS	–	120	80	4653	1983

Re	436 141	Re4/4	141 VHB		SLM/BBC/MFO/SAAS	–	120	80	4653	1983
Re	436 181	Re4/4	181 SMB		SLM/BBC/MFO/SAAS	–	120	80	4653	1983
Re	456 142	-	- VHB	GUTENBURG	SLM/SGP/ABB		130	68	3200	1993
Re	456 143	-	- VHB		SLM/SGP/ABB		130	68	3200	1993
RBDe 566 221		RBDe4/4221	EBT		SWS/SAAS	56	125	71	1340	1973
RBDe 566 222		RBDe4/4222	EBT		SWS/SAAS	56	125	71	1340	1974
RBDe 566 223		RBDe4/4223	EBT		SWS/SAAS	56	125	71	1340	1974
RBDe 566 224		RBDe4/4224	EBT		SWS/SAAS	56	125	71	1340	1974
RBDe 566 225		RBDe4/4225	EBT		SWS/SAAS	56	125	71	1340	1974
RBDe 566 226		RBDe4/4226	EBT		SWS/SAAS	56	125	71	1340	1974
RBDe 566 227		RBDe4/4227	EBT	EMMENTAL	SWS/BBC	56	125	71	1340	1984
RBDe 566 228		RBDe4/4228	EBT	GERLAFINGEN	SWS/BBC	56	125	71	1340	1985
RBDe 566 229		RBDe4/4229	EBT	HASLE-RÜEGSAU	SWS/BBC	56	125	71	1340	1985
RBDe 566 230		RBDe4/4230	EBT	OBERDIESSBACH	SWS/BBC	56	125	71	1340	1985
RBDe 566 231		RBDe4/4231	EBT	KIRCHBERG-ALCHENFLÜH	SWS/BBC	56	125	71	1340	1985
RBDe 566 232		RBDe4/4232	EBT	GROSSHÖCHSTETTEN	SWS/BBC	56	125	71	1340	1985
RBDe 566 233		RBDe4/4233	EBT	LÜTZELFLÜH	SWS/BBC	56	125	71	1340	1985
RBDe 566 261		RBDe4/4261	VHB		SWS/SAAS	56	125	71	1340	1973
RBDe 566 262		RBDe4/4262	VHB	SUMISWALD	SWS/BBC	56	125	71	1340	1985
RBDe 566 263		RBDe4/4263	VHB	ROHRBACH	SWS/BBC	56	125	71	1340	1985
RBDe 566 264		RBDe4/4264	VHB	ZELL	SWS/BBC	56	125	71	1340	1985
RBDe 566 265		RBDe4/4265	VHB	MADISWIL	SWS/BBC	56	125	71	1340	1985
RBDe 566 281		RBDe4/4281	SMB		SWS/SAAS	56	125	71	1340	1973
RBDe 566 282		RBDe4/4282	SMB	LANGENDORF	SWS/BBC	56	125	71	1340	1985
RBDe 566 283		RBDe4/4283	SMB	CRÉMINES	SWS/BBC	56	125	71	1340	1985
BDe	576 201	BDe4/4^{II} 201	EBT	BURGDORF	SIG/BBC	32	110	73	2060	1966
BDe	576 240	BDe2/4 240	EBT	*	SWS/SIG/BBC/MFO	30	80		588	1932
BDe	576 251	BDe4/4^{II} 251	VHB	HUTTWIL	SIG/BBC	32	110	73	2060	1966
BDe	576 252	BDe4/4^{II} 252	VHB	WILLISAU	SIG/BBC	32	110	73	2060	1966
De	586 235	De4/4 235	EBT		SWS/SIG/BBC/MFO	–	80	67	1177	1981
De	586 236	De4/4 236	EBT		SWS/SIG/BBC/MFO	–	80	67	1177	1981
De	586 266	De4/4 266	VHB		SWS/SIG/BBC/MFO	–	80	67	1177	1981
De	586 267	De4/4 267	VHB		SWS/SIG/BBC/MFO	–	80	67	1177	1981
Ee	936 131	Ee3/3 131	EBT		SLM/BBC/MFO/SAAS	–	45	44	508	1967
Ee	936 132	Ee3/3 132	EBT		SLM/ABB	-	75	45	663	1992
Ee	936 133	Ee3/3 133	EBT		SLM/ABB	-	75	45	663	1992
Ee	936 134	Ee3/3 134	EBT		SLM/ABB	-	75	45	663	1992
Ee	936 135	Ee3/3 135	EBT	(ex SBB 16312)	SLM/BBC	–	40	45	428	1928
Ee	936 151	Ee3/3 151	VHB		SLM/ABB	-	75	45	663	1992

* Historic car.

FERROVIE AUTOLINEE REGIONALI TICINESE (620)   FART
SOCIETA SUBALPINA DI IMPRESE FERROVIARIE (620)   SSIF

This international light railway links Locarno in Switzerland with Domodossola in Italy, traversing very spectacular scenery. The SSIF is an Italian company operating the western half of the line, although the through services are jointly operated and the stock is numbered in a common series. The route through Lugano was reconstructed on a new underground alignment in 1990.

Gauge: 1000 mm.
Electrical System: 1200 V d.c.
Depots: Locarno, Ponte Brolla, Camedo (FART), Domodossola, Re (SSIF).

Class	No.	Co.	Name	Builder	Seats	km/h	Tonnes	kW	Built
ABDe4/4	1	FART		MAN/BBC	12/32	45	28	180	1907 (64)
Xe2/4	4	SSIF		MAN/MFO	–	60	15.2	100	1911
Xe2/4	5	SSIF		MAN/MFO	–	60	15.2	100	1911
Xe2/2	6	FART		MAN/BBC/FART	–	40	11	60	1908 (75)
Ce2/2	7	FART	*	MAN/BBC	18	40	11	60	1908
Tm2/2	9	FART		RACO/DZ	–		21		1989
ABDe4/4	12	SSIF		CET/BBC	6/30	45	30	310	1923
ABDe4/4	13	SSIF		CET/BBC	6/30	45	30	310	1923

Class	No.	Owner		Name	Builder	Seats	km/h	Tonnes	kW	Built
ABDe4/4	16	SSIF			CET/BBC/SSIF	6/30	45	30	310	1923 (75)
BCFe4/4	17	FART	*		CET/BBC	6/30	45	30	310	1923
ABDe4/4	18	SSIF			CET/BBC	6/30	45	30	310	1923
ABe8/8	21	SSIF		ROMA	SWP/TIBB	28/85	60	59	725	1959
ABe8/8	22	FART		TICINO	SWP/TIBB	28/85	60	59	725	1959
ABe8/8	23	SSIF		OSSOLA	SWP/TIBB	28/85	60	59	725	1959
ABe8/8	24	SSIF		VIGEZZO	SWP/TIBB	28/85	60	59	725	1959
ABDe6/6	31	FART		BERNA	SWP/TIBB	18/45	60	45	365	1963
ABDe6/6	32	FART		VALLESE	SWP/TIBB	18/45	60	45	365	1963
ABe6/6	33	SSIF		SEMPIONE	SWP/TIBB	10/72	60	45.5	545	1968
ABe6/6	34	SSIF		PIEMONTE	SWP/TIBB	10/72	60	45.5	545	1968
ABe6/6	35	SSIF		VERBANO	SWP/TIBB	10/72	60	45.5	545	1968
ABe4/6	51	FART			ACMV		80		640	1992
ABe4/6	52	FART			ACMV		80		640	1992
ABe4/6	53	FART			ACMV		80		640	1993
ABe4/6	54	FART			ACMV		80		640	1993
ABe4/6	55	FART			ACMV		80		640	1993
ABe4/6	56	FART			ACMV		80		640	1993
Ae4/6	57	FART			ACMV		80		640	1993
Ae4/6	58	FART			ACMV		80		640	1993
ABe4/6	61	SSIF			ACMV		80		640	1992
ABe4/6	62	SSIF			ACMV		80		640	1992
ABe4/6	63	SSIF		MALESGO	ACMV		80		640	1993
ABe4/6	64	SSIF			ACMV		80		640	1993

* Historic cars.

FORCHBAHN (731)   **FB**

Once a tramway basically operated as a rural extension of the Zürich system, this light railway has been upgraded mostly to roadside running, but with some sections of private right-of-way. The cars still run over the Zürich tram tracks from the terminus at Stadelhofen (adjacent to the SBB station) to Rehalp.

Gauge: 1000 mm.
Electrical System: 1200 V d.c. (600 V over VBZ tram tracks).
Depot: Forch.

Class	No.		Name	Builder	Seats	km/h	Tonnes	kW	Built
CFe2/2	4	*		SWS/MFO	24	36	20.2	150	1912
Xe4/4	9			SWS/MFO/VBZ	–	70	26	300	1948 (82)
CFe4/4	10	*		SWS/MFO	40	70	26.5	300	1948
BDe4/4	11			SWS/MFO	40	65	29.4	375	1959
BDe4/4	12			SWS/MFO	40	65	29.4	375	1959
BDe4/4	13			SWS/MFO	40	65	29.4	375	1959
BDe4/4	14			SWS/MFO	40	65	29.4	375	1959
BDe4/4	15			SWS/MFO	40	65	29.4	375	1966
BDe4/4	16			SWS/MFO	40	65	29.4	375	1966
Be8/8	21+22			SWS/SWP/BBC	86	65	42	610	1976
Be8/8	23+24			SWS/SWP/BBC	86	65	42	610	1976
Be8/8	25+26			SWS/SWP/BBC	86	65	42	610	1976
Be8/8	27+28			SWS/SWP/BBC	86	65	42	610	1981
Be8/8	29+30			SWS/SWP/BBC	86	65	42	610	1981
Be8/8	31+32			SWS/SWP/BBC	86	65	42	610	1986
Be4/4	51			SWP/SIG/ABB	46	65	24.5	500	1993
Be4/4	52			SWP/SIG/ABB	46	65	24.5	500	1993
Be4/4	53			SWP/SIG/ABB	46	65	24.5	500	1993
Be4/4	54			SWP/SIG/ABB	46	65	24.5	500	1993
Be4/4	55			SWP/SIG/ABB	46	65	24.5	500	1993
Be4/4	56			SWP/SIG/ABB	46	65	24.5	500	1993
Be4/4	57			SWP/SIG/ABB	46	65	24.5	500	1993
Be4/4	58			SWP/SIG/ABB	46	65	24.5	500	1993

* Historic cars.

FERROVIA LUGANO–PONTE TRESA (635) FLP

The only survivor of several light railways in the Lugano area, the FLP has been modernised and new cars purchased.

Gauge: 1000 mm.
Electrical System: 1000 V d.c.
Depots: Agno, Ponte Tresa.

Class	No.	Name	Builder	Seats	km/h	Tonnes	kW	Built
Tm	1		GLEIS					1994
Be4/4	21	LEMA	SIG/BBC	128	60	48.7	330	1978
Be4/4	22	MALCANTONE	SIG/BBC	128	60	48.7	330	1979
Be4/4	23	VEDEGGIO	SIG/BBC	128	60	48.7	330	1979
Be4/4	24	MAGLIASENA	SIG/BBC	128	60	48.7	330	1979
Be4/4	25	CERESIO	SIG/BBC	128	60	48.7	330	1979
Be4/4	41*		SIG/BBC	112	60	46	335	1979
Be4/4	42*		SIG/BBC	112	60	46	335	1979

* Ex FART 41/2 in 1993.

FURKA OBERALP (610) FO

Forming the only east–west rail link across the south of the country, for many years the section of the FO over the Furka pass was only open during the summer. However, in 1982 the new Furka tunnel was opened, facilitating all-year-round operation, but eliminating the spectacular section over the pass itself. Several stretches of rack remain on this scenic line. Through coaches operate from Zermatt (BVZ) to Chur & St. Moritz (RhB).

Gauge: 1000 mm.
Electrical System: 11 kV $16^2/_3$ Hz a.c.
Depots: Brig Glisergrund, Andermatt.

Class	No.	Name	Builder	Seats	km/h	Tonnes	kW	Built
HGe4/4	31		SLM/MFO	-	55/30	46.6	912	1941
HGe4/4	32		SLM/MFO	-	55/30	46.6	912	1941
HGe4/4	33		SLM/MFO	-	55/30	46.6	912	1941
HGe4/4	34		SLM/MFO	-	55/30	46.6	912	1941
HGe4/4	36		SLM/MFO	-	55/30	46.6	912	1949
HGe4/4	37		SLM/MFO	-	55/30	46.6	912	1956
BDeh2/4	41		SLM/BBC	40	55/30	37	427	1941
BDeh2/4	42		SLM/BBC	40	55/30	37	427	1941
BDeh2/4	44		SLM/BBC	40	55/30	37	427	1942
BDeh2/4	45		SLM/BBC	40	55/30	37	427	1942
Deh4/4	51	DISENTIS/MUSTÉR	SIG/SLM/BBC	–	60/30	48	1032	1972
Deh4/4	52	TAVETSCH/TUJETSCH	SIG/SLM/BBC	–	60/30	48	1032	1972
Deh4/4	53	URSERN	SIG/SLM/BBC	–	60/30	48	1032	1972
Deh4/4	54	GOMS	SIG/SLM/BBC	–	60/30	48	1032	1972
Deh4/4	55	BRIG	SIG/SLM/BBC	–	60/30	48	1032	1972
HGm4/4	61		SLM/BBC/MFO/CUM	–	50/30	54	1134	1968
HGm4/4	62		SLM/BBC/MFO/CUM	–	50/30	54	1134	1968
Gm4/4	71	ELCH	JUNG/MWM	–	40	37.6	652	1966
Ge4/4III	81	WALLIS	SLM/BBC	–	90	50	1700	1980
Ge4/4III	82	URI	SLM/BBC	–	90	50	1700	1980
Deh4/4II	91	GÖSCHENEN	SLM/BBC	–	60/30	51	1032	1979
Deh4/4II	92	REALP	SLM/BBC	–	60/30	51	1032	1980
Deh4/4II	93	OBERWALD	SLM/BBC	–	60/30	51	1032	1980
Deh4/4II	94	FIESCH	SLM/BBC	–	60/30	51	1032	1980
Deh4/4II	95	ANDERMATT	SLM/BBC	–	60/30	51	1032	1984
Deh4/4II	96	MÜNSTER	SLM/BBC	–	60/30	51	1032	1984
HGe4/4II	101	SITTEN/VILLE DE SION	SLM/BBC	–	90/30	64	1932	1986
HGe4/4II	102	ALTDORF	SLM/BBC	–	90/30	64	1932	1986
HGe4/4II	103	CHUR/MARCAU DE CUERA	SLM/BBC	–	90/30	64	1932	1986
HGe4/4II	104	FURKA*	SLM/BBC	–	90/30	64	1932	1986
HGe4/4II	105	OBERALP†	SLM/BBC	–	90/30	64	1932	1986

FO. Furka-Oberalp Bahn Deh 4/4 No. 54 'GOMS' at Göschenen on 1st August 1994 is a motor baggage van used on push-pull services. **T.M. Wallis**

HGe4/4ⁱⁱ	106	ST GOTTHARD	SLM/ABB	–	90/30	64	1932	1989
HGe4/4ⁱⁱ	107	GRIMSEL	SLM/ABB	–	90/30	64	1932	1989
HGe4/4ⁱⁱ	108	NOVENA	SLM/ABB	–	90/30	64	1932	1989
Te2/2	4926		SLM/SAAS	–	30	12.7	96	1946
Xrote	4931		SLM/SIG/MFO	–		16	405	1941
Xrote	4932		SLM/SIG/MFO	–		16	405	1943
Xrote	4933		SLM/SIG/MFO	–		16	405	1945
Xrotm	4934		BEIL/DZ/JMR	–	60	32	670	1980
Xrotm	4935		BEIL	–				1986
Tm2/2	4971		SCH/DZ	–	33	21.8	170	1960
Tm2/2	4972		SCH/DZ	–	33	21.8	170	1960
Tm2/2	4973 §		RUHR	–	45	23	176	1958
Ta2/2	4982			–	15	6.5		1994

* ex SBB 1951 in 1990.
† ex SBB 1952 in 1990.
§ ex DB 333.902 in 1984.

FRAUENFELD–WIL (841)   FW

Once threatened with closure, this light railway has now been modernised with new stock and a new depot. The line is mostly roadside running, with street running in Frauenfeld.

Gauge: 1000 mm.
Electrical System: 1200 V d.c.
Depots: Wil.

Class	No.	Name	Builder	Seats	km/h	Tonnes	kW	Built
Be4/4	11	FRAUENFELD	FFA/BBC					1985
Be4/4	12	MATZINGEN	FFA/BBC					1985
Be4/4	13	WÄNGI	FFA/BBC					1985
Be4/4	14	MÜNCHWILEN	FFA/BBC					1985
Be4/4	15	STADT WIL	FFA/BBC					1985
Be4/4	16	KUFSTEIN	STAD/ABB					1992
Be4/4	17		STAD/ABB					1992
Be4/4	205		SWS/MFO	54	65	29.5	460	1947
Be4/4	206		SWS/MFO	54	65	29.5	460	1947

▲ **GFM.** Metre gauge Gruyère Fribourg Morat Be 4/4 No. 151 at Bulle on 1st September 1994.

J.D. Davis

▼ **GFM.** Gruyère Fribourg Morat standard gauge RABDe 4/4 No. 173 also at Bulle on the same day.

J.D. Davis

GRUYÈRE–FRIBOURG–MORAT (CHEMINS DE FER FRIBOURGEOIS) (253, 254, 255, 256)　　GFM

This system operates both standard and metre gauge lines. There are two separate standard gauge branches, Fribourg–Ins and Bulle–Romont, plus an extensive metre gauge system centred on Bulle. Connection is made with the MOB at Montbovon.

Gauges: 1435/1000 mm.
Electrical System: 15 kV $16^2/_3$ Hz a.c. (1435 mm), 800 V d.c. (1000 mm).
Depots: Bulle, Fribourg (1435 mm), Bulle, Châtel St. Denis, Montbovon (1000 mm).

Metre Gauge Stock:

Class	No.	Name	Builder	Seats	km/h	Tonnes	kW	Built
Te2/2	11		MFO	-	30	16.5	88	1913
Te2/2	12		CEG/ALIOTH	-	50	9	774	1913
Te4/4	13		CEG/ALIOTH	-	45	23	148	1901 (27)
Te4/4	14		CEG/ALIOTH	-	50	21.5	264	1901 (33)
Tm2/2	15		SCH/DZ	-	35	24	168	1971
Tm2/2	16		CFD	-	-	-	-	-
GDe4/4	101	VILLE DE BULLE	SLM/BBC	-	90	48.2	1053	1983
GDe4/4	102	NEIRIVUE	SLM/BBC	-	90	48.2	1053	1983
Be4/4	107		SWS/ALIOTH	40	60	27	264	1903
Be4/4	111		SWS/ALIOTH	44	60	27	264	1903
Be4/4	115		SWS/ALIOTH	44	60	29.5	296	1905
Be4/4	116 †		SWS/MFO	58	75	35	486	1922
BDe4/4	121	REMAUFENS	ACMV/ABB		90		640	1992
BDe4/4	122	LATOURDETRÔME	ACMV/ABB		90		640	1992
BDe4/4	123	BROC	ACMV/ABB		90		640	1995
BDe4/4	124	VAUDENS	ACMV/ABB		90		640	1995
Be4/4	131		SWS/BBC	48	75	33	408	1943
Be4/4	133		SWS/BBC	48	75	33	408	1943
BDe4/4	141	GRUYÈRES	SWP/SAAS	46	70	38	648	1972
BDe4/4	142	SEMSALES	SWP/SAAS	46	70	38	648	1972
Be4/4	151	LA GRUYÈRE	SIG/SAAS	44	80	32	448	1977
Be4/4	152	CHÂTEL ST. DENIS	SIG/SAAS	44	80	32	448	1977

Standard Gauge Stock:

Number		Class	Name	Builder	Seats	km/h	Tonnes	kW	Built
Te	217 052	Te2/2		SLM/SAAS	–	20	11.5	44	1947
Te	217 091	Te2/2		SIG/BBC	–	75	30	242	1960
Tm	237 081	Tm2/2		RACO/SAU	–	30	10.3	81	1943
Tm	237 082	Tm2/2		RACO/VR/MB	–	45	33	236	1964
Tm	237 085	Tm2/2		MOYSE	–	40			
Tm	237 086	Tm2/2		MOYSE	–	40			
Ae	417 191	*		LEW/STAD	–	100	82	2920	1967
Ae	417 192	*	VAULRUZ	LEW/STAD	–	100	82	2920	1969
ABDe	537 155	ABDe2/4		SIG/BBC	16/39	90	48.8	442	1931
ABDe	537 161	ABDe4/4		SIG/BBC	18/34	100	56	736	1946
ABDe	537 162	ABDe4/4		SIG/BBC	18/34	100	56	736	1946
ABDe	537 163	ABDe4/4		SIG/BBC	18/34	100	56	736	1947
ABDe	537 165	ABDe4/4		SIG/BBC	18/34	100	56	736	1947
ABDe	537 166	ABe4/4		SIG/BBC	18/58	100	57	736	1947
ABDe	537 167	ABe4/4		SIG/BBC	18/58	100	57	736	1948
RABDe	537 171	RABDe4/4	LA SARINE	SIG/SWS/BBC	12/31	125	70	1700	1983
RABDe	537 172	RABDe4/4	VULLY	SIG/SWS/BBC	12/31	125	70	1700	1983
RABDe	537 173	RABDe4/4 ‡		SIG/SWS/BBC	15/28	125	70	1700	1983
RABDe	537 181	RBDe4/4	CRESSIERSURMORAT	SIG/SWS/ABB	55	125	69.7	1700	1991
RABDe	537 182	RBDe4/4	COURTEPIN	SIG/SWS/ABB	55	125	69.7	1700	1991
Em	837 084	Tm3/3		KRUPP/MAN	-	40	45.5	324	1963

* ex DB 142 110/45 in 1995.
† renumbered ex 121 in 1992.　　‡ ex RVT 104 in 1991.

JB. Jungfraubahn BDhe 2/4 No. 206 photographed below the Eiger on 7th September 1992.

Mervyn Turvey

GORNERGRATBAHN (142) GGB

A pure rack mountain railway starting from Zermatt. This line and the Jungfraubahn are the only Swiss railways electrified on the 3-phase system which requires two overhead wires.

Gauge: 1000 mm.
Electrical System: 725 V 50 Hz 3-phase.
Depot: Zermatt.

Class	No.	Name	Builder	Seats	km/h	Tonnes	kW	Built
He2/2	3001		SLM/SIG/BBC	-	9	13.3	184	1898
He2/2	3002		SLM/SIG/BBC	-	9	13.3	184	1898
He2/2	3003		SLM/SIG/BBC	-	9	11.4	184	1898
Bhe2/4	3011		SLM/BBC	56	14.5	18	190	1947
Bhe2/4	3012		SLM/BBC	56	14.5	18	190	1947
Bhe2/4	3013		SLM/BBC	56	14.5	18	190	1952
Bhe2/4	3014		SLM/BBC	56	14.5	18	190	1952
Bhe2/4	3015		SLM/BBC	56	14.5	18	190	1954
Bhe2/4	3016		SLM/BBC	56	14.5	18	190	1954
Bhe2/4	3017		SLM/BBC	56	14.5	18	190	1958
Bhe2/4	3018		SLM/BBC	56	14.5	18	190	1958
Bhe2/4	3019		SLM/BBC	56	14.5	18	190	1961
Bhe2/4	3020		SLM/BBC	56	14.5	18	190	1961
Bhe2/4	3021		SLM/BBC	56	14.5	18	190	1961
Bhe2/4	3022		SLM/BBC	56	14.5	18	190	1961
Bhe4/8	3041		SLM/BBC	120	14.5	35.7	380	1965
Bhe4/8	3042		SLM/BBC	120	14.5	35.7	380	1965
Bhe4/8	3043		SLM/BBC	120	14.5	35.7	380	1967
Bhe4/8	3044		SLM/BBC	120	14.5	35.7	380	1967
Bhe4/8	3051		SLM/ABB	124	28	48.85	804	1993
Bhe4/8	3052		SLM/ABB	124	28	48.85	804	1993
Bhe4/8	3053		SLM/ABB	124	28	48.85	804	1993
Bhe4/8	3054		SLM/ABB	124	28	48.85	804	1993
Bhe4/4	3061		SLM/BBC	28	15.3	27.2	380	1981
Bhe4/4	3062		SLM/BBC	28	15.3	27.2	380	1981
Xrote	3931		SLM/MFO	-				1944
Xrote	3932		SLM/BBC	-				1970

JUNGFRAUBAHN (311, 312) JB

This rack line starting at Kleine Scheidegg, where it connects with the WAB, climbs mostly in tunnel through the Eiger and Mönch to its upper terminus at Jungfraujoch below the summit of the Jungfrau. There are superb views here, the highest railway station in Europe.

Gauge: 1000 mm.
Electrical System: 1125 V 50 Hz 3-phase a.c.
Depots: Eigergletscher, Kleine Scheidegg.

Class	No.	Name	Builder	Seats	km/h	Tonnes	kW	Built
He2/2	6		SLM/BBC	-	11.5	15	324	1904
He2/2	8		SLM/BBC	-	18.5	15	280	1912
He2/2	9		SLM/BBC	-	18.5	15	280	1912
He2/2	10		SLM/BBC	-	18.5	15	280	1912
He2/2	11	*	SLM/BBC	-	18.5	15	280	1924
Xrote	51		SLM/MFO	-	12	14	376	1937
BDhe2/4	201		SLM/BBC	41	24	25	440	1955
BDhe2/4	202		SLM/BBC	41	24	25	440	1955
BDhe2/4	203		SLM/BBC	41	24	25	440	1960
BDhe2/4	204		SLM/BBC	41	24	25	440	1960
BDhe2/4	205		SLM/BBC	41	24	25	440	1961
BDhe2/4	206		SLM/BBC	41	24	25	440	1961
BDhe2/4	207	LAKE BIWA/OTSU	SLM/BBC	41	24	25	440	1964
BDhe2/4	208		SLM/BBC	41	24	25	440	1964
BDhe2/4	209		SLM/BBC	41	24	25	440	1964
BDhe2/4	210		SLM/BBC	41	24	25	440	1964

BDhe4/8	211	SLM/ABB	108	27/14	44.8	804	1992
BDhe4/8	212	SLM/ABB	108	27/14	44.8	804	1992
BDhe4/8	213	SLM/ABB	108	27/14	44.8	804	1992
BDhe4/8	214	SLM/ABB	108	27/14	44.8	804	1992

* Historic Locomotive.

LAUSANNE–ECHALLENS–BERCHER (102)   LEB

A light railway serving the area to the north of Lausanne, recently modernised with new stock. The railway is to be extended from the present inconveniently located terminus at Lausanne Chauderon to a new terminus at Flon, nearer the town centre and with an interchange with the LG/LO; the first stage, a new underground station at Chauderon opened in 1995.

Gauge: 1000 mm.
Electrical System: 1500 V d.c.
Depots: Eschallens, Lausanne Chauderon.

Class	No.	Name	Builder	Seats	km/h	Tonnes	kW	Built
Tm2/2	1		DIEMA/DEUTZ	-				1966
Tm2/2	2		RACO/CUMM	-	25			1988
BDe4/4	21	*	SWS/SAAS	40	60	30	324	1935
BDe4/4	25		SWS/SAAS	40	60	30	324	1947
Be4/4	26		SWS/SAAS	40	80	35	588	1966
Be4/4	27		SWS/SAAS	40	80	35	588	1966
Be4/8	31	LAUSANNE	ACMV/SIG/BBC	58+66	80	54.5	752	1985
Be4/8	32	ESCHALLENS	ACMV/SIG/BBC	58+66	80	54.5	752	1985
Be4/8	33	BERCHER	ACMV/SIG/BBC	58+66	80	54.5	752	1985
Be4/8	34	PRILLY	ACMV/SIG/ABB	56+64	80	54.5	752	1991
Be4/8	35	ROMANEL	ACMV/SIG/ABB	56+64	80	54.5	752	1991
Be4/8	36	CHESEAUX	ACMV/SIG/ABB	56+64	80	54.5	752	1991

* Historic car.

LAUSANNE–GARE (104)   LG
LAUSANNE–OUCHY (103)   LO

Two short rack lines, originally funiculars, now owned by the municipality. The LO provides a link between the town centre (Flon), the SBB station and Ouchy on Lake Geneva. The LG provides a supplementary service between the town and the station. Plans exist to convert the line to a rubber-tyred metro, and extend it northwards to Epalinges. This will require new stock.

Gauge: 1435 mm.
Electrical System: 650 V d.c.
Depot: Ouchy.

Number	Class	Old No.	Co.	Builder	Seats	km/h	Tonnes	kW	Built
He 298821	He2/2	121	LO	SLM/MFO	-	32	18.1	464	1958
He 298822	He2/2	122	LO	SLM/MFO	-	32	18.1	464	1958
He 298823	He2/2	123	LO	SLM/MFO	-	32	18.1	464	1958
Bhe 598811	Bhe2/2	111	LG	SLM/SIG/MFO	*	32	18.5	464	1964
Bhe 598812	Bhe2/2	112	LG	SLM/SIG/MFO	*	32	18.5	464	1964

* Accommodates 154 standing passengers (no seats).

LOOKOOP AG   LOKOOP

This is a recently established company jointly owned by the Mittel Thurgau Bahn and Sudostbahn. It owns no track but operates a fleet of former DB Class 142 electric locomotives. These are used on the lines of the owning railways, and are available for hire to other railways which are short of motive power. All LOKOOP locomotives entered service with new computer numbers, but these have already been changed; however, not all locomotives carry the latest numbers. The locomotives were all refurbished by Stadler prior to entering service.

▲ **AB.** Appenzellerbahnen BDe 4/4 No. 32 'HERISAU' at Weissbad on 8th October 1995.
Siltex Ltd/Andrew Milliken

▼ **AL.** Aigle Leysin BDeh 4/4 No. 304 'OLLON' at Aigle in July 1992 is one of three modern cars on the line.
Eric Sawford

▲ **BT.** Bodensee Toggenburg RBDe No. 566.072 at Wattwil on 7th April 1996. This is one of the modern generation of BT railcars. **C.R. Appleby**

▼ **BD.** Bremgarten Dietikon Be 4/8 No. 24 at Bremgarten is one of a new generation of light rail cars. **J.D Davis**

▲ **BRB.** The Brienz Rothorn Bahn is still steam worked and has some new oil-fired one person operated locomotives. No. 12 is seen here at Brienz on 8th September 1992. **Mervyn Turvey**

▼ **CJ.** Chemins de Fer du Jura Xe 2/4 No. 503 restored as museum car BCe 2/4 No. 70 at Saigne Légier depot on 17th May 1996. **Brian Leighton**

▲ **CEV.** Chemins de Fer Electriques Veveysans Bt No. 224 + BDeh 2/4 No. 73 at Blonay on 21st July 1991 is one of a batch that operate all regular services.   **Bob Sweet**

▼ **CMN.** Chemins de Fer des Montagnes Neuchâtel BDe 4/4 No. 5 at Les Brenets on 12th May 1996 is one of the Italian-built cars dating from the electrification of the system.   **Brian Leighton**

▲ **EBT.** Emmental Burgdorf Thun Re No. 436.112 at Huttwil on 9th April 1996 is similar to the SBB Re 4/4 III class. It is in the latest unusual livery.   **C.R Appleby**

▼ **FART.** Ferrovie e Autolinee Regionali Ticinese ABe 4/8 No. 54 seen at Domodossola depot in Italy on 16th June 1995 is one of 12 stylish low-floor cars recently delivered to this international line.
                                                                                        Ray Smith

Paul Russenberger

FO. Furka Oberalp Deh 4/4 No. 55 'Brig' at Oberalp-Passhohe in August 1992

▲ **FW.** Frauenfeld Wil Bt 111 "STETTFURT" and Be 4/4 15 "STADT WIL" arrive at Wil forming the 09.57 from Frauenfeld on 22nd October 1994.   **Murdoch Currie**

▼ **LSE.** Three Luzern Stans Engelberg BDEh 4/4s Nos. 2, 6 and 1 at Engelberg on 8th April 1996.
                                                                                                                    C.R. Appleby

▲ **MThB.** Mittel Thurgau Bahn ABDe No. 536 613-3 'KREUZINGEN' at Kreuzingen forming part of the 12.47 ex-Engen on 20th October 1994.   **Murdoch Currie**

▼ **NStCM.** The Nyon St Cergue Morez was an international railway but the French part was closed in the 1950s. The line now terminates at La Cure on the French border where Be 4/4 No. 205 was observed on 13th July 1991.   **Bob Sweet**

▲ **OC.** Orbe Chavornay Be 2/2 No. 14 (now renumbered Be 557 614) at Orbe on 18th May 1996.
Brian Leighton

▼ **OeBB.** Oensingen Balsthal Bahn Ce 2/2 No. 102 (now renumbered Ce 217 262) at Oensingen on 9th April 1996. **C.R. Appleby**

RB. The Rigi Bahnen were formed in 1992 with the combination of the Arth Rigi Bahn and the Vitznau Rigi Bahn. The photograph above shows ex ARB BDhe 2/4 No. 11 at Arth Goldau on 16th September 1995, whilst that below shows ex VRB No. 31 at Rigi–Kulm on the same day.   **T.N. Hall (2)**

▲ **OSST.** Oberaargau Solothurn Seeland Transport Be 4/4 No. 103 ex RVO at Solothurn on 5th April 1996. **C.R. Appleby**

▼ **RBS.** Regional Bahn Solothurn ABe 4/12 No. 72 at Solothurn on 9th April 1996.
C.R. Appleby

▲ **SATEB.** The odd little diesel-worked line of the S.A. des Transports Emosson Barbarine with Ta 2/2 No. 7 at Emosson on 30th August 1993.   **C.R. Appleby**

▼ **SOB.** Schweizerische Sudostbahn Re No. 446 447 (ex SBB 10103) at Arth-Goldau on 16th September 1995.   **T.N. Hall**

▲ **TB.** Trogener Bahn BDe 4/8 No. 25 leaves Trogen on 22nd October 1995 with the 14.02 to St Gallen.
Siltex Ltd/Andrew Milliken

▼ **WSB.** Wynental und Suhrentalbahn Bt No. 77 with an unidentified power car at Aarau on 29th August 1994.   **J.D. Davis**

▲ Sihltalbahn 0–6–0T No. 2 at Bouveret on 29th August 1993 with a train for Evian-les-Bains operated
by "Trains de Rive Bleu."   **C.R. Appleby**

▼ P.S. 'STADT LUZERN' at Vitznau on the Vierwaldstättersee (Lake Lucerne), 8th April 1996.
                                                                             C.R. Appleby

▲ The Basel tramway undertaking was the only one in Switzerland which veered away from Swiss-built trams for a while in favour of the standard Duewag product from Germany. Six-axle car **632**, one of a batch dating from 1972, passes in front of the SBB station, with the entrance to the SNCF station on the right. **M.R. Taplin**

▼ The trams in the Swiss capital, Bern, present a very conservative image, despite some attempt at livery modernisation. Eight-axle car **711** dates from 1973, and is seen in the city centre passing a set of Swiss Standard cars. **M.R. Taplin**

CLASS 477   Bo–Bo

Built: 1967–76 for DR as Class 242. Reclassified 142 by DB.
Builder: LEW.
One Hour Rating: 2920 kW.**Weight in Full Working Order**: 82 tonnes.
Continuous Rating: 2740 kW.**Length over Buffers**: 16.26 m.
Maximum Tractive Effort: 245 kN.**Maximum Speed** 100 km/h.
Driving Wheel Dia.: 1350 mm.**Electric Brake**: Rheostatic.

Number	Old No.	DB No.	Built	Number.	Old No.	DB No.	Built
477 900-5	476 470-0	142 130-4	1967	477 907-0	476 477-5	142 118-9	1967
477 901-3	476 471-8	142 150-2	1968	477 908-8	476 478-3	142 126-2	1967
477 902-1	476 472-6	142 132-0	1967	477 909-6	476 479-1	142 128-8	1967
477 903-9	476 473-4	142 133-8	1967	477 910-4	476 465-0	142 103-1	1967
477 904-7	476 474-2	142 159-3	1969	477 911-2	476 466-8	142 197-3	1972
477 905-4	476 475-9	142 191-6	1971	477 912-0	476 467-6	142 199-9	1972
477 906-2	476 476-7	142 157-7	1968	477 913-8	476 469-2	142 272-4	1976

All ex DB in 1993–5; some locos arrived still carrying their old DR numbers (class 242).

LUZERN–STANS–ENGELBERG (480)   LSE

Once an isolated 3-phase line connecting the lake steamers at Stansstad with the towns of Stans and Engelberg, this railway was modernised and upgraded in the 1960s. A link was built from Stansstad to join the SBB Brunig line at Hergiswil, and most trains now run through to Luzern. At the same time, the electrical system was changed to the SBB standard. There is rack operation near the Engelberg end of the line, although a deviation is planned to eliminate this.

Gauge: 1000 mm.
Electrical System: 15 kV $16^2/_3$ Hz a.c.
Depots: Stansstad, Engelberg.

Class	No.	Name	Builder	Seats	km/h	Tonnes	kW	Built
BDeh4/4	1		SWP/SLM/BBC	40	75/20	48	745	1964
BDeh4/4	2		SWP/SLM/BBC	40	75/20	48	745	1964
BDeh4/4	3		SWP/SLM/BBC	40	75/20	48	745	1964
BDeh4/4	4		SWP/SLM/BBC	40	75/20	48	745	1964
BDeh4/4	5		SWP/SLM/BBC	40	75/20	48	745	1964
BDeh4/4	6		SWP/SLM/BBC	40	75/20	48	745	1970
BDeh4/4	7		SWP/SLM/BBC	40	75/20	48	745	1970
BDeh4/4	8		SWP/SLM/BBC	40	75/20	48	745	1980
Tm^I	100	*	RACO/DZ	-	30	6.3	30	1931
Tm^{II}	101	†	RACO/SAU	-	45	10	70	1964
Tm^{II}	102		RACO/DZ/VR	-	45	10.4	80	1961
Tm^{II}	103		RACO/DZ/VOITH	-	50	15.2	115	1967
Gm4/4	111	JUMBO	JUNG/MAN	-	40	36	375	1950
De4/4	121	‡	SLM/STAD/BBC	-	75	40	930	1942
De4/4	122	‡	SLM/STAD/BBC	-	75	40	930	1942

* Ex No. 101 in 1994.
† Ex SBB 734 in 1994 (rebuilt from standard gauge by WWOlten).
‡ Ex SBB 905/7 in 1991 (rebuilt from Deh4/6 by Stadler).

Facing Page Top: Genève led the way with low-floor trams in 1984, and converted its whole route (12) in 1987–9. In 1995 a second route, 13, was opened to provide a link to the Cornavin railway station, and some of the Vevey/Duewag six-axle cars received a new centre section with a small-wheel bogie to maintain the low-floor design. 845 is en-route to Bachet; in June 1997 this service was extended to Les Palettes.
                                                                    C.J. Wansbeek

Facing Page Middle: Neuchâtel's light rail line links the town centre at Place Pury with the lakeside villages of Auvernier, Colombier, Areuse and Boudry. The line is single-track with crossing loops, but a very slick service is provided using coupled sets of Swiss-built cars.   **M.R. Taplin**

Facing Page Bottom: Public transport patronage in Zürich is the highest per head of population in any European city, and is achieved with the highly-efficient surface tramway, backed up by trolleybuses and buses. Swiss standard cars 2012 + 2310 are seen approaching Triemli terminus on one of the few sections of reserved track on the system, with the blind already set for the return journey to Seebach.   **M.R. Taplin**

MARTIGNY–CHÂTELARD (132)   MC

This rack and adhesion line possesses a number of unusual features. From Martigny SBB to Vernayez overhead current collection is used, but the remainder of the line to Châtelard, which includes the rack sections, has 3rd rail. However the 3rd rail is being gradually converted to overhead. At Châtelard, the MC links with the metre gauge SNCF line from St. Gervais, which uses a similar 3rd rail system.

The MC and the SNCF have recently purchased five new railcar sets to enable a joint through service to be operated.

Gauge: 1000 mm.
Electrical System: 800 V d.c.
Depots: Vernayez, Finhaut, Le Châtelard.

Class	No.		Builder	Seats	km/h	Tonnes	kW	Built
BDeh4/4	4		SWP/SAAS	52	50/25	37.9	560	1957
BDeh4/4	5		SWP/SAAS	52	50/25	37.9	560	1957
BDeh4/4	6		SWP/SAAS	52	50/25	37.9	560	1957
BDeh4/4	7		SWP/SAAS	52	50/25	37.9	560	1964
BDeh4/4	8		SWP/SAAS	52	50/25	37.9	560	1964
BDeh4/4	14	‡	SLM/SWS/MFO	48	35/9	36.3	176	1908
BDe4/4	22		SWS/SAAS	40	45	22.6	110	1908
Te2/2	91	†	SWS/MFO/MC	-	40	16.6	108	1962(81)
Te2/2	92	†	SWS/MFO/MC	-	40	16.6	108	1962(84)
Tm2/2	204	*	BEIL	-	50	16	149	1982
BDeh4/4	501		SWP/SLM/BBC	44	65/24	41.1	716	1979
BDeh4/8	821+822		ACMV/SLM/AD	48+48	70	72	1000	1996
BDeh4/8	823+824		ACMV/SLM/AD	48+48	70	72	1000	1996

* Can be fitted with rotary snowplough, when classification becomes Xtm2/2.
‡ Historic car.
† ex VBZ 1906/7 in 1974.

MONTE GENEROSO (636)   MG

The only mountain rack line south of the Gotthard pass, the MG was electrified as late as 1982. For many years prior to this, the line was diesel operated. Some of the old diesel stock still remains on the line, either stored or for works or reserve use.

Gauge: 800 mm.
Electrical System: 650 V d.c.
Depot: Capolago.

Class	No.		Builder	Seats	km/h	Tonnes	kW	Built
Hm2/3	1	*	SLM/MG/VM	-	11.5	11.5	280	1953
Hm2/3	2	*	SLM/MG/VM	-	11.5	11.7	280	1954
Bhm2/4	4		SIG/BÜS/SAU/MAN	60	18	15.6	335	1957
Hm2/2	7		BÜH/PLEI/MG	-	14	9.8	280	1975
Bhe4/8	11		SLM/SE	96	14	34.1	810	1982
Bhe4/8	12		SLM/SE	96	14	34.1	810	1982
Bhe4/8	13		SLM/SE	96	14	34.1	810	1982
Bhe4/8	14		SLM/SE	96	14	34.1	810	1982

* Built on the frames of steam locos 5/6 (new 1890).

MEIRINGEN–INNERTKIRCHEN BAHN (474)   MIB

Originally built in 1926 as a construction railway for a hydro-electric scheme, this line was opened to the public in 1946. For many years the line was battery operated, and was only electrified in 1977 using second-hand cars from the OEG (Mannheim).

Gauge: 1000 mm.
Electrical System: 1200 V d.c.
Depot: Innertkirchen.

Class	No.		Builder	Seats	km/h	Tonnes	kW	Built
Bem4/4	6	*	FUCHS/BBC(M)/VW/SBB(MR)	34	65	22	240	1952 (77)

Bem4/4	7	*	FUCHS/BBC(M)/VW/SBB(MR)	34	65	22	240	1952 (77)
Be4/4	8		STAD/SIG/ABB	40	75	24.5	360	1996

* ex OEG (Mannheim, Germany) 63, 65 in 1977.

MARTIGNY ORSIÈRES (133)   MO

A standard gauge light railway serving an area to the south of the Rhône Valley.

Gauge: 1435 mm.
Electrical System: 15 kV 16$^2/_3$ Hz a.c.
Depots: Orsières, Martigny Croix.

Number	Class	Old No.	Name	Builder	Seats	km/h	Tonnes	kW	Built
Tm 237 512	Tm2/2	512		DZ	–	34	21	96	1960
ABDe 537 505	ABDe4/4	5		ACMV/BBC	24	60	52	736	1955
ABDe 537 506	ABDe4/4	6	OOZIÈRES	SIG/SWS/SAAS/BBC/MFO	6/47	100	64	1076	1965
ABDe 537 507	ABDe4/4	7	MARTIGNY	SIG/SWS/SAAS/BBC/MFO	6/47	100	64	1076	1965
ABDe 537 508	ABDe4/4	8	BAGNES	SIG/SWS/SAAS/BBC/MFO	6/47	100	64	1076	1965
ABDe 537 509	ABDe4/4	9	SEMBRANCHER	SIG/SWS/SAAS/BBC/MFO	6/47	100	64	1076	1965

MONTREUX OBERLAND BERNOIS (120, 321) MOB

The MOB is a lengthy metre gauge railway linking Montreux with Zweisimmen, where connections can be made for Interlaken. There is also a branch from Zweisimmen to Lenk. The climb out of Montreux is one of the world's steepest adhesion worked lines, and excellent views can be had over Lake Geneva. It is intended to convert the line from Zweisimmen to Interlaken (SEZ/BLS owned) to mixed gauge to enable through trains to operate to Luzern over the Brünig line.

Gauge: 1000 mm.
Electrical System: 850 V d.c.
Depots: Chernex, Montreux, Zweisimmen.

Class	No.	Name	Builder	Seats	km/h	Tonnes	kW	Built
Tm2/2	1		OK	-	12	7	30	1938
Tm2/2	2 a		DZ	-	30	15.7	92	1953
Tm2/2	3 b		DZ	-	30	16	88	1954
Tm	4 c		DMG/PUCH/SAU	-	35	10.4	48	1934
ABDe4/4	11		SIG/ALIOTH		50	29	250	1904

MOB. Montreux Oberland Bernois Be 4/4 No. 1004 at the Vevey depot of the CEV on 31st August 1994.
J.D. Davis

Class	No.	Name	Builder	Seats	km/h	Tonnes	kW	Built
BDe4/4	18		SIG/ALIOTH	28	50	27.6	192	1905
BDe4/4	20		SIG/ALIOTH	28	35	27.6	192	1906
Xe4/4	22		SIG/ALIOTH	-	50	29.6	192	1906
BDe4/4	27		SIG/BBC	14	50	36.2	388	1924
BDe4/4	28		SIG/BBC	14	50	36.2	388	1924
BDe4/4	36	d	SIG/BBC	40	65	26.7	368	1913
BDe4/4	37	d	SIG/MFO	40	60	25	218	1913
Be4/4	1001	e	ACMV/BBC/SWS/MFO	64	45	30.4	308	1955
Be4/4	1002	f	SWS/SAAS	56	60	29	176	1951
Be4/4	1003	g	SWS/SAAS/SLM/BBC	56	55	31	244	1958
DZe6/6	2001	h	SIG/BBC	-	65	62.8	738	1932
Gm4/4	2003	MONTBOVON	MOY/POY/CFD	-	80	44	515	1976
Gm4/4	2004	ALBEUVE	MOY/POY/CFD	-	80	44	515	1982
BDe4/4	3001	ROUGEMONT	SIG/BBC	42	75	35.7	440	1944
BDe4/4	3002	CHÂTEAU D'OEX	SIG/BBC	42	75	35.7	440	1944
BDe4/4	3003		SIG/BBC	32	75	35.7	440	1944
BDe4/4	3004		SIG/BBC	32	75	35.7	440	1944
BDe4/4	3005		SIG/BBC	24	75	36	440	1946
BDe4/4	3006		SIG/BBC	24	75	36	440	1946
ABDe8/8	4001	SUISSE	SIG/BBC/SAAS	86	70	60	880	1968
ABDe8/8	4002	VAUD	SIG/BBC/SAAS	86	70	60	880	1968
ABDe8/8	4003	BERN	SIG/BBC/SAAS	86	70	60	880	1968
ABDe8/8	4004	FRIBOURG	SIG/BBC/SAAS	86	70	60	880	1968
BDe4/4	5001	MONTREUX	SIG/SAAS	48	80	32	448	1976
BDe4/4	5002	ZWEISIMMEN	SIG/SAAS	48	80	32	448	1976
BDe4/4	5003	LENK	SIG/SAAS	48	80	32	448	1979
BDe4/4	5004	ST STEPHAN	SIG/SAAS	48	80	32	448	1979
GDe4/4	6001	VEVEY	SLM/BBC	-	90	48.2	1053	1983
GDe4/4	6002	ROSSINIÈRE	SLM/BBC	-	90	48.2	1053	1983
GDe4/4	6003	SAANEN	SLM/BBC	-	90	48.2	1053	1983
GDe4/4	6004	INTERLAKEN	SLM/BBC	-	90	48.2	1053	1983
Ge4/4	8001		SLM/ABB	-	120	64	2000	1995
Ge4/4	8002		SLM/ABB	-	120	64	2000	1995
Ge4/4	8003		SLM/ABB	-	120	64	2000	1995
Ge4/4	8004		SLM/ABB	-	120	64	2000	1995

a 2 ex Inselbahn Juist (Germany) in 1993.
b 3 ex Verkehrsbetriebe Grafschaft Hoya (Germany) in 1984.
c 4 ex RhB Xm2/2 9913 in 1995.
d 36/7 ex VBW 36/7 in 1988.
e 1001 ex LCD 9 in 1972.
f 1002 ex BA 4 in 1973.
g 1003 ex FLP 5 in 1981.
h Historic car.

MONTREUX–TERRITET–GLION–NAYE (121)   MTGN

The MTGN was formed in 1992 by the merger of the Montreux Glion Naye (MGN) rack line with the Territet–Glion funicular. Both lines had been under the management of the MOB for many years. The MGN itself was the result of a 1987 merger between the Montreux–Glion (MGI) and Glion–Naye (GN) railways which had been operated as a single entity for almost 50 years. Although electrification had been completed in 1938, a new steam locomotive was purchased in 1992 for summer tourist trains. A pure rack line giving excellent views over Lake Geneva.

Gauge: 800 mm.
Electrical System: 850 V d.c.
Depot: Glion.

Class	No.	Name	Builder	Seats	km/h	Tonnes	kW	Built
H 11/3	1	*	SLM	-	14	16	300	1992
HGe2/2	2		SLM/MFO	-	13	14.2	162	1909
xrote	3		RACO/Beil/MFO	-		7.5		1954
Hm	4	‡	RC/BÜH/CAT/PLEI/MG	-	14	12.3	415	1973
HGe2/2	101		SLM/MOB/MFO	-	13	14.5	162	1909 (76)
Bhe2/4	201		SLM/BBC	52	17.5	15.5	150	1938
Bhe2/4	202		SLM/BBC	52	17.5	15.5	150	1938

Bhe2/4	203		SLM/BBC		52	17.5	15.5	150	1938
Bhe2/4	204		SLM/BBC		52	17.5	15.5	150	1938
Bhe2/4	205		SLM/BBC		52	17.5	15.5	150	1938
Bhe2/4	206		SLM/BBC		52	17.5	15.5	150	1947
Bhe2/4	207		SLM/BBC		52	17.5	15.5	150	1949
Bhe2/4	208		SLM/BBC		52	17.5	15.5	150	1966
Bhe4/8	301	MONTREUX	SLM/SE		96	22	34	800	1983
Bhe4/8	302	VEYTAUX	SLM/SE		96	22	34	800	1983
Bhe4/8	303	VILLENEUVE	SLM/SE		96	22	34	800	1983
Bhe4/8	304		SLM/SE		96	22	34	800	1991

* Steam locomotive.
‡ ex BRB No. 8 in 1996.

MITTEL THURGAU BAHN (830)   MThB

A standard gauge line in north east Switzerland linking Wil and Kreuzlingen. After many years of quiet existance with services only extending beyond their own line for the short distance from Kreuzlingen to Konstanz (Germany), the operations have expanded considerably over recent years. Under contract to the local authority, the local service in Germany from Konstanz to Engen via Singen is now operated by the MThB, and combined as a through service to Kreuzlingen or Wil. In 1996, a further service, Radolfzell to Stockach commenced - this line was previously freight only, and resulted in the purchase of diesel railcars. The SBB service from Schaffhausen to Romanshorn is to be taken over by the MThB in 1997.

Gauge: 1435 mm.
Electrical System: 15 kV $16^2/_3$ Hz a.c.
Depot: Weinfelden.

Number		Class	Old No.	Name	Builder	Seats	km/h	Tonnes	kW	Built
Tm	236 651	Tm2/2	51	SEPPLI	STAD/BBC	–	60	29	315	1966
Tm	236 661	Tm"	61		RACO/SAU	–	45	10	70	1969
Re	426 621	Re4/4"	21		SLM/BBC/MFO/SAAS	–	140	80	4650	1969
ABDe	536 611	ABDe4/4	11	WIL	SIG/SWS/SAAS/BBC/MFO	12/39	100	64	1076	1965
ABDe	536 612	ABDe4/4	12	WEINFELDEN	SIG/SWS/SAAS/BBC/MFO	12/39	100	64	1076	1965
ABDe	536 613	ABDe4/4	13	KREUZLINGEN	SIG/SWS/SAAS/BBC/MFO	12/39	100	64	1076	1965
ABDe	536 614	ABDe4/4	14	KONSTANZ	SIG/SWS/SAAS/BBC/MFO	12/39	100	64	1076	1965
ABDe	536 615	ABDe4/4	15	BERG	SIG/SWS/SAAS/BBC/MFO	12/39	100	64	1076	1965
ABDe	536 616	ABDe4/4	16 ‡		SIG/SWS/SAAS/BBC/MFO	12/31	100	64	1076	1966
RBDe	566 631	-		-	SWG/SIG/ABB	–/65	140	25	1650	1994
RBDe	566 632	-		-	SWG/SIG/ABB	–/65	140	25	1650	1994
RBDe	566 633	-		-	SWG/SIG/ABB	–/65	140	25	1650	1994
RBDe	566 634	-		- ENGEN	SWG/SIG/ABB	–/65	140	25	1650	1994
Bm	596 671	-		-	STAD/SLM/AD	–/118	130	47.5	420	1996
Bm	596 672	-		-	STAD/SLM/AD	–/118	130	47.5	420	1996
Bm	596 673	-		- SEEHÄSLE	STAD/SLM/AD	–/118	130	47.5	420	1997
Em	826 641	Em2/2	41	ROLFLI	STAD/BBC	–	60	30	315	1972
Ee	936 618	Ee3/3	16318 *		SLM/BBC	–	40	45	428	1928

On order – 8 x Be2/6 STAD/SLM/AD.
* ex SBB 16318.
‡ ex GFM 171 in 1983.

NYON–ST. CERGUE–MOREZ (155)   NStCM

Once an international line linking Nyon on Lake Geneva with Morez in France, the French section was closed as long ago as 1958. Recently under threat of closure, the line has now been modernised with new rolling stock.

Gauge: 1000 mm.
Electrical System: 1500 V d.c.
Depots: Nyon Les Plantaz, St. Cergue.

Class	No.	Builder	Seats	km/h	Tonnes	kW	Built
Be4/4	201	ACMV/BBC/SAAS	40	65	33	752	1985
Be4/4	202	ACMV/BBC/SAAS	40	65	33	752	1985
Be4/4	203	ACMV/BBC/SAAS	40	65	33	752	1985

Be4/4	204		ACMV/BBC/SAAS	40	65	33	752	1985
Be4/4	205		ACMV/BBC/SAAS	40	65	33	752	1986
BDe4/4	211		ACMV/ABB	40	65	33	752	1991
BDe4/4	221	‡	SWS/SAAS	40	60	30	324	1935
Tm2/2	251	*	BEIL	-	50	22.1	149	1984
Tm2/2			OK					

* Can be fitted with rotary snowplough when classification becomes Xtm2/2.
‡ ex LEB 22 in 1991.

ORBE CHAVORNAY (211)   OC

A short branch line north of Lausanne which is the only Swiss private standard gauge adhesion line with d.c. electrification. As a consequence, it has been used for testing stock built for export. The two elderly railcars which operated all passenger services have now been replaced by a new 4-wheel car built by Stadler.

Gauge: 1435 mm.
Electrical System: 700 V d.c.
Depots: Orbe, Les Granges.

Number		Class	Old No.	Builder	Seats	km/h	Tonnes	kW	Built
Be	557 614	Be2/2	14	STAD/ABB	40	80	20	160	1990
De	587 632	De2/2	32	SWS/MFO	-	45	15.4	106	1902
Em	837 603	Em3/3	3	HEN	-	50	60	550	1985
Ee	927 601	Ee2/2	1	SIG/MFO	-	55	40	456	1970
Ee	927 602	Ee2/2	2	SIG/MFO	-	55	40	456	1970

OENSINGEN BALSTHAL BAHN (412)   OeBB

A short branch line connecting with the SBB at Oensingen and using a motley selection of mostly second hand stock.

Gauge: 1435 mm.
Electrical System: 15 kV 16$^2/_3$ Hz a.c.
Depot: Balsthal.

Number		Class	Old No.	Builder	Seats	km/h	Tonnes	kW	Built
Ce	217 262	Ce2/2	102	SLM/SAAS	-	60	28	257	1944
Ce	217 263	Ce2/2	103	SLM/SAAS	-	60	28	257	1947
ABDe	537 244	ABDe4/8	244	c SIG/SAAS	18/120	125	69.7	1700	1946
ABDe	537 245	ABDe4/8	245	c SIG/SAAS	18/120	125	69.7	1700	1945
Be	547 201	Be2/4	201	a SIG/BLS/BBC	60	90	34	220	1935
RBe	547 202	RBe2/4	202	b SLM/BBC/MFO/SAAS	67	125	38	394	1938
De	607 266	De6/6	15301	e SLM/BBC	-	50	73	862	1926
		RFe4/4	601	d SLM/BBC/MFO/SAAS	-	90	47	1000	1940

a ex BLS 721 in 1958.
b ex SBB 1007 in 1974.
c ex GBS/SEZ 744/5 in 1991/2.
d ex SZU De4/4 51 in 1993, restored to its original identity as SBB RFe4/4 601.
e ex SBB 15301.

OBERAARGAU SOLOTHURN SEELAND TRANSPORT   OSST

This is the group name for three light railways to the north and west of Bern, these being:
BIEL–TÄUFFELEN–INS (261)   BTI
REGIONALVERKEHR OBERAARGAU (413)   RVO
SOLOTHURN NIEDERBIPP BAHN (413).   SNB

The RVO was the OJB (Oberaargau Jura Bahn) until July 1990.

There is now a common numbering system. New stock now delivered to the BTI is expected to result in transfers of stock to the other lines.

Gauge: 1000 mm.
Electrical System: 1200 V d.c.

Depots: Langenthal (RVO), Täufflen (BTI), Wiedlisbach (SNB).

Class	No.	Name	Builder	Seats	km/h	Tonnes	kW	Built
Be4/4	101		SWS/MFO/BBC	52	60	32	368	1966
Be4/4	102		SWS/MFO/BBC	52	60	32	368	1966
Be4/4	103		SWS/OJB/SAAS	52	60	32	308	1973
Be4/4	108	MELCHNAU	SWS/OJB/MFO/SAAS	40	60	26	308	1913 (69)
Be4/4	109		SWS/SAAS	58	55	28	280	1963
Bre4/4	116		RING/ALIOTH	30	50	23.2	216	1907
De4/4	121		STAD/SIG/ABB	–	65	45	1040	1987
Ge4/4	126		SIG/BBC	–	35	20	206	1917
Tm	141		RACO/DZ	–	75	19	177	1985
Tm	142		RACO/PER	–	28	5.3	41	1933
Be4/4	301		SWS/MFO/BBC	52	60	32	368	1966
Be4/4	302		SWS/MFO/BBC	52	60	32	368	1966
Be4/4	303	SOLOTHURN	SWS/BBC	52	60	32	368	1971
Be4/4	304	WIEDLISBACH	SWS/MFO/BBC	52	60	32	368	1978
BDe4/4	311		SWS/MFO/SAAS	46	60	25.5	308	1918
BDe4/4	312		SWS/MFO	46	45	25	216	1918
De4/4	321		SZB/MFO	–	50	30.1	264	1957
Be4/4	501		SWS/MFO	48	65	33.7	368	1965
Be4/4	502		SWS/MFO	48	65	33.7	368	1965
Be4/4	503		SWS/MFO	48	65	33.7	368	1965
Be4/4	504		SWS/MFO	48	65	33.7	368	1970
Be4/4	505		SWS/MFO	48	65	33.7	368	1970
BDe4/4	511		SWS/MFO	40	60	34.1	264	1924
BDe4/4	513	*	SWS/MFO	40	60	26	282	1947
Tm	541		RACO/DZ	–	75	19	177	1985
Tm	542		RJ/RACO/ZÜR	–	45	4.8	22	1929(92)
Be2/6	5011+5010+5012		STAD/SLM/AD					1997
Be2/6	5021+5020+5022		STAD/SLM/AD					1997
Be2/6	5031+5030+5032		STAD/SLM/AD					1997
Be2/6	5041+5040+5042		STAD/SLM/AD					1997
Be2/6	5051+5050+5052		STAD/SLM/AD					1997
Be2/6	5061+5060+5062		STAD/SLM/AD					1997
Be2/6	5071+5070+5072		STAD/SLM/AD					1997

Note: 101–142 RVO, 301–321 SNB, 501–542 & 5011-5072 BTI.
* Restored to its original identity as BTI 6.
The OSST also owns Em 837.826, a standard gauge shunter.

PILATUS BAHN (473)   PB

The world's steepest rack railway, requiring the "Locher" rack system, comprising a double-sided horizontal rack rail, the railcars having two pinions, one on each side of the rack.

Gauge: 800 mm.
Electrical System: 1550 V d.c.
Depot: Alpnachstad.

Class	No.	Builder	Seats	km/h	Tonnes	kW	Built
Bhe1/2	21	SLM/MFO	40	12	9.65	155	1937
Bhe1/2	22	SLM/MFO	40	12	9.65	155	1937
Bhe1/2	23	SLM/MFO	40	12	9.65	155	1937
Bhe1/2	24	SLM/MFO	40	12	9.65	155	1937
Bhe1/2	25	SLM/MFO	40	12	9.65	155	1937
Bhe1/2	26	SLM/MFO	40	12	9.65	155	1937
Bhe1/2	27	SLM/MFO	40	12	9.65	155	1937
Bhe1/2	28	SLM/MFO	40	12	9.65	155	1937
Bhe1/2	29	SLM/MFO	40	12	9.6	155	1962
Bhe1/2	30	SLM/MFO	40	12	10.5	175	1968
Ohe1/2	31	SLM/MFO	–	12	8.3	155	1954
Xhm1/2	32	SLM/STAD/BBC	–	12	11.3	320	1981

Note: Only one underframe exists for cars 29 & 31, the bodies being exchanged as required. Hence, only one of these two cars can be in use at any one time.

PONT BRASSUS BAHN (201)   PBr

A somewhat remote line in the west of the country, the PBr was for many years operated by the SBB and its predecessors. The PBr never owned any motive power until tractor 101 was purchased from the SBB in 1982. Services have always run through to Vallorbe, but from 1989 these have been extended to Lausanne using railcars 2184–5, numbered in the SBB list and operated by them, but financed by the local canton and lettered for the PBr (Vallée de Joux) – these were numbered into PBr stock in 1996.

Gauge: 1435 mm.
Electrical System: 15 kV 16^2/$_3$ Hz a.c.
Depot: Le Brassus.

Number		Class	Old No.	Builder	Seats	km/h	Tonnes	kW	Built
		Te2/2	101	* SLM/MFO	–	45	12	90	1946
Tm	283 302	Tm2/2	102	† CMR	-	45	10	66	
Tm	283 303	Tm2/2	103	RACO/DZ	-	80	27	176	1992
RBDe	568 384	RBDe4/4	2184	FFA/SIG/SWP/ABB	-/65	140	70	1650	1989
RBDe	568 385	RBDe4/4	2185	FFA/SIG/SWP/ABB	-/65	140	70	1650	1989

* ex SBB Te^I 957 in 1982.
† ex SBB Tm^I 420.

POST TELEPHON TELEGRAPH   PTT

Not a private railway, the Swiss Post Office is included since it uses shunting locos at a number of locations, often involving operation into SBB stations. Locations of locos are shown in the last column.

Class	No.	Builder	km/h	Tonnes	kW	Built	Location
Te^{III}	3	SLM/SAAS	60	28	250	1952	Lausanne
Ee3/3	4	SLM/BBC/MFO/SAAS	45	45	502	1962	Luzern
Te^{III}	5	SLM/MFO	60	28	245	1965	Lausanne
Em3/3	6	HEN	60	45	375	1965	Zürich Mülligen
Ee3/3	7	SLM/BBC	40	45	428	1928	Zürich Mülligen
Ee3/3	8	SLM/BBC	60	48	660	1985	Zürich Mülligen
Ee3/3	9	SLM/BBC	60	48	660	1985	Zürich Mülligen
Ee3/3	10	SLM/BBC	60	48	660	1985	Daniken
Ee3/3	11	SLM/BBC	60	48	660	1985	Bern
Tm	12	SCH	23	14	81	1958	Ostermundigen
Tm	13	UNIMOG/MERC	20	6.8	92	1978	Kriens
Ee3/3	14	SLM/ABB	60	48	660	1992	Luzern

RIGIBAHNEN   RB

The RB were formed in 1992 by the merger of the Arth Rigi Bahn (ARB) and Vitznau Rigi Bahn (VRB). The VRB was the very first Swiss mountain rack line, opened in 1871. It connects with the steamers on Lake Lucerne at Vitznau, while the former ARB connects with the Gotthard main line at Arth Goldau. The two lines run side by side for some distance at the summit of the Rigi mountain, and were under common management for many years prior to the merger. Both lines are pure rack. Since the merger, the two lines have retained their separate liveries, but there has been considerable inter-working of the stock.

Gauge: 1435 mm.
Electrical System: 1500 V d.c.
Depots: Arth Goldau, Vitznau, Rigi Kulm.

Class	No.		Builder	Seats	km/h	Tonnes	kW	Built
Bhe2/4	1	†	SLM/BBC	64	19	16.7	335	1937
Bhe2/4	2	†	SLM/BBC	64	19	16.7	335	1937
Bhe2/4	3	†	SLM/BBC	64	19	16.7	335	1937
Bhe2/4	4	†	SLM/BBC	64	19	18.2	335	1953
Bhe4/4	5	†	SLM/SIG/BBC	62	30	35	870	1965
CFhe2/3	6	*‡	SWS/MFO	60	15	23.5	395	1911
BDhe2/4	7	*	SIG/MFO	60	15	25.5	455	1925
He2/3	8	*	SLM/MFO	-	15	30.4	455	1930

BDhe2/4	11	*	SLM/SAAS	60	21	26.5	485	1949
BDhe2/4	12	*	SLM/SAAS	60	21	26.5	485	1949
BDhe2/4	13	*	SLM/SAAS	60	21	26.5	485	1954
BDhe2/4	14	*	SLM/SAAS	60	21	26.5	485	1967
Bhe4/4	15	*	SLM/BBC	60	18.6	30.3	835	1982
He2/2	18	†	SLM/BBC	-	18	13.6	335	1938
Bhe4/4	21	†	SLM/BBC	74		30.5	824	1986
Bhe4/4	22	†	SLM/BBC	74		30.5	824	1986
Ta2/2	1	†§	RACO/STAD/MFO/BBC	-	8	7.5	7	1982a
Xrotm	1	†§						1974

* ex ARB (same nos.).
† ex VRB (same nos.).
‡ Historic car.
§ Number duplicated.
a Built from parts of SBB Tm 540 (new 1949).

Note: No renumbering took place at the time of the 1992 merger since the existing numbers did not clash (apart from the three No.1s already owned by the VRB!).

REGIONALVERKEHR BERN–SOLOTHURN (293, 294, 295, 420)   RBS

Once two separate railways, under common management for many years, the former SZB (Solothurn Zollikofon Bern) and VBW (Vereinigte Bern Worb Bahnen) were merged as the RBS in 1985. The railway provides frequent suburban services from Bern, and at one time all routes entered the town over the urban tram tracks. A new line, terminating in an underground station below Bern HB was opened in 1965, and is used by all Solothurn line trains, plus those on the ex VBW route from Worb via Bolligen. The other ex VBW route to Worb via Muri still enters Bern over the urban tram tracks, and for many years terminated at the inconveniently located Helvetiaplatz. Due to the width and weight of the existing rolling stock, the cars could not continue further. Therefore, new tramway type cars have been purchased for this route which was extended to Bern Casinoplatz in 1997. The voltage of this line was lowered from 800 V to 600 V to be fully compatible with the tramways.

Gauge: 1000 mm.
Electrical System: 1250 V d.c. (Bern–Muri–Worb 600 V d.c.).
Depots: Solothurn, Worblaufen, Worb (2 depots), Boll–Utzigen.

Class	No.		Builder	Seats	km/h	Tonnes	kW	Built
BDre4/4	1		SWS/MFO	36	75	36.4	512	1916
BDre4/4	3		SWS/MFO	36	75	35.5	512	1929
BDre4/4	4		SWS/MFO	44	75	34.6	512	1950
BDe4/4	6		SWS/MFO	40	75	34.6	512	1950
CFe4/4	11	‡	SWS/MFO	36	75	33.3	264	1916
BDre4/4	21		SWS/MFO	40	75	34	512	1955
BDre4/4	22		SWS/MFO	40	75	34	512	1955
BDre4/4	23		SWS/MFO	40	75	34	512	1955
Be4/8	41		SIG/BBC	136	75	48.7	326	1974
Be4/8	42		SIG/BBC	136	75	48.7	326	1974
Be4/8	43		SIG/BBC	136	75	48.7	326	1974(87)
Be4/8	44		SIG/BBC	136	75	48.7	326	1974
Be4/8	45		SIG/BBC	136	75	48.7	326	1974
Be4/8	46		SIG/BBC	136	75	48.7	326	1974
Be4/8	47		SIG/BBC	136	75	48.7	326	1974
Be4/8	48		SIG/BBC	136	75	48.7	326	1974
Be4/8	49		SIG/BBC	136	75	48.7	326	1974
Be4/8	50		SIG/BBC	136	75	48.7	326	1974
Be4/8	51		SIG/BBC	136	75	48.7	326	1974
Be4/8	52		SIG/BBC	136	75	48.7	326	1974
Be4/8	53		SIG/BBC	136	75	48.7	326	1978
Be4/8	54		SIG/BBC	136	75	48.7	326	1978
Be4/8	55		SIG/BBC	136	75	48.7	326	1978
Be4/8	56		SIG/BBC	136	75	48.7	326	1978
Be4/8	57		SIG/BBC	136	75	48.7	326	1978
Be4/8	58		SIG/BBC	136	75	48.7	326	1978
Be4/8	59		SIG/BBC	136	75	48.7	326	1978
Be4/8	60		SIG/BBC	136	75	48.7	326	1978

▲ **RHB.** Rorschach Heiden Bahn ABD eh 2/4 No. 24 (now BDeh No. 578 724) with a train of veteran coaches at Rorschach on 3rd August 1994.   **T.M. Wallis**

▼ **RHB.** Rorschach Heiden Bahn DZeh 2/4 No. 21 (now DZeh No. 588 721) at Heiden on 28th August 1994.   **J.D. Davis**

Class/No.		Builder					
Be4/8	61		SIG/BBC	136	75	48.7	326	1978
Be4/8	62		SWA/SIG/ABB	-/120	90	57	640	1993
Be4/8	63		SWA/SIG/ABB	-/120	90	57	640	1993
Be4/8	64		SWA/SIG/ABB	-/120	90	57	640	1993
ABe4/12	65	§	SWA/SIG/ABB	16/184	90	80	640	1992(94)
ABe4/12	66	§	SWA/SIG/ABB	16/184	90	80	640	1992(94)
ABe4/12	67	§	SWA/SIG/ABB	16/184	90	80	640	1992(94)
ABe4/12	68	§	SWA/SIG/ABB	16/184	90	80	640	1992(94)
ABe4/12	69	§	SWA/SIG/ABB	16/184	90	80	640	1992(94)
ABe4/12	70	§	SWA/SIG/ABB	16/184	90	80	640	1992(94)
ABe4/12	71	§	SWA/SIG/ABB	16/184	90	80	640	1992(94)
ABe4/12	72	§	SWA/SIG/ABB	16/184	90	80	640	1992(94)
Be4/4	74	*	SWS/MFO	36	65	28	240	1961
Be4/8	81	*	SWP/SIG/BBC	74	60	36.5		1987
Be4/8	82	*	SWP/SIG/BBC	74	60	36.5		1987
Be4/8	83	*	SWP/SIG/BBC	74	60	36.5		1987
Be4/8	84	*	SWP/SIG/BBC	74	60	36.5		1987
Be4/8	85	*	SWP/SIG/BBC	74	60	36.5		1987
Be4/8	86	*	SWP/SIG/BBC	74	60	36.5		1987
Be4/8	87	*	SWP/SIG/BBC	74	60	36.5		1987
Be4/8	88	*	SWP/SIG/BBC	74	60	36.5		1987
Be4/8	89	*	SWP/SIG/BBC	74	60	36.5		1988
De4/4	101		SZB/MFO	–	50	34	264	1961
De4/4	102		SZB/MFO	–	50	34.7	264	1965
De4/4	103		SZB/BBC/AEG	–	40	40	548	1973
De4/4	105	†	SIG/SZB/MFO	–	50	32	412	1924
Ge4/4	111	†	AEG	–	35	34	470	1927
Ge4/4	112	†	AEG	–	35	34	470	1927
Gem4/4	121		SIG/MFO/DZ	–	45	23	132/96	1912
Xm1/2	151		LÜTHI/VBW/VW	–	40	3.5	25	1925
Tm	162		RACO/DZ	–	30	3.2	37	1932
Tmf2/2	165		RACO/RhB	–	60	25		1996
Tmf2/2	166		RACO/RhB	–	60	25		1996

* 600 V d.c. cars.
† dual voltage stock.
§ Built as ABe4/8, lengthened 1994 with new centre car to ABe4/12.
‡ Historic car, renumbered ex BDe4/4 24.

RORSCHACH HEIDEN BAHN (857)   RHB

A short rack and adhesion line running into the hills above Rorschach, with through running over the SBB to Rorschach Hafen.

Gauge: 1435 mm.
Electrical System: 15 kV 16²/₃ Hz a.c.
Depots: Heiden, Rorschach.

Number		Class	Old No.	Builder	Seats	km/h	Tonnes	kW	Built
ABDeh	538 723	ABDeh2/4	23	SLM/BBC	7/50	25	42.3	550	1953
BDeh	578 724	ABDeh2/4	24	SLM/BBC	7/50	25	42.3	550	1967
DZeh	588 721	DZeh2/4	21	SLM/MFO	–	25	42.8	420	1930
DZeh	588 722	DZeh2/4	22	SLM/MFO	–	25	42.8	420	1930

On order 1 x BDeh3/6 STAD/SLM/AD.

RHEINECK WALZENHAUSEN (858)   RhW

Once a tramway with a connecting funicular, the whole line was converted to rack and adhesion operation in 1958. This is one of the smallest Swiss railways, less than 2 km long with just one item of motive power.

Gauge: 1200 mm.
Electrical System: 600 V d.c.
Depot: Ruderbach (but car normally stables overnight in Walzenhausen station).

Class	No.	Builder	Seats	km/h	Tonnes	kW	Built
BDeh1/2	1	SLM/FFA/BBC	28	30/20	14.7	215	1958

RÉGIONAL DE VAL DE TRAVERS (221)   RVT

A secondary line in the west of the country, through services running over the SBB to Neuchâtel.
The Fleurier to St. Sulpice branch is freight only, but does see occasional use for steam specials.

Gauge: 1435 mm.
Electrical System: 15 kV 16²/₃ Hz a.c.
Depot: Fleurier.

Number	Class	Old No.	Name	Builder	Seats	km/h	Tonnes	kW	Built
Tm 237 302	Tm	12		RACO/DZ	–	75	19	177	1983
Be 407 301	Be4/4	1		ACMV/SAAS	–	75	45	690	1951
ABDe 537 311	ABDe2/4	101		SWS/BBC	59	75	40	412	1944
ABDe 537 312	ABDe2/4	102		SWS/BBC	59	75	40	412	1945
ABDe 537 313	ABDe2/4	*		SIG/SWS	18/120	125	69.7	1700	1945
RBDe 567 315	RABDe4/4	105	FLEURIER	SIG/SWS/BBC	43	125	70	1700	1983
RBDe 567 316	RBDe4/4	106	COUVET	SWS/BBC	55	125	70	1700	1985
RBDe 567 317	RBDe4/4	107		SIG/SWS/BBC	55	125	70	1700	1991

* ex BN 743.

S.A. DES TRANSPORTS EMOSSON BARBARINE (1143)   SATEB

A most unusual line, originally built to provide access to a hydro-electric scheme. Connecting with
the MC at Le Châtelard–Giétroz, there is a funicular to Château d'Eau and a narrow gauge line from
here to Emosson. From Emosson a second funicular continues to Barrage.

Gauge: 600 mm.
Electrical System: not electrified.
Depot: Château d'Eau.

Class	No.	Builder	Seats	km/h	Tonnes	kW	Built
Tm2/2	4	LISTER	–	7.4	3.6	12	1940
Ta2/2	5	SSW	–	12	6	30	1952
Ta2/2	6	SSW	–	12	6	30	1952
Ta2/2	7	SSW	–	12	6	30	1952
Ta2/2	8	SSW	–	12	6	30	1952

SOB. Schweizerische Sudostbahn Driving trailer 901 at Samstagern on 17th June 1995.   **Ray Smith**

SCHWEIZERISCHE SUDOSTBAHN (670, 671, 672)   SOB

This line running from Arth Goldau on the Gotthard line to Rapperswil provides the middle section of the Luzern to Romanshorn route, over which a through service is operated jointly with the SBB and BT. There are also branches to Einsiedeln and Wädenswil and a surprisingly frequent service is operated.

Gauge: 1435 mm.
Electrical System: 15 kV 16^2/$_3$ Hz a.c.
Depot: Samstagern.

Number		Class	OldNo.	Name	Builder	Seats	km/h	Tonnes	kW	Built
Te	216 451	Te^{III}	51		SLM/SAAS	–	60	28.5	260	1943
Te	216 452	Te^I	52 ‡		SLM/MFO	–	45	12	90	1950
Te	216 453	Te^I	53 §		SLM/MFO	–	45	12	90	1950
Tm	236 432	Tm2/2	32	SCHNARCHLI	JUNG/DBZ	–	14	12	30	1958
Tm	236 433	Tm2/2	33	WILEN	STAD/CAT	–	60	37.7	565	1983
Tm	236 434	Tm2/2	34	*MANDARINLI	JUNG/KAEL	–	45	16	95	1960
Re	446 445		- a		SLM/BBC	-	160	80	4960	1982
Re	446 446		- a		SLM/BBC	-	160	80	4960	1982
Re	446 447		- a		SLM/BBC	-	160	80	4960	1982
Re	446 448		- a		SLM/BBC	-	160	80	4960	1982
Ae	476 468		- b		LEW/STAD	-	100	82	2920	1964
ABe	526 405	ABe4/4	5		SLM/SWS/BBC/MFO/SAAS	53	80	44	745	1939
ABe	526 411	ABe4/4	11	BURGHALDEN	SLM/SWS/BBC/MFO/SAAS	50	80	46.5	745	1940
ABe	526 413	ABe4/4	13	RICHTERSWIL	SLM/SIG/BBC/MFO/SAAS	50	80	46.5	745	1940
ABe	526 414	ABe4/4	14	GRÜNFELD	SLM/SIG/BBC/MFO/SAAS	50	80	46.5	745	1940
RBDe	566 400	-	-	BEZIRK SCHWYZ	SWG/SIG/ABB	65	140	70	1650	1995
RBDe	566 401	-	-	BEZIRK HÖFE	SWG/SIG/ABB	65	140	70	1650	1995
RBDe	566 402	-	-		SWG/SIG/ABB	65	140	70	1650	1995
RBDe	566 403	-	-		SWG/SIG/ABB	65	140	70	1650	1995
BDe	576 480	BDe4/4	80	EINSIEDELN	SIG/BBC	32	110	71.5	1595	1959
BDe	576 481	BDe4/4	81	WÄDENSWIL	SIG/BBC	32	110	72	2135	1959
BDe	576 482	BDe4/4	82	RAPPERSWIL	SIG/BBC	32	110	72	2135	1966
BDe	576 483	BDe4/4	83	STEINERBERG	SIG/SWP/BBC	32	110	72	2135	1978
BDe	576 484	BDe4/4	84	SATTEL	SIG/BBC	32	110	72	2135	1979
BDe	576 485	BDe4/4	85	FEUSISBERG	SIG/BBC	32	110	72	2135	1979
BDe	576 486	BDe4/4	86	WOLLERAU	SIG/BBC	32	110	72	2135	1979
BDe	576 487	BDe4/4	87	FREIENBACH	SIG/BBC	32	110	72	2135	1979
Am	846 461	Am4/4	61 †		KRUPP/AEG/CAT	-	100	68	990	1964

* ex DB 323 812 in 1984.
§ ex SBB Te^I 959 in 1987.
‡ ex SBB Te^I 951 in 1989.
a ex SBB Re4/4IV 10101–4 in 1994–6.
† ex Mainischen Ebn (Germany) DE 1500 in 1991; originally demonstrator DE1500, on loan to DB as 201 001.
b ex DB 142 042 in 1995.
BDE 576 483 was rebuilt in 1991.

SCHYNIGE PLATTE BAHN (314)   SPB

Another member of the BOB group, this pure rack mountain line connects with the BOB at Wilderswil near Interlaken. It appears to the 'poor relation' of the group, since all trains are operated by elderly 4-wheel electric locomotives dating from the time of electrification, some being second hand from the WAB. Transfers between the two lines continue, but recent ones have not been renumbered. Its rolling stock is lettered 'BOB'.

Gauge: 800 mm.
Electrical System: 1500 V d.c.
Depot: Wilderswil.

Class	No.	Name	Builder	Seats	km/h	Tonnes	kW	Built
He2/2	11	WILDERSWIL	SLM/BBC	–	12	16.3	220	1914
He2/2	12	GSTEIGWILER	SLM/BBC	–	12	16.3	220	1914

SPB. Schynige Platte Bahn He 2/2 No. 20 stands at the summit station with a pair of coaches on 6th September 1992. **Mervyn Turvey**

He2/2	13	MATTEN	SLM/BBC	–	12	16.3	220	1914
He2/2	14	GÜNDLISCHWAND	SLM/BBC	–	12	16.3	220	1914
He2/2	16	ANEMONE	SLM/ALIOTH	–	12	16	220	1910
He2/2	17		SLM/ALIOTH	–	12	16	220	1910
He2/2	18	KROKUS	SLM/ALIOTH	–	12	16	220	1910
He2/2	19	FLUHBLUME	SLM/ALIOTH	–	12	16	220	1911
He2/2	20	EDELWEIS	SLM/ALIOTH	–	12	16	220	1911
He2/2	61	ENZIAN	SLM/ALIOTH	–	12	16	220	1912
He2/2	62	ALPENROSE	SLM/ALIOTH	–	12	16	220	1912
He2/2	63	SILBERDISTER	SLM/ALIOTH	–	12	16	220	1912

Note: SPB 16–20, 61-3 were originally WAB 56-63.

SURSEE TRIENGEN   ST

A branch off the SBB Luzern to Olten line, the ST lost its passenger service in 1971. Now freight only, the occasional steam special is operated.

Gauge: 1435 mm.
Electrical System: not electrified.
Depot: Triengen.

Number	Class	Old No.	Name	Builder	km/h	Tonnes	kW	Built
Em 828 501	Em2/2	1	LISI	SIG/BBC/SAU	65	39	243	1965
Em 828 502	Em2/2	2		SLM/MAN	60	30	280	1976

SENSETALBAHN (257)   STB

A branch line linking the SBB at Flamatt to the BN at Gümmenen via the town of Laupen. Most of the stock is second hand. A recent development is a through Bern to Laupen service, using SBB RBDe4/4 railcars with intermediate trailers owned by the STB. However the Laupen–Gümmenen section closed to passengers in 1993 and has since been dewired.

Gauge: 1435 mm.
Electrical System: 15 kV $16^2/_3$ Hz a.c.
Depot: Laupen.

Number	Class	Old No.	Name	Builder	Seats	km/h	Tonnes	kW	Built
Tm 238 111	Tm2/2	11		STAD/BBC/SAU	–	55	23.5	185	1969
Tm 238 114	Tm2/2	14		STAD/MB/ABB	–	80	29	350	1994
Be 548 106	Be4/4	106		SLM/SIG/BBC/MFO/SAAS	64	80	44	736	1939
BDe 578 102	BDe4/6	102	LAUPEN	SIG/SAAS	128	110	82	708	1938
BDe 578 103	BDe4/6	103	NEUENEGG	SIG/SAAS	128	110	82	708	1938

SIHLTAL ZÜRICH UETLIBERG (712, 713)   SZU

Formerly two separate lines, merged in 1973. The Sihltalbahn provides a suburban service from Zürich to Langnau and Sihlbrugg and is electrified on high voltage a.c. The Uetlibergbahn climbs up the hills above Zürich to a terminus at Uetliberg and is electrified on d.c. To enable trains from both lines to use the common section from Zürich HB to Giesshübel, the d.c wires are offset to one side, resulting in the tracks on this section having two sets of overhead wires, and giving the d.c. stock an odd appearance with off-centre pantographs. From May 1990, the line has been extended from the inconveniently located Selnau terminus to a new underground terminus at the Hauptbahnhof using platforms built for the never constructed U-Bahn.

Gauge: 1435 mm.
Electrical System: 15 kV 16²/₃ Hz a.c. and 1200 V d.c.‡
Depots: Giesshübel, Sihlwald.

Number	Class	Old No.	Name	Builder	Seats	km/h	Tonnes	kW	Built
De 016 541	De3/4	41		SIG/MFO	–	50	48	495	1926
FCe 026 584	FCe2/4	84	†	SWS/MFO	50	50	43	330	1924
Tm 236 508	Tm	8		Robel					1994
Tm 236 510	Tm2/2	10	(ex SBB 536)	RACO/MB	–	45	7.5	35	1949
Re 456 542				SLM/SGP/ABB	–	130	68	3200	1992
Re 456 543				SLM/SGP/ABB	–	130	68	3200	1993
Re 456 544				SLM/SGP/ABB	–	130	68	3200	1993
Re 456 545				SLM/SGP/ABB	–	130	68	3200	1993
Re 456 546	Re4/4	46		SLM/ABB	–	130	68	3200	1987
Re 456 547	Re4/4	47	RED DEVIL	SLM/ABB	–	130	68	3200	1987
Ce 556 502	Ce2/2	2	*	SWS/MFO	24	35	17.5	150	1923
Be 556 521	Be4/4‡	21		SWS/SE	64	70	39.8	544	1992
Be 556 522	Be4/4‡	22		SWS/MFO	64	70	39.8	544	1992
Be 556 523	Be4/4‡	23		SLM/SE	64	70	39.8	544	1992
Be 556 524	Be4/4‡	24		SLM/SE	64	70	39.8	544	1992
Be 556 525	Be4/4‡	25		SLM/SE	64	70	39.8	544	1992
Be 556 526	Be4/4‡	26		SLM/SE	64	70	39.8	544	1992
Be 556 527	Be4/4‡	27		SLM/SE	64	70	39.8	544	1992
Be 556 528	Be4/4‡	28		SLM/SE	64	70	39.8	544	1993
Be 556 531	Be8/8‡	31	ZÜRICH	SWS/SE	162	60	60.4	850	1978
Be 556 532	Be8/8‡	32	UITIKON	SWS/SE	162	60	60.4	850	1978
BDe 576 513	BDe4/4‡	13		SWS/MFO	48	50	28	330	1960
BDe 576 514	BDe4/4‡	14		SWS/MFO	48	50	28	330	1960
BDe 576 592	BDe4/4	92	HORGEN	SWS/MFO	56	70	52.4	645	1968
BDe 576 593	BDe4/4	93	THALWIL	SWS/MFO	56	70	52.4	645	1968
BDe 576 594	BDe4/4	94	LANGNAU A/A	SWS/MFO	56	70	53	645	1971
BDe 576 595	BDe4/4	95	ADLISWIL	SWS/MFO	56	70	53	645	1971
BDe 576 596	BDe4/4	96	ZÜRICH	SWS/MFO	56	70	53	645	1971
Em 826 507	Em2/2	7	MUTZ	SIG/BBC/SAU	–	55	39	245	1961
Em 836 506	Em3/3	6	LEU	SLM/SAAS/BBC	–	65	49	445	1962

† restored as FCe2/4 84.
* ex Be2/2 22 restored to its original condition as Uetliburgbahn Ce2/2.

TROGENER BAHN (859)   TB

Originally an interurban tramway running from St. Gallen to Trogen, the TB has been upgraded to a light railway, mostly with roadside running, although there is still street running in St. Gallen.

Gauge: 1000 mm.
Electrical System: 1000 V d.c.
Depot: Speicher.

Class No.		Builder	Seats	km/h	Tonnes	kW	Built	
BDe4/4	6	SWP/MFO	30		65	27	385	1952
BDe4/4	7	SWP/MFO	30		65	27	385	1952
BDe4/4	8	SWP/MFO	30		65	27	385	1953
BDe4/8	21	FFA/BBC	72		65	39	405	1975
BDe4/8	22	FFA/BBC	72		65	39	405	1975
BDe4/8	23	FFA/BBC	72		65	39	405	1975
BDe4/8	24	FFA/BBC	72		65	39	405	1977
BDe4/8	25	FFA/BBC	72		65	39	405	1977
Xrotm2/2	72	RACO/BEIL/DZ	–		30	15	150	1974

WENGERNALPBAHN (311, 312)   WAB

Another member of the BOB group, this railway operates the middle section of the route to the Jungfrau, connecting the BOB at Lauterbrunnen and Grindelwald to the JB at Kleine Scheidegg. No through operation is possible due to the different gauges.

Gauge: 800 mm.
Electrical System: 1500 V d.c.
Depots: Lauterbrunnen, Grindelwald Grund.

Class	No.		Builder	Seats	km/h	Tonnes	kW	Built
Xrote	11		SLM/MFO	–	11	14	138	1928
Xrote	12		SLM/MFO	–	11	14	228	1945
He2/2	15	*	SLM/ALIOTH	–	12	16	220	1910
HGe2/2	31		STAD/ABB	-	25/15	16	460	1995
HGe2/2	32		STAD/ABB	-	25/15	16	460	1995
He2/2	51		SLM/ALIOTH	–	12	16	220	1909
He2/2	52		SLM/ALIOTH	–	12	16	220	1909
He2/2	53		SLM/ALIOTH	–	12	16	220	1909
He2/2	54		SLM/ALIOTH	–	12	16	220	1909
He2/2	64		SLM/BBC	–	12	16.5	236	1926
He2/2	65		SLM/MFO	–	12	17	236	1929
BDhe4/4	101		SLM/BBC	52	25	23.5	440	1947
BDhe4/4	102		SLM/BBC	52	25	23.5	440	1947
BDhe4/4	103		SLM/BBC	52	25	23.5	440	1948
BDhe4/4	104		SLM/BBC	52	25	23.5	440	1951
BDhe4/4	105		SLM/BBC	52	25	23.5	440	1951
BDhe4/4	106		SLM/BBC	52	25	23.5	440	1954
BDhe4/4	107		SLM/BBC	52	25	23.5	440	1954
BDhe4/4	108		SLM/BBC	52	25	23.5	440	1958
BDhe4/4	109		SLM/BBC	52	25	23.5	440	1958
BDhe4/4	110		SLM/BBC	52	25	23.5	440	1960
BDhe4/4	111		SLM/BBC	52	25	23.5	440	1960
BDhe4/4	112		SLM/BBC	52	25	23.5	440	1963
BDhe4/4	113		SLM/BBC	52	25	23.5	440	1963
BDhe4/4	114		SLM/BBC	52	25	23.5	440	1963
BDhe4/4	115		SLM/BBC	52	25	23.5	440	1963
BDhe4/4	116		SLM/BBC	52	25	23.5	440	1963
BDhe4/4	117		SLM/BBC	52	25	23.5	440	1964
BDhe4/4	118		SLM/BBC	52	25	23.5	440	1964
BDhe4/4	119		SLM/SIG/BBC/SAAS	48	25	25.7	440	1970
BDhe4/4	120		SLM/SIG/BBC/SAAS	48	25	25.7	440	1970
BDhe4/4	121		SLM/SIG/BBC/SAAS	48	25	25.7	440	1970
BDhe4/4	122		SLM/SIG/BBC/SAAS	48	25	25.7	440	1970
BDhe4/4	123		SLM/SIG/BBC/SAAS	48	25	25.7	440	1970
BDhe4/4	124		SLM/SIG/BBC/SAAS	48	25	25.7	440	1970
BDhe4/8	131		SLM/ABB	64	28/16.5	42.4	804	1988
BDhe4/8	132		SLM/ABB	64	28/16.5	42.4	804	1988
BDhe4/8	133		SLM/ABB	64	28/16.5	42.4	804	1988
BDhe4/8	134		SLM/ABB	64	28/16.5	42.4	804	1988

* ex SPB 15; originally WAB 55.
On order: 4 Bhe3/6 from STAD/AD.

WALDENBURGERBAHN (502) WB

Unique for Switzerland in being 750 mm gauge, the WB is a mainly roadside light railway with some street running. New stock has been purchased recently to enable an improved service to be introduced.

Gauge: 750 mm.
Electrical System: 1500 V d.c.
Depot: Waldenburg.

Class	No.	Name	Builder	Seats	km/h	Tonnes	kW	Built
BDe4/4	11		SWP/SIG/BBC	–				1985
BDe4/4	12		SWP/SIG/BBC	–				1986
BDe4/4	13		SWP/SIG/BBC	–				1986
BDe4/4	14		SWP/SIG/BBC	–				1986
BDe4/4	15	BUBENDORF	SWP/SIG/ABB	–				1993
BDe4/4	16	LIESTAL	SWP/SIG/ABB	–				1993
BDe4/4	17	WALDENBURG	SWP/SIG/ABB	–				1993

WYNENTAL UND SUHRENTALBAHN (643,644) WSB

Once two separate unconnected lines, a new station alongside the SBB one at Aarau connected to both lines was opened in 1967. The lines are mainly a mixture of roadside and street running.

Gauge: 1000 mm.
Electrical System: 750 V d.c.
Depots: Aarau, Schöftland.

Class	No.	Name	Builder	Seats	km/h	Tonnes	kW	Built
Tm	1		ROBEL/DZ	–	63	7.5	67	1969
De4/4	6		SWS/BBC	–	65	27.5	286	1947
Be4/4	9	HIRSCHTHAL	SWS/BBC	48	80	29	448	1966
Be4/4	10	HOLZIKEN	SWS/BBC	48	80	29	448	1966
Be4/4	11	DÜRRENÄSCH	SWS/BBC	48	80	29	448	1966
Be4/4	12	ZETZWIL	SWS/BBC	48	80	29	448	1966
Be4/4	13	LEIMBACH	SWS/BBC	48	80	29	448	1966
Be4/4	14	BURG	SWS/BBC	48	80	29	448	1966
Be4/4	15	AARAU	SWS/BBC	52	80	31	442	1979
Be4/4	16	SUHR	SWS/BBC	52	80	31	442	1979
Be4/4	17	GRÄNICHEN	SWS/BBC	52	80	31	442	1979
Be4/4	19	UNTERKULM	SWS/BBC	52	80	31	442	1979
Be4/4	20	OBERKULM	SWS/BBC	52	80	31	442	1979
Be4/4	21	GONTENSCHWIL	SWS/BBC	52	80	31	442	1979
Be4/4	22	REINACH	SWS/BBC	52	80	31	442	1979
Be4/4	23	MENZIKEN	SWS/BBC	52	80	31	442	1979
Be4/4	24	UNTERENTFELDEN	SWS/BBC	52	80	31	442	1979
Be4/4	25	OBERENTFELDEN	SWS/BBC	52	80	31	442	1979
Be4/4	26	MUHEN	SWS/BBC	52	80	31	442	1979
Be4/4	27	SCHÖFTLAND	SWS/BBC	52	80	31	442	1979
Be4/8	28		SWA/SIG/ABB	120	90		600	1993
Be4/8	29		SWA/SIG/ABB	120	90		600	1993
Be4/8	30		SWA/SIG/ABB	120	90		600	1993
Be4/8	31		SWA/SIG/ABB	120	90		600	1993
Be4/8	32		SWA/SIG/ABB	120	90		600	1993
Be4/8	33		SWA/SIG/ABB	120	90		600	1993
Be4/8	34		SWA/SIG/ABB	120	90		600	1993
De4/4	42		SWS/SSW/BBC	–	50	27.5	280	1904
De4/4	43		SWS/SE/BBC	–	60	46	536	1974
De4/4	44		SWS/SE/BBC	–	60	46	536	1974
De4/4	45		SWS/SE/BBC	–	60	46	536	1974
Te2/2	47		SWS/MFO/WSB	–	55	13.9	108	1954
Te2/2	48		SWS/MFO/WSB	–	55	13.9	108	1955
Te2/2	49		SWS/MFO/WSB	–	55	13.9	108	1957
Te2/2	50		SWS/VBZ/MFO	–	40	15.4	108	1915
ASe4/4	116		SWS/BBC	33	65	28.3	286	1901

5. SWISS TRAMWAY SYSTEMS

INTRODUCTION

Switzerland had numerous urban tramways, almost all being built to metre gauge. In general, those in the smaller and medium sized towns have closed, many being replaced by trolleybuses. The larger systems have survived and been modernised, but in some towns (Genève and Neuchâtel), only a small part of a much larger system remains in use. Several systems have recently built or planned extensions, and there is one completely new system at Lausanne. It is often difficult to differentiate between tramways and light railways; the systems detailed in this section are those that are legally classified as tramways. In spite of this some have no street running, despite this being a feature of several of the railways.

Most of the systems have museum cars that are used for specials or tourist operations; these are included in the list of preserved trams.

5.1. BASELLAND TRANSPORT   BLT

The BLT was created in 1974 to operate or co-ordinate transport in the Canton of Basel Land which excludes the city itself. Of the four tram routes that extend beyond the city boundary, two (to Aesch and Prateln) were operated by the BVB, one (the Birseckbahn to Dornach) was an independant operation, and the other (the Birsigtalbahn to Rodersdorf) was a light railway. The latter line is unusual in that it passes through French territory at Leymen. New trams have been purchased, and all the services fully integrated; however the Prateln route continues to be operated by the BVB in compensation for BTB trams carrying passengers within the city on the other routes. The BLT is also reponsible for the Waldenburgerbahn; this is detailed separately as a railway.

Gauge: 1000 mm.
Electrical System: 600 V d.c.
Depots: Hüslimatt, Ruchfeld, Rodersdorf, Aesch.

CLASS Be4/6   Bo–2–Bo

These cars were built for the Birseckbahn, and passed to the BLT on its formation in 1974.

Built: 1971–6.
Builder–Mech Parts: SWP.
Builder–Elec Parts: BBC/Siemens.
One Hour Rating: 300 kW.
Weight: 22.4 tonnes.
Overall Length: 19.20 m.
Max Speed: 60 km/h.
Seats: 47.
Multiple Working: Within class and with 200 series.

101	104	107	110	113
102	105	108	111	114
103	106	109	112	115

CLASS Be4/6 (Be4/8*)   Bo–2–Bo (Bo–2–2–Bo*)

These cars operate most BLT services. The cars indicated * have been lengthened with new low-floor centre sections. They can operate in multiple (often with the 100 series) and can also haul ex-BVB 3-axle trailers.

Built: 1978–81 (rebuilt 1987–95 by SWP *) (some cars did not enter service until 1984).
Builder–Mech Parts: SWP.
Builder–Elec Parts: Siemens.
One Hour Rating: 300 kW (300 kW*).
Weight: 25 tonnes (31 tonnes*).
Overall Length: 19.8 m (25.4 m*).
Max Speed: 65 km/h (65 km/h*).
Seats: 45 (60*).
Multiple Working: Within class and with 100 series.

201	*	215	*	228		241		254	*
202	*	216	*	229		242	*	255	*
203	*	217	*	230		243		256	*
204	*	218	*	231	*	244	*	257	
205	*	219	*	232	*	245	*	258	
206	*	220	*	233	*	246	*	259	
207	*	221	*	234		247	*	260	*
208	*	222	*	235		248	*	261	
209	*	223		236	*	249	*	262	*
210	*	224		237	*	250	*	263	*
211	*	225		238	*	251	*	264	*
212	*	226		239		252	*	265	*
213	*	227		240	*	253	*	266	*
214	*								

CLASS B3   3-axle TRAILER

Used for transporting bicycles.

Built: 1943.
Builder: SIG/SLM.
Weight: 7.4 tonnes.
Overall Length:
Max Speed: 60 km/h.

1326	1328	

CLASS B3   3-axle TRAILER

Built: 1956–8 (1960–4*).
Builder: SLM/BVB.
Weight: 8.0 (7.7*) tonnes.
Overall Length:
Max Speed: 60 km/h.
Seats: 25.

1333		1336		1339	*	1341	*	1343	*
1334		1337		1340	*	1342	*	1344	*
1335		1338							

WORKS CARS

Class.	Number	Builder	Date
Xe2/2	112	SWS/BBC	1905
Xe2/3	113	Bautzen/Alioth/SLM	1902

5.2. BASLER VERKEHRSBETRIEBE   BVB

Today this is the second largest tram system in Switzerland, and apart from some short sections across the borders into France and Germany, very little has been closed. The operation is complicated in that Baselland Transport operate over the BVB tracks into the city.

Gauge: 1000 mm.
Electrical System: 600 V d.c.
Depots: Allschwilerstrasse, Dreispitz, Klybeck (workshops), Wiesenplatz.

CLASS Be4/4   Bo–Bo

These are 'Swiss Standard' bogie cars; the earlier examples are now being withdrawn. They normally operate with bogie trailers.

Built: 1948–51 (1958*, 1967–8†).
Builder–Mech Parts: SWP.
Builder–Elec Parts: BBC (BBC/Siemens†).
One Hour Rating: 190 kW.
Weight: 19.3 tonnes (20 tonnes*).
Overall Length: 13.95m (13.74m *†).
Max Speed: 60 km/h.
Seats: 28.

401	417	433	447		465	†
402	419	434	454	*	466	†
404	421	435	455	*	467	†
405	422	437	456	*	468	†
406	423	444	457	†	469	†
408	424	445	458	†	470	†
410	425	447	459	†	471	†
411	426	449	460	†	472	†
412	427	450	461	†	473	†
413	428	451	462	†	474	†
414	429	452	463	†	475	†
415	430	453	464	†	476	†
416	431					

CLASS Be4/4   B–B

These modern bogie cars are unusual in being asymmetric; the nearside taper is less severe than that on the offside to accommodate the wide doorways. The usually operate in multiple with the 659–686 series.

Built: 1986–7.
Builder–Mech Parts: SWP/SIG.
Builder–Elec Parts: BBC/Siemens.
One Hour Rating: 300 kW.
Weight: 20 tonnes.
Overall Length: 13.79 m.
Max Speed: 60 km/h.
Seats: 28.

477	483	488	493	498
478	484	489	494	499
479	485	490	495	500
480	486	491	496	501
481	487	492	497	502
482				

CLASS Be4/6   Bo–2–Bo

A prototype for a new fleet of articulated cars. However, the design was not adopted since cheaper German-built cars were purchased instead.

Built: 1961–2.

Builder–Mech Parts: SIG.
Builder–Elec Parts: BBC.
One Hour Rating: 230 kW.
Weight: 25.9 tonnes.
Overall Length: 20.17 m.
Max Speed: 60 km/h.
Seats: 37.

602 |

CLASS Be4/6   Bo–2–Bo

As noted under the 601 series, the standard Düwag design of articulated car was adopted by Basel for financial reasons. All the Basel articulated cars normally operate with bogie trailers.

Built: 1967 (1972–3*).
Builder–Mech Parts: Düwag.
Builder–Elec Parts: Siemens.
One Hour Rating: 261 kW.
Weight: 22.5 tonnes (23.5 tonnes*).
Overall Length: 19.18 m.
Max Speed: 60 km/h.
Seats: 40.

603	615		626	*	637	*	648	*
604	616		627	*	638	*	649	*
605	617		628	*	639	*	650	*
606	618		629	*	640	*	651	*
607	619		630	*	641	*	652	*
608	620		631	*	642	*	653	*
609	621		632	*	643	*	654	*
610	622		633	*	644	*	655	*
611	623	*	634	*	645	*	656	*
612	624	*	635	*	646	*	657	*
613	625	*	636	*	647	*	658	*
614								

CLASS Be4/6   Bo–2–Bo

Modern articulated cars, usually operated in multiple with the 477–502 series. New low-floor centre sections from SWG-P are to be added to these cars. They will be of lightweight fibreglass construction and have single axles at each end replacing the centre bogie making the wheel arrangement Bo–1–1–Bo.

Built: 1990/1.
Builder–Mech Parts: SWP/SIG.
Builder–Elec Parts: BBC/Siemens.
One Hour Rating: 300 kW.
Weight: 26.5 tonnes.
Overall Length: 20.37 m.
Max Speed: 60 km/h.
Seats: 43.

659	665	671	677	682
660	666	672	678	683
661	667	673	679	684
662	668	674	680	685
663	669	675	681	686
664	670	676		

CLASS B4   BOGIE TRAILER

Built: 1946–8.
Builder: FFA.
Weight: 9.3 tonnes.
Overall Length: 13.8 m.
Max Speed: 60 km/h.
Seats: 26.

1401	1407	1409	*	1411	*	1413	*
1404	1408	1410	*	1412	*	1415	*
1405							

CLASS B4 — BOGIE TRAILER

Built: 1961–72.
Builder: FFA.
Weight: 10.2 tonnes.
Overall Length: 13.8 m.
Max Speed: 60 km/h.
Seats: 26.

1416	1435	1453	1471	1489
1417	1436	1454	1472	1490
1418	1437	1455	1473	1491
1419	1438	1456	1474	1492
1420	1439	1457	1475	1493
1421	1440	1458	1476	1494
1422	1441	1459	1477	1495
1423	1442	1460	1478	1496
1424	1443	1461	1479	1497
1425	1444	1462	1480	1498
1426	1445	1463	1481	1499
1427	1446	1464	1482	1500
1428	1447	1465	1483	1501
1429	1448	1466	1484	1502
1430	1449	1467	1485	1503
1431	1450	1468	1486	1504
1432	1451	1469	1487	1505
1433	1452	1470	1488	1506
1434				

WORKS CARS

Class.	Number	Builder	Date	Details
Xe2/2	2017	SIG/BBC	1930	Depot shunter, ex Be2/2 200
Xe2/2	2018	SWS/BBC	1919	Depot shunter, ex Be2/2 156
Xe2/2	2019	SWS/BBC	1921	Depot shunter, ex Be2/2 170
Xe2/2	2021	SWS/BBC	1921	Transport wagen/snowplough
Xe2/2	2022	SWS/BBC	1926	Transport wagen/snowplough
Xe2/2	2023	SWS/BBC	1931	Transport wagen/snowplough
Xe4/4	2330	WINDHOFF	1995	Rail scrubber

5.3. STÄDTISCHE VERKEHRSBETRIEBE BERN   SVB

The capital of Switzerland has three tram routes remaining from a once larger system. Several routes were abandoned during 1940–65, most being replaced by trolleybuses. However, the remainder of the system has been modernised. There was once extensive working into city over the tram tracks by the light railways (all now part of the RBS). One route from Worb still enters the city in this manner.

Gauge: 1000 mm.
Electrical System: 600 V d.c.
Depots: Eigerplatz, Burgernziel, Weissenbühl.

CLASS B4   BOGIE TRAILER

Built: 1951.
Builder: FFA.
Weight: 9.7 tonnes.
Overall Length: 13.8 m.
Max Speed: 50 km/h.
Seats: 21.

321	323	325	327	329
322	324	326	328	330

CLASS B4   BOGIE TRAILER

Built: 1960–1.
Builder: SIG/SWS.
Weight: 10 tonnes.
Overall Length: 13.8 m.
Max Speed: 50 km/h.
Seats: 21.

331	334	335	337	340

CLASS B4   BOGIE TRAILER

Built: 1947–8.
Builder: FFA.
Weight: 9.3 tonnes.
Overall Length: 13.8 m.
Max Speed: 60 km/h.
Seats: 26.

ex BVB 1402/3/6 in 1994.

341	342	343	

CLASS Be4/4   Bo–Bo

These elderly 'Swiss Standard' cars are now mainly in reserve. They normally work with bogie trailers.

Built: 1947–8.
Builder–Mech Parts: SWS.
Builder–Elec Parts: BBC/MFO.
One Hour Rating: 166 kW.
Weight: 17.4 tonnes.
Overall Length: 14.10 m.
Max Speed: 50 km/h.
Seats: 27.

604	605	607	613	614

CLASS Be4/4   Bo–Bo

These are more modern 'Swiss Standard' cars, also normally used with bogie trailers.

Built: 1960–1.
Builder–Mech Parts: SWS.
Builder–Elec Parts: BBC/MFO.
One Hour Rating: 188 kW.
Weight: 17.8 tonnes.
Overall Length: 14.00 m.
Max Speed: 50 km/h.
Seats: 26.

621	623	625	627	629
622	624	626	628	630

CLASS Be4/8   B–2–2–B

Articulated cars operating singly.

Built: 1973.
Builder–Mech Parts: SWS.
Builder–Elec Parts: BBC/SAAS.
One Hour Rating: 310 kW.
Weight: 34 tonnes.
Overall Length: 26.2 m.
Max Speed: 60 km/h.
Seats: 52.

711	715	718	721	724
712	716	719	722	725
713	717	720	723	726

CLASS Be4/8   B–2–2–B

Modern low-floor cars operating singly.

Built: 1989–90.
Builder–Mech Parts: ACMV/Duewag.
Builder–Elec Parts: ABB.
One Hour Rating: 302 kW.
Weight: 33 tonnes.
Overall Length: 31.14 m.
Max Speed: 60 km/h.
Seats: 68.

731	734	737	739	741
732	735	738	740	742
733	736			

WORKS CARS

Class	Number	Builder	Date	Details
Xe2/2	501	SWS/MFO	1910	Snowplough
Xe2/2	502	SWS/MFO	1920	Snowplough
Xe4/4	503	SIG/MFO	1936 (rebt 1975)	Railgrinder, ex Be4/4 148

5.4. TRAMWAYS DE NEUCHÂTEL   TN

This was once a mostly street tramway with seven routes. All but one of the routes were replaced by trolleybuses during 1940–76, but the remaining route to Boudry has been upgraded to a light railway (it was already mostly on a private right of way), and all remaining street running eliminated. New stock has been purchased; the original 1902 stock operated many services until then.

Gauge: 1000 mm.
Electrical System: 630 V d.c.
Depots: Neuchâtel Evole, Boudry.

CLASS Be4/4   Bo–Bo

These are light rail cars, and operate in various formations with driving trailers Bt 551–4.

Built: 1981 (1988*).
Builder–Mech Parts: SWS (SWP/SIG*).
Builder–Elec Parts: BBC.
One Hour Rating:
Weight: .
Overall Length: .
Max Speed: .
Seats: .

501	Boudry		504		Cortaillod
502	Auvernier		505	*	Ville de Neuchâtel
503	Colombier		506	*	Ville de Neuchâtel

CLASS Bt   BOGIE DRIVING TRAILER

Built: 1981.
Builder–Mech Parts: SWS.
Builder–Elec Parts: BBC.
Weight: 17.3 tonnes.
Overall Length:
Max Speed: km/h.
Seats: 46.

551	552	553	554	

5.5. TRANSPORTS PUBLICS GENÈVOIS   TPG

This was once the largest Swiss tram system in terms of mileage, and included several long rural routes, plus a network extending into France. Abandonments started in the 1930s, and by 1969, just one tram route remained. However, this was by far the busiest transport route in the city, and has now been modernised. The system has now started to expand again, and there are now two routes and a third is under construction.

Gauge: 1000 mm.
Electrical System: 600 V d.c.
Depot: Bachet de Pesay

CLASS Be4/6 (Be4/8*)   B–2–B (B–2–2–B)

The entire fleet of 'Swiss Standard' cars has been replaced by these modern articulated cars. Instead of purchasing new cars for recent route extensions, many of the cars have been lengthened with new centre sections.

Built: 1987–9 (1984†).
Builder–Mech Parts: ACMV/Duewag.
Builder–Elec Parts: BBC.
One Hour Rating: 300 kW.
Weight: 27 tonnes.
Overall Length: 21 m.
Max Speed: 60 km/h.
Seats: 48.

Note: 847–9 were renumbered from 828/9/4 to separate the series of 6-axle and 8-axle cars.

801	Gaillard	825		Choulex
802	Lancy	826		Confignon
803	Carouge	827		Cologny
804	ChÛne-Bougeries	830	*	Corsier
805	Thônex	831	*	Gy
806	ChÛne-Bourg	832	*	Hermance
807	Céligny	833	*	Perly-Certoux
808	Onex	834	*	Jussy
809	Aire-la-Ville	835	*	Grand-Saconnex
810	Ville de Genève	836	*	Puplinge
811	Collonge Bellerive	837	*	Meyrin
812	Avully	838	*	Troinex
813	Avusy	839	*	Russin
814	Bardonnex	840	*	Laconnex
815	Bellevue	841	*	Plan-les-Ouates
816	Vernier	842	*	Pregny-Chambésy
817	Dardagny	843	*	Presinge
818	Satigny	844	*	Meinier
819	Anières	845	*	Soral
820	Cartigny	846	*	Vandoeuvres
821	Bernex	847	*	Veyrier
822	Chancy	848	*	Genthod
823	Collex-Bossy	849	*	Versoix

WORKS CAR

Class	Number	Builder	Date	Details
Xe4/4	T01	Herbrand/CGTE/AEG/SAAS	1901	(reb 1972) ex Be4/4 70

5.6. TRAMWAY DE SUD-OUEST LAUSANNOIS TSOL

The old metre gauge tram system in Lausanne finally closed in 1964. However, this new line from Flon (interchange with LG/LO, and also in the future with the LEB) to Renens (interchange with SBB) opened in 1991. It is the the only standard gauge Swiss tramway, and is mostly roadside running, but with a lengthy subway section at the Flon end.

Gauge: 1435 mm.
Electrical System: 750 V d.c.
Depot: EPFL.

CLASS Bem4/6   B–2–B

These trams incorporate a diesel engine since the depot area is not electrified. They are also numbered in the national computerised system for railway stock, although the operation is at present self-contained. They often operate in pairs.

Built: 1990–1 (1995*).
Builder–Mech Parts: ACMV/Duewag.
Builder–Elec Parts: ABB.
One Hour Rating: 376 kW (88 kW on diesel traction).
Weight: 41 tonnes.
Overall Length: 31.00 m.
Max Speed: 80 km/h.
Seats: 66.

558 201-0	558 206-9	558 210-1	558 214-3 *
558 202-8	558 207-7	558 211-9	558 215-0 *
558 203-6	558 208-5	558 212-7	558 216-8 *
558 204-4	558 209-3	558 213-5 *	558 217-6 *
558 205-1			

WORKS VEHICLES

Class	Number	Builder	Date	Details
Tm2/2	6101	CFD/Baudouin	1977	Tractor
Xm1/2	6102	Robel/Deutz	1957	Ex DB Köf

5.7. VERKEHRSBETRIEBE DER STADT ZÜRICH   VBZ

This is the largest tram system in Switzerland. Although some of the longer routes were cut back many years ago, most of the system has survived, and since the late 1970s has been expanding again. The decision not to construct the proposed U-Bahn has been a major factor in this. The Forchbahn uses VBZ tracks to enter the city.

Gauge: 1000 mm.
Electrical System: 600 V d.c.
Depots: Altstetten (workshops), Burgwies, Elisabethenstrasse, Hard, Kalkbreite, Irchel, Oerlikon, Wollishofen.

CLASS B4   BOGIE TRAILER

Built: 1945–53.
Builder: SIG.
Weight: 9.4 tonnes.
Overall Length: 13.8 m.
Max Speed: 55 km/h.
Seats: 21.

725	741	757	764	767
727	750	760	765	768
729	751	761	766	770

CLASS B4   BOGIE TRAILER

Built: 1959–60.
Builder: SIG.
Weight: 11 tonnes.
Overall Length: 13.8 m.
Max Speed: 60 km/h.
Seats: 33.

771	775	778	781	784
772	776	779	782	785
773	777	780	783	786
774				

CLASS B4   BOGIE TRAILER

Built: 1962.
Builder: FFA/SIG.
Weight: 11 tonnes.
Overall Length: 13.8 m.
Max Speed: 60 km/h.
Seats: 25.

787	790	793	795	797
788	791	794	796	798
789	792			

CLASS B4   BOGIE TRAILER

Built: 1973.
Builder: FFA/SWP.
Weight: 10.2 tonnes.
Overall Length: 13.8 m.
Max Speed: 60 km/h.
Seats: 27.

799	800	801	

CLASS Be4/4   Bo–Bo

These are the last survivors of a large fleet of 'Swiss Standard' cars. They normally operate with bogie trailers, but nowadays are usually held in reserve.

Built: 1949–52.
Builder–Mech Parts: SWS.
Builder–Elec Parts: MFO/BBC (MFO*).
One Hour Rating: 252 kW.
Weight: 18.8 tonnes (18.5 tonnes*).
Overall Length: 13.95 m.
Max Speed: 55 km/h.
Seats: 27.

1381 *	1397	1408	1409	1410
1392 *	1400			

CLASS Be4/4   Bo–Bo

A more modern development of the 'Swiss Standard' car, normally operating with bogie trailers.

Built: 1959–60.
Builder–Mech Parts: SWS.
Builder–Elec Parts: MFO.
One Hour Rating: 252 kW.
Weight: 23 tonnes.
Overall Length: 13.95 m.
Max Speed: 60 km/h.
Seats: 29.

1416	1419	1422	1425	1428
1417	1420	1423	1426	1429
1418	1421	1424	1427	1430

CLASS Be4/6   Bo–2–Bo

These cars are of an unusual 3-section design, but with only 3 bogies. They normally operate in pairs, or with bogie trailers.

Built: 1966–69.
Builder–Mech Parts: SIG (SWS*†, SWP§).
Builder–Elec Parts: BBC/MFO/SAAS.
One Hour Rating: 400 kW.
Weight: 25.8 tonnes (23.2 tonnes§).
Overall Length: 20.90 m.
Max Speed: 60 km/h.
Seats: 43 (39†, 47§).

§ These cars have no driving cabs, and are used as trailing units in multiple formations.

1601		1618		1635	*	1652	†	1669	†
1602		1619	*	1636	*	1653	†	1670	†
1603		1620	*	1637	*	1654	†	1671	†
1604		1621	*	1638	*	1655	†	1672	†
1605		1622	*	1639	*	1656	†	1673	†
1606		1623	*	1640	*	1657	†	1674	†
1607		1624	*	1641	*	1658	†	1675	†
1608		1625	*	1642	*	1659	†	1676	†
1609		1626	*	1643	*	1660	†	1677	
1610		1627	*	1644	*	1661	†	1678	
1611		1628	*	1645	*	1662	†	1679	
1612		1629	*	1646	*	1663	†	1680	
1613		1630	*	1647		1664	†	1681	
1614		1631	*	1648		1665	†	1682	
1615		1632	*	1649		1666	†	1683	
1616		1633	*	1650		1667	†	1684	
1617		1634	*	1651	†	1668	†	1685	

1686		1695	§	1703	§	1711	§	1719	§
1687		1696	§	1704	§	1712	§	1720	§
1688		1697	§	1705	§	1713	§	1721	§
1689		1698	§	1706	§	1714	§	1722	§
1690		1699	§	1707	§	1715	§	1723	§
1691	§	1700	§	1708	§	1716	§	1724	§
1692	§	1701	§	1709	§	1717	§	1725	§
1693	§	1702	§	1710	§	1718	§	1726	§
1694	§								

CLASS Be6/6   Bo–Bo–Bo

This car was the prototype for the later 1601 series, from which it differs in having all axles powered.

Built: 1961.
Builder–Mech Parts: SIG.
Builder–Elec Parts: BBC.
One Hour Rating: 400 kW.
Weight: 28.5 tonnes.
Overall Length: 20.45 m.
Max Speed: 60 km/h.
Seats: 40.

1801

CLASS Be4/6   B–2–B

These are the most modern type currently in service in Zürich, known as the 'Tram 2000'. They normally operate in pairs, or with the non-driving 2300 and 2400 series cars.

Built: 1976–8.
Builder–Mech Parts: SWS/SWP.
Builder–Elec Parts: BBC.
One Hour Rating: 278 kW.
Weight: 26.5 tonnes.
Overall Length: 21.4 m.
Max Speed: 65 km/h.
Seats: 50.

2001	Höngg	2016		2031	
2002	Seebach	2017		2032	
2003	Unterstrass	2018		2033	
2004		2019		2034	
2005	Industriequartier	2020		2035	
2006	Fluntern	2021	Albisrieden	2036	
2007	Enge	2022		2037	Oberstrass
2008	Friesenberg	2023		2038	Witikon
2009	Triemli	2024		2039	Rennweg
2010	Wipkingen	2025		2040	Rechts der Limmat
2011	Oerlikon	2026		2041	Hottingen
2012	Wipkingen	2027		2042	Altstetten
2013		2028		2043	
2014		2029		2044	Wollishofen
2015		2030	Hirslanden	2045	Reisbach

CLASS Be4/6   B–2–B

Development of 2000 series with higher-powered motors.

Built: 1985–7 (1991–2*).
Builder–Mech Parts: SIG/SWS/SWP (SWS/SWP*).
Builder–Elec Parts: BBC.
One Hour Rating: 300 kW.
Weight: 26.5 tonnes.
Overall Length: 21.4 m.
Max Speed: 65 km/h.
Seats: 50.

2046	2062	2077	2092		2107	*
2047	2063	2078	2093		2108	*
2048	2064	2079	2094		2109	*
2049	2065	2080	2095		2110	*
2050	2066	2081	2096		2111	*
2051	2067	2082	2097		2112	*
2052	2068	2083	2098		2113	*
2053	2069	2084	2099	*	2114	*
2054	2070	2085	2100	*	2115	*
2055	2071	2086	2101	*	2116	*
2056	2072	2087	2102	*	2117	*
2057	2073	2088	2103	*	2118	*
2058	2074	2089	2104	*	2119	*
2059	2075	2090	2105	*	2120	*
2060	2076	2091	2106	*	2121	*
2061						

CLASS Be4/6   B–2–B

These cars are similar to the 2000 series, but have no driving cabs, and are used as trailing units in multiple formations.

Built: 1978.
Builder–Mech Parts: SWS/SWP.
Builder–Elec Parts: BBC.
One Hour Rating: 278 kW.
Weight: 26 tonnes.
Overall Length: 21.4 m.
Max Speed: 65 km/h.
Seats: 50.

2301	2304	2307	2310	2313
2302	2305	2308	2311	2314
2303	2306	2309	2312	2315

CLASS Be2/4   2–B

These bogie cars also have no driving cabs, and are used as trailing units in multiple formations with 2000 series cars.

Built: 1985–7 (1992*).
Builder–Mech Parts: SWS/SWP.
Builder–Elec Parts: BBC.
One Hour Rating: 150 kW.
Weight: 18.5 tonnes.
Overall Length: 15.4 m.
Max Speed: 65 km/h.
Seats: 35.

2401	2408	2415		2422	*	2429	*
2402	2409	2416		2423	*	2430	*
2403	2410	2417		2424	*	2431	*
2404	2411	2418		2425	*	2432	*
2405	2412	2419		2426	*	2433	*
2406	2413	2420		2427	*	2434	*
2407	2414	2421	*	2428	*	2435	*

CARS ON ORDER

17 'Cobra' low-floor Class Be5/6 cars have been ordered from SWS/SIG/Fiat/ADtranz. 6 are due in 1999, and the remaining 11 in 2002; there is an option for a further 58 cars.

WORKS CARS

Class	Number	Builder	Date	Details
Xe4/4	1921	SWS/VBZ/MFO	1940 (reb 1980)	Snowplough (reb ex Be4/4 1351)
Xe4/4	1922	SWS/VBZ/MFO	1940 (reb 1981)	Snowplough (reb ex Be4/4 1352)
Xe4/4	1923	SWS/VBZ/MFO	1941 (reb 1981)	Snowplough (reb ex Be4/4 1353)
Xe4/4	1924	SWS/VBZ/MFO	1942 (reb 1981)	Snowplough (reb ex Be4/4 1354)
Xe4/4	1925	SWS/VBZ/MFO	1942 (reb 1981)	Snowplough (reb ex Be4/4 1355)
Xe4/4	1926	SWS/VBZ/MFO	1945 (reb 1981)	Snowplough (reb ex Be4/4 1356)
Xe4/4	1927	SWS/VBZ/PIFO	1942 (reb 1981)	Snowplough (reb ex Be4/4 1357)
Xe4/4	1928	SWS/VBZ/MFO	1942 (reb 1981)	Snowplough (reb ex Be4/4 1358)
Xe4/4	1929	SWS/VBZ/MFO	1942 (reb 1982)	Snowplough (reb ex Be4/4 1359)
Xe2/2	1951	SWS/MFO/BBC	1924	Crane car
Xe2/2	1953	Crede/VBZ/Kiepe	1963 (reb 1979)	Crane car

6. PADDLE STEAMERS

The details of these steam operations are covered since most are included witihin the availability of the Swiss Pass, and can be easily combined with other railway visits. Generally, the steamers only operate from June to September; full details of the steam services are shown in the SBB Timetable. The services below operate daily unless noted otherwise. There are numerous diesel ships also operating on these lakes, and diesel substitutions do occasionally take place.

BRIENZERSEE

Two return trips operate from Interlaken Ost to Brienz (connection the the Brienz-Rothorn and Brünig lines).

Ship: LÖTSCHBERG   Escher Wyss 1914

LAC LEMAN (Lake Geneva)

Four paddle steamers operate one return trip for the full length of the lake from Geneve to Bouveret, two circular trips from Lausanne covering the east end of the lake (one clockwise, one anticlockwise), and additional sailings operating from Lausanne to Thonon and Evian. Calls are made at numerous piers, several of which are in France. Round trips can be made in conjunction with the Train de Rive Bleu operation between Evian and Bouveret. Note there are a further four paddle steamers here that have been converted to diesel operation; in appearance they look very similar to their steam operated sisters.

Ships:

LA SUISSE	Sulzer	1910
SAVOIE	Sulzer	1914
SIMPLON	Sulzer	1920
RHÔNE	Sulzer	1927

The diesel conversions are MONTREUX (1904), VEVEY (1907), ITALIE (1908) and HELVETIE (1926).

THUNERSEE

One return sailing operates from Thun to Interlaken West via Spiez.

Ship: BLÜMLISALP   Escher Wyss   1906

VIERWALDSTÄTTERSEE (Lake Lucerne)

Five paddle steamers operate on this lake. The principal route is from Luzern to Fluelen (on the Gotthard main line), a 3 hour trip each way with up to four sailings per day. En route calls are made at the pier adjacent to the Swiss Transport Museum, and at Vitznau (terminus of the Rigibahnen). Numerous other calls are made. There are also up to two sailings per day to Alpnachstad (connection with the Brünlg and Pilatus Railways) calling at Stansstad (connection with the line to Engelberg).

Ships:

URI	Sulzer	1901
UNTERWALDEN	Escher Wyss	1902
SCHILLER	Sulzer	1906
GALLIA	Escher Wyss	1913
STADT LUZERN	Sachsenberg	1928

ZÜRICHSEE

The two paddle steamers cover two return trips from Zürich to Rapperswil, with a third on Wednesdays and Saturdays operating the full length of the lake from Zürich to Schmerikan.
Ships:

STADT ZÜRICH	Escher Wyss 1909
STADT RAPPERSWIL	Escher Wyss 1914

In additional to the above, there are paddle steamers on the Bodensee (HOHENTWIEL) based in Austria, but operting to Germany and Switzerland, Lago Maggiore (PIEMONTE) based in Italy, but operating to Lugano, plus a small steam screw ship (GREIF) on the Greifensee at Uster. These ships operate various public excursions, but are not shown in the timetable.

7. PRESERVED LOCOMOTIVES RAILCARS & TRAMS

In this section, all preserved locomotives and railcars from Swiss public railways are shown. In the case of steam locomotives, all known surviving locomotives from these railways are shown, since many of those not actually preserved will no doubt be the subject of future preservation attempts. Not detailed are industrial locomotives, trams, and items imported for preservation from countries outside Switzerland. The current status of the motive power is indicated as follows:

IA   Industrial use, still active.
M   Museum, on display (not active).
MA   Museum, active.
MR   Museum, under repair.
MS   Museum, stored.
P   Plinthed.
S   Stored.

Steam Locomotives & Railcars

The system for describing steam locomotives used here is the one which is in general use in Germany. Firstly, letters and numbers are used to describe the wheel arrangement as follows: This is then followed by 'h' for superheated locos (from the German 'heizdampf'), or 'n' for saturated locos (from the German 'nassdampf'). The number of cylinders follow, then codes for various features, i.e.

v   compound.
z   rack locomotive with 1 pinion.
zz   rack locomotive with 2 pinions.
t   tank locomotive.
e.g.: 1C1h2t is a superheated 2–6–2 tank locomotive with 2 cylinders.

Rly.	Gauge	Class	No.	Details	Status	Date	Location
SBB	1000	G3/3	109 (BAM 6)	Cn2t	MA	1901	Chaulin
SBB	1000	G3/4	203	1Ch2t	S	1912	Volos (Greece)
SBB	1000	G3/4	204	1Ch2t	S	1912	Pirgos (Greece)
SBB	1000	G3/4	205	1Ch2t	S	1912	Pirgos (Greece)
SBB	1000	G3/4	208	1Ch2t	MA	1913	Meiringen
SBB	1435	A3/5	705	2Ch4v	MA	1904	Biel/Bienne
SBB	1000	HG3/3	1055	Czn4vt	S	1906	Volos (Greece)
SBB	1000	HG3/3	1058	Czn4vt	S	1908	Volos (Greece)
SBB	1000	HG3/3	1063	Czn4vt	M	1909	VHS
SBB	1000	HG3/3	1067	Czn4vt	MA	1910	Meiringen
SBB	1000	HG3/3	1068	Czn4vt	P	1926	Meiringen
SBB	1435	B3/4	1367	1Ch2	MA	1916	Zürich (VHS)
SBB	1435	C5/6	2958	1Eh4v	MR	1915	Sulgen
SBB	1435	C5/6	2965	1Eh4v	M	1916	VHS
SBB	1435	C5/6	2969	1Eh4v	P	1916	Winterthur
SBB	1435	C5/6	2978	1Eh4v	MA	1917	St Sulpice (SBB)
SBB	1435	Eb2/4	5469	2Bn2t	MA	1891	Basel
SBB	1435	Eb3/5	5810	1C1h2t	S	1911	Fribourg
SBB	1435	Eb3/5	5811	1C1h2t	S	1911	Glarus
SBB	1435	Eb3/5	5819	1C1h2t	MA	1912	Zürich (VHS)
SBB	1435	Eb3/5	5886 (BT 6)	1C1h2t	P	1910	Degersheim
SBB	1435	Eb3/5	5889 (BT 9)	1C1h2t	MA	1910	Herisau
SBB	1435	Ed2x2/2	7696 (SCB 196)	BBn4vt	MA	1893	Balsthal
SBB	1435	E3/3	8410	Cn2t	P	1901	Zürich Altstetten
SBB	1435	E3/3	8463	Cn2t	MR	1904	Mendrisio
SBB	1435	E3/3	8474	Cn2t	S	1907	Koblenz
SBB	1435	E3/3	8476	Cn2t	IA	1907	Uetikon
SBB	1435	E3/3	8479 (ST 5)	Cn2t	MA	1907	Triengen
SBB	1435	E3/3	8481	Cn2t	IA	1907	Rheinfelden
SBB	1435	E3/3	8483	Cn2t	MS	1907	Haltingen (Germany)
SBB	1435	E3/3	8485	Cn2t	S	1907	Koblenz
SBB	1435	E3/3	8487	Cn2t	P	1909	Buchs
SBB	1435	E3/3	8491	Cn2t	MA	1909	Kriens

SBB	1435	E3/3	8492	Cn2t	IA	1909	Perlen
SBB	1435	E3/3	8494	Cn2t	MA	1909	Le Pont
SBB	1435	E3/3	8500	Cn2t	MS	1910	Haltingen (Germanyf
SBB	1435	E3/3	8501	Cn2t	MA	1910	Mendrisio
SBB	1435	E3/3	8507	Cn2t	S	1910	Sierre
SBB	1435	E3/3	8511	Cn2t	MA	1911	St Sulpice
SBB	1435	E3/3	8512	Cn2t	M	1911	VHS
SBB	1435	E3/3	8516	Cn2t	MA	1911	Zürich
SBB	1435	E3/3	8518	Cn2t	MA	1913	Uster
SBB	1435	E3/3	8522 (ST 8522)	Cn2t	MA	1913	Triengen
SBB	1435	E3/3	8523	Cn2t	MA	1915	Le Pont
SBB	1435	E3/3	8527	Cn2t	S	1915	Kaufdorf
SBB	1435	E3/3	8532	Cn2t	MA	1915	Kandern (Germany)
SBB	1435	E3/3	8551	Cn2t	P	1894	Kleinhuningen (Basel)
SBB	1435	E3/3	8554	Cn2t	P	1894	Dietikon
SBB	1435	E3/3	8573	Cn2t	MA	1890	Laupen
SBB	1435	E3/3	8575	Cn2t	MA	1890	St Sulpice
SBB	1435	E3/3	8651 (KLB 1)	Cn2t	MA	1909	Balsthal
SBB	1435	Xrot	100	rotary	M	1896	VHS
BLS	1435	E2/2	72 (Bodelibahn3)	Bn2t	MA	1874	Spiez
BLS	1435	E3/3	77 (GTB 3)	Cn2t	MA	1901	Spiez
RhB	1000	G3/4	1	1Cn2t	MA	1889	Landquart
RhB	1000	G3/4	11	1Cn2t	MA	1902	Zweilütschinen
RhB	1000	G3/4	14	1Cn2t	MA	1902	Herisau
RhB	1000	G4/5	107	1Dh2	MA	1906	Landquart
RhB	1000	G4/5	108	1Dh2	MA	1906	Landquart
RhB	1000	G4/5	118 (RSR 340)	1Dh2	P	1912	Chiangmai (Thailand)
RhB	1000	G4/5	122 (RSR 338)	1Dh2	S	1913	Makkasan (Thailand)
RhB	1000	Xrotd	R12	rotary	MR	1913	Realp
RhB	1000	Xrotd6/6	9214	rotary	MA	1912	Chaulin
BSB	1435	Ed3/4	51	1Cn2t	P	1906	Schwarzenburg
EB	1435	Ed3/3	3	Cn2t	M	1881	VHS
EBT	1435	Ed4/5	8	1Dh2t	MA	1914	Burgdorf
FO	1000	HG3/4	1 (DFB 1)	1Czzh4vt	MA	1913	Realp
FO	1000	HG3/4	2	1Czzh4vt	MS	1913	Goldau
FO	1000	HG3/4	3	1Czzh4vt	MA	1913	Chaulin
FO	1000	HG3/4	4	1Czzh4vt	MS	1413	Münster
FO	1000	HG3/4	8	1Czzh4vt	MS	1914	Goldau
FO	1000	HG3/4	9 (DFB 2)	1Czzh4vt	MA	1914	Realp
FW	1000	G3/3	2	Cn2t	P	1887	Wil
GB	1435	E2/2	11	Bn2t	M	1881	VHS
GGB	800	HII/3	8	B1zzh2t	MA	1892	Ribas de Freser (Spain)
HWB	1435	E3/3	5	Ch2t	MA	1936	Huttwil (VHS)
HWB	1435	E3/3	8	Cn2t	S	1898	Porrentruy
LEB	1000	03/3	5	Cn2t	MA	1890	Chaulin
LEB	1000	G3/3	8	Cn2t	MA	1910	Eschallens
LHB	1435	Ed3/4	11	1Ch2t	MA	1908	Huttwil
WG	800	HII/3	2	B1zzn2t	MA	1890	Capolago
MThB	1435	Ed3/5	3	1C1h2t	MA	1912	Weinfelden
NOB	1435	DI	1	2An2	MA	1947	VHS (Replica of 1847 loco)
OeBB	1435	E3/3	2	Cn2t	MA	1899	Balsthal
PB	800	Bhm	9	railcar	M	1889	VHS
PB	800	Bhm	10	railcar	M	1900	München (Germany)
RdB	1000	G3/3	1	Cn2t	MA	1890	Chaulin
RdB	1000	G3/3	2	Cn2t	P	1890	Les Brenets
RdB	1000	G3/3	3	Cn2t	M	1892	Le Locle (incomplete)
RSG	1435	Ed3/4	2	1Ch2t	MA	1903	Uster
SCB	1435	Ec2/5	28	B3n2t	M	1858	VHS
SiTB	1435	E3/3	2	Cn2t	MA	1893	Bouveret
SiTB	1435	E3/3	3	Cn2t	P	1897	Horgen
SiTB	1435	E3/3	4	Cn2t	P	1897	Adliswil
SiTB	1435	E3/3	5	Cn2t	MA	1899	Zürich Giesshubel
SMB	1435	Ed3/4	1	1Cn2t	MR	1907	Uster

Rly.	Gauge	Class	No.			Status	Date	Location
SMB	1435	Ed3/4	2		1Cn2t	MA	1907	Huttwil
SMB	1435	Ec4/5	11		1Dh2t	MA	1911	Burgdorf
SOB	1435	E3/3			Cn2t	MR	1887	Uster
SOB	1435	E2/2	1 (KLB 2)		Bn2t	S	1891	Rorschach
SPB	800	HII/3	5		B1zzh2t	MA	1894	Wilderswil
STB	1435	Ed3/3	3		Cn2t	MA	1884	Beromunster
UeBB	1435	CZm1/2	31		railcar	MA	1907	Zürich
UeBB	1435	E3/3	401		Ch2t	MA	1901	Uster
VRB	1435	HI/2	7		1Azn2t	MA	1873	Vitznau (VHS)
VRB	1435	HII/S	16		B1zzh2t	MA	1923	Vitznau
VRB	1435	HII/S	17		B1zzh2t	MA	1925	Vitznau
VZ	1000	HG2/3	6		B1zzh4vt	MA	1902	Realp
VZ	1000	HG2/3	7		B1zzh4vt	MA	1906	Visp
WB	750	G3/3	5		Cn2t	MA	1902	Waldenburg
WB	750	G3/3	6		Cn2t	M	1912	VHS
YSC	1000	G4/4	4		Dh2t	S	1911	Volos (Greece)

Diesel & Electric Locomotives & Railcars

Rly.	Gauge	Class	No.		Status	Date	Location
SBB	1435	Re4/4[I]	10042		M	1951	VHS
SBB	1435	Ae3/6[II]	10448		S	1925	CR
SBB	1435	Ae3/6[I]	10601		P	1921	Baden
SBB	1435	Ae3/6[I]	10639		P	1925	CR
SBB	1435	Ae3/6[I]	10693		P	1927	CR
SBB	1435	Ae4/7	10902		S	1927	CR
SBB	1435	Ae4/7	10908		S	1928	CR
SBB	1435	Ae4/7	10914		S	1928	CR
SBB	1435	Ae4/7	10922		S	1928	CR
SBB	1435	Ae4/7	10943		S	1931	CR
SBB	1435	Ae4/7	10948		S	1931	CR
SBB	1435	Ae4/7	10949		M	1931	VHS
SBB	1435	Ae4/7	10950		S	1931	CR
SBB	1435	Ae4/7	10951		S	1931	CR
SBB	1435	Ae4/7	10961		S	1931	CR
SBB	1435	Ae4/7	10987		S	1932	CR
SBB	1435	Ae4/7	10997		S	1933	CR
SBB	1435	Ae4/7	10999		S	1933	CR
SBB	1435	Ae4/7	11000		S	1934	CR
SBB	1435	Ae4/7	11001		S	1934	CR
SBB	1435	Ae4/7	11002		S	1934	CR
SBB	1435	Ae4/7	11010		S	1932	CR
SBB	1435	Ae4/7	11016		S	1933	CR
SBB	1435	Ae4/7	11018		S	1932	SBB (location unknown)
SBB	1435	Ae4/7	11022		S	1933	CR
SBB	1435	Ae4/7	11026		S	1934	Zürich Oerlikon
SBB	1435	Ae8/1	11852		M	1940	Erstfeld
SBB	1435	Be4/6	12332		M	1922	VHS
SBB	1435	Be4/6	12339		S	1923	Voghera (Italy)
SBB	1435	Be6/8[II]	13254		M	1920	VHS
SBB	1435	Be6/8[II]	13257		MS	1920	Wien (Austria)
SBB	1435	Be6/8[III]	13302		MA	1925	Rapperswil
SBB	1435	Ce4/4	13501 (SW 1)		M	1904	VHS
SBB	1435	Ce4/4	13502 (SW 2)		M	1904	VHS (stored elsewhere)
SBB	1435	Ce6/8[I]	14201		M	1920	VHS (stored elsewhere)
SBB	1435	Ce6/8[II]	14267		M	1921	Speyer (Germany)
SBB	1435	Ce6/8[II]	14270		P	1921	Erstfeld
SBB	1435	Ce6/8[II]	14276		MS	1922	Mendrisio
SBB	1435	Ce6/8[II]	14282		M	1922	Sinsheim (Germany)
SBB	1435	Te[I]	47		MA	1950	Zürich
SBB	1435	Te[I]	52		MA	1954	Zürich
SBB	1435	Te[III]	221		S	1927	SBB (location unknown)
SBB	1435	Tm	438		MA	1928	St Sulpice
SBB	1435	Tm	464		M	1931	VHS

SBB	1435	Tm	873	S	1925	Langenthal
SBB	1435	Tm	899	MA	?	St Sulpice
SBB	1435	Te'	960	MA	1950	Zürich
SBB	1435	Ta	971	M	1927	VHS
SBB	1435	RCe2/4	203 (1003)	M	1936	VHS
SBB	1435	RAe4/8	1021	MA	1939	Samstagern
SBB	1435	Fe4/4	18518 (1678)	M	1928	VHS
BLS	1435	Be5/7	151	M	1912	VHS
BLS	1435	Ae6/8	206	S	1939	CR
BLS	1435	Ae6/8	208	S	1943	CR
GBS	1435	Ce4/4	312 (SZU 49)	MS	1920	Mendrisio
BLS	1435	Ce4/4	315	S	1924	CR
BLS	1435	De4/5	796	MS	1929	St Sulpice
RhB	1000	Tm2/2	68	MA	1948	Realp
RhB	1000	Ge4/4	181	MA	1916	Chaulin
RhB	1000	Ge4/4	182	MS	1928	La Mure (France)
RhB	1000	Ge2/4	205	P	1913	Winterthur
RhB	1000	Ge2/4	207	M	1913	VHS
RhB	1000	Ge4/6	391	M	1913	Berlin (Germany)
RhB	1000	Ge6/6	402	M	1921	VHS
RhB	1000	Ge6/6	406	P	1921	Zürich Oerlikon
RhB	1000	Ge6/6	407	P	1922	Bergün
RhB	1000	ABDe4/4	453	S	1907	Grono
RhB	1000	ABDe4/4	454	MS	1909	Mendrisio
AG	1000	CFeh3/3	1 (SGA 16)	M	1911	VHS
ASD	1000	ABDe4/4	3	MS	1913	La Mure (France)
ASD	1000	ABDe4/4	12	MS	1913	La Mure (France)
BN	1435	Ce4/4	315	S	1924	CR
BN	1435	Ce2/4	727	M	1935	VHS
BOB	1000	HGe3/3	26	S	1915	Zweilütschinen
BT	1435	Be4/4	13	MA	1932	Uster (VHS)
BT	1435	Be4/4	14	MA	1932	Samstagern
BT	1435	Be4/4	15	MA	1932	Uster
BTB	1435	De2/2	1	M	1899	München (Germany)
BTB	1435	De2/2	2	M	1899	VHS
BTB	1435	Be4/4	7	S	1923	Oberwil
CJ	1000	Tm	506	MA	1953	Realp
EZB	1435	Ce4/6	307	MA	1920	Spiez
FLP	1000	Ce4/4	3	MA	1912	Grono
FO	1000	CFm2/2	21	MA	1927	Realp (VHS)
FW	1000	Ce4/4	1	S	1921	La Chaux de Fonds
JB	1000	He2/2	1	M	1898	VHS
LEB	1000	Te2/2	2	MA	1896	Chaulin
LJB	1000	Ce2/2	12	MA	1907	Chaulin
LLB	1000	BCFeh4/4	10	MA	1914	Chaulin
MC	1000	ABDeh4/4	15	MA	1909	Martigny
MC	1000	ABDeh4/4	31	MA	1921	Martigny
MC	1000	ABDeh4/4	32	MA	1921	Martigny
MCM	1000	BCFeh4/4	6	MA	1909	Chaulin
MIB	1000	Ta2/2	3	MA	1931	Bruchhausen Vilsen (Germany)
MIB	1000	CFa2/2	4	M	1939	VHS
MIB	1000	CFa2/2	5	P	1949	Innertkirchen
MOB	1000	BDe4/4	16	S	1905	Niederscherli
MOB	1000	BCFe4/4	20	MA	1905	Chaulin
MOB	1000	De4/4	26	P	1912	Saanen
NStCM	1000	ABDe4/4	1	MS	1916	La Mure (France)
NStCM	1000	ABDe4/4	5	MS	1916	La Mure (France)
NStCM	1000	ABDe4/4	10	MS	1918	La Mure (France)
NStCM	1000	ABDe4/4	11	MS	1918	La Mure (France)
OC	1435	CFe2/2	11	MS	1894	VHS (stored elsewhere)
OeBB	1435	ABDe2/8	203 (GBS 704)	P	1937	Balsthal
OeBB	1435	BDe4/12	204	S	1935	Stuttgart (Germany)
PTT	1435	Tm	1	S	1930	Olten

Rly.	Gauge	Class	No.	Status	Date	Location
RBS	1000	Gem4/4	122	MA	1916	Pré Petitjean
RVO	1000	De4/4	122	S	1917	Niederscherli
RVO	1000	Xe4/4	131	MR	1913	Zug
RVT	1435	BCm2/5	9	M	1914	VHS
SeTB	1000	BDe2/2	4	MA	1928	Chaulin
SGA	1000	CHeh2/3	17	S	1911	Wasserauen
StEB	1000	HGe2/2	1	M	1898	VHS
SZU	1435	Tm	8	MA	1975	Uster
TB	1000	CFe4/4	1	P	1903	Meilen
VBW	1000	Be4/4	30	MS	1910	Ungersheim (France)
VBW	1000	BDe4/4	38	MS	1913	Ungersheim (France)
WB	750	BDe4/4	1	MS	1953	Prora (Germany)
WB	750	BDe4/4	3	MS	1953	Prora (Germany)

Steam Trams

Rly.	Gauge	Class	No.	Details	Status	Date	Location
SSB	1000	G3/3	12	Bn2t	M	1894	Winterthur
SSB	1000	G3/3	18	Bn2t	M	1894	VHS

Electric Trams

Rly.	Gauge	Class	No.	Status	Date	Location
BEB	1000	Ce2/2	9	M	1921	Sehnde-Wehmingen (Germany)
BEB	1000	Be2/4	12	MA	1916	Ruchfeld
BEB	1000	Be2/4	13	MA	1916	Ruchfeld
BVB	1000	Ce2/2	4	MA	1900	Basel Wiesenplatz
BVB	1000	Ce2/2	31	MS	1898	Klagenfurt (Austria)
BVB	1000	Ce2/2	37	MS	1898	Klagenfurt (Austria)
BVB	1000	Be2/2	114	P	1904	Pfäffikon
BVB	1000	Ce2/2	126	MA	1908	Basel Eglisee
BVB	1000	Ce2/2	160	M	1919	Sehnde-Wehmingen (Germany)
BVB	1000	Be2/2	163	MA	1914	Basel Eglisee
BVB	1000	Be2/2	181	MA	1925	Basel Wiesenplatz
BVB	1000	Ce2/2	182	MA	1927	Chaulin
BVB	1000	Be2/2	185	P	1925	Allschwil
BVB	1000	Be2/2	190	MA	1927	Basel Wiesenplatz
BVB	1000	Be2/2	192	MA	1927	Basel Wiesenplatz
BVB	1000	Be2/2	199	MA	1930	Basel Wiesenplatz
BVB	1000	Ce2/2	202	M	1931	VHS
BVB	1000	Be2/2	203	MA	1931	Basel Eglisee
BVB	1000	Be2/2	205	MA	1931	Basel Wiesenplatz
BVB	1000	Be2/2	209	S	1933	Hochwald
BVB	1000	Be2/2	213	M	1933	Skjoldenaesholm (Denmark)
BVB	1000	Be2/2	215	MA	1933	Basel Wiesenplatz
BVB	1000	Be4/4	400	MA	1914	Basel Eglisee
BVB	1000	Xe2/2	2014	MR	1900	Basel Eglisee
LSB	1000	Ce2/2	10	MA	1900	Zürich Wartau/Höngg †
RhV	1000	Be2/2	6	P	1898	Altstatten
RhV	1000	Ce2/2	31	MA	1914	Chaulin
RhV	1000	Be2/4	40	P	1920	Steinebrunn
RiT	800	Ce2/2	–	S	1899	Riffelalp
RiT	800	Fe2/2	–	S	1899	Riffelalp
SVB	1000	Ce2/2	37	MA	1910	Bern Burgernziel
SVB	1000	Ce2/2	52	MA	1914	Chaulin
SVB	1000	Be4/4	145	MA	1935	Bern Burgernziel
SVB	1000	Be4/4	147	MA	1936	Bern Burgernziel
SVB	1000	Be4/4	149	MA	1936	Bern Burgernziel
TEM	1000	Be2/2	3	S	1910	Stabio
TF	1000	Ce2/2	1	MA	1897	Chaulin
TF	1000	Be2/2	4	M	1898	Olmstedt Falls (USA)
TF	1000	Be2/2	5	M	1900	Schepdaal (Belgium)
TF	1000	Be2/2	6	MS	1900	Bulle
TF	1000	Ce2/2	7	MA	1909	Chaulin

TF	1000	Be2/2	10	P	1913	Villars les Joncs
TL	1000	Be2/2	27	M	1908	Karlsruhe (Germany)
TL	1000	Ce2/3	28	MA	1913	Chaulin
TLoc	1000	Be2/2	6	S	1910	Agno
TN	1000	Be2/4	41	MS	1902	La Voulte sur Rhône (France)
TN	1000	Ce2/4	43	M	1902	VHS
TN	1000	Ce2/4	44	M	1902	Paris St Mandé
TN	1000	Be2/4	45	MS	1902	Neuchâtel
TN	1000	Ce2/4	46	M	1902	Sehnde-Wehmingen (Germany)
TN	1000	Be2/4	47	MS	1902	Sentheim (Germany)
TN	1000	Be2/2	72	M	1921	Detroit (USA)
TN	1000	Be2/2	73	MS	1921	Neuchâtel
TN	1000	Ce2/2	74	M	1921	Lille (France)
TN	1000	Be2/2	76	MS	1928	Montbovon
TN	1000	Ce2/2	78	M	1928	Paris St Mandé
TN	1000	Be4/4	582	M	1947	VHS
TN	1000	Be4/4	583	MS	1947	Neuchâtel
TN	1000	Be4/6	592	MS	1942	Le Locle
TPG	1000	Ce4/4	63	M	1901	Paris St Mandé
TPG	1000	Ce4/4	65	M	1901	Lille (France)
TPG	1000	Ce4/4	66	M	1901	Lille (France)
TPG	1000	Be4/4	67	MA	1901	Genève Moillesulaz
TPG	1000	Be4/4	69	P	1901	Genève Le Lignon
TPG	1000	Ce2/2	125	MA	1920	Chaulin
TPG	1000	Fe4/4	151	MA	1911	Chaulin
TPG	1000	Be4/4	729	MA	1952	Genève Moillesulaz
TrB	1000	Xe2/2	1	MA	1915	Chaulin
VBZ	1000	Ce2/2	2	MA	1928	Zürich Wartau/Höngg
VBZ	1000	Ce2/2	9	MA	1928	Zürich
VBZ	1000	Ce2/2	16	MA	1929	Zürich
VBZ	1000	Ce2/2	18	MA	1929	Zürich
VBZ	1000	Ce2/2	25	MA	1929	Zürich
VBZ	1000	Ce2/3	32	M	1939	VHS
VBZ	1000	Ce2/2	102	MA	1900	Zürich Wartau/Höngg
VBZ	1000	Ce2/2	146	MS	1907	Klagenfurt (Austria)
VBZ	1000	Ce2/2	176	MA	1909	Zürich Wartau/Höngg
VBZ	1000	Ce4/4	321	MA	1930	Zürich Wartau/Höngg
VBZ	1000	Xe2/2	925	MA	1914	Zürich Wartau/Höngg
VBZ	1000	Xe2/2	952	MA	1928	Zürich Wartau/Höngg
VBZ	1000	Xe2/2	926	MA	1935	Chaulin
VBZ	1000	Be2/2	1019	M	1929	Viernheim (Germany)
VBZ	1000	Ce2/2	1208	MA	1913	Zürich
VBZ	1000	Ce4/4	1326	MA	1430	Zürich
VBZ	1000	Ce4/4	1330	MA	1930	Zürich
VBZ	1000	Ce4/4	1350	MA	1931	Zürich
VBZ	1000	Be4/4	1360	MA	1942	Zürich Wartau/Höngg
VBZ	1000	Be4/4	1379	M	1947	Paris St Mandé
VBZ	1000	Be4/4	1506	P	1943	Schlieren
VBZ	1000	Be6/6	1802	MA	1960	Zürich
VMCV	1000	Ce1/2	4	M	1888	VHS
ZOS	1000	Ce2/2	1	MA	1897	Zürich Wartau/Höngg

† Falsely restored as SSZ Ce2/2 93.

Additional Abbreviations

AG	Alstatten Gais
BSB	Bern Schwarzenburg Bahn
BTB	Burgdorf Thun Bahn
BTB*	Birsigtalbahn
CR	Classic Rail (locos stored at various locations)
EB	Emmental Bahn
ESZ	Elektrische Strassenbahn Zug
EZB	Erlenbach Zweisimmen Bahn
GB	Gotthard Bahn

HWB	Huttwil Wolhusen Bahn
LHB	Langenthal Huttwil Bahn
LJB	Langenthal Jura Bahn
LLB	Leuk Leukerbad Bahn
LSB	Limmattal Strassenbahn
MCM	Monthey Champery Morgins
NOB	Nordostbahn
RdB	Regional des Brenets
RhV	Rheintalische Verkehrsbetnëbe
RiT	Riffelalp Tramway
RSG	Regional Saignelegier Glovelier
RSR	Royal State Railway (Siam)
SCB	Schweizerischen Central Bahn
SeTB	Sernftalbahn
SGA	St Gallen Gais Appenzell
SiTB	Sihltalbahn
SSB	Städtische Strassenbahn Bern
STB	Seetalbahn (not Sensetalbahn, which is now the STB)
StEB	Stansstad Engelberg Bahn
SW	Seebach Wettingen
TF	Tramways de Fribourg
TL	Tramways Lausannois
TLoc	Tramvie di Locarno
TrB	Trambahn Biel
UeBB	Uerikon Bauma Bahn
VHS	Verkehrshaus der Schweiz (Luzern Transport Museum)
VHX	Vietnam Hoa Xa
VMCV	Vevey Montreux Chillon Villeneuve
VZ	Visp Zermatt
WPI	Wetzikon Meilen
ZOS	Zürich Oerlikon Seebach

8. MUSEUMS AND MUSEUM LINES

There are few museum lines as such in Switzerland, due to the fact that very few lines have been closed by either the SBB or the various private railways. However, a number of steam locomotives belonging to the Swiss Transport Museum at Luzern are in working order and these run public excursions on certain weekends, often in association with special events. As detailed in the SBB section, a number of old electric locomotives have been retained as official museum locomotives, and these have limited regular diagrams on freight trains. They are also used on specials, and appear at open days etc. Several of the private railways have retained steam locomotives, or older examples of modern traction, and these either operate at weekends, or are available for private hire.

The Swiss Transport Museum is located at Luzern, and is well worth a visit. It covers all aspects of communications, not just railways. The best known museum line operated by enthusiasts is the Blonay-Chamby near Montreux, but there are a number of other operations, often over the lines of private railways.

The Swiss National Tourist Office produces an annual booklet 'Steam in Switzerland' detailing all regular steam operations. Some of these are also detailed in the SBB timetable.

Also of interest are the paddle steamers operating on the Brienzersee, Lac Leman (Lake Geneva), Thunersee, Vierwaldstättersee (Lake Lucerne) and Zürichsee. These are also detailed in the SBB timetable.

It should be noted that all the above operations are summer only, usually from May to September.

The list below of museum operations is arranged into alphabetical order of Cantons.

AARGAU

Brugg

The 'Mikado 1244' Club operate ex SNCF 141R 1244 on occasional public excursions over SBB main lines.

Rheinfelden

Not really a museum operation, but the Feldschlossen Brewery near the station still owns 2 steam locos, nowadays mainly for publicity. A diesel normally carries out the regular shunting. A set of coaches is available to take parties from the SBB station to the brewery.
2 steam.

Schinznach Bad

A 600 mm gauge line operating at weekends around a nursery.
6 steam, 7 diesel.

APPENZELL

Herisau

The Appenzellerbahnen have one steam locomotive available for charter.

Herisau

The Bodensee Toggenburg Bahn has one steam locomotive available for charter.

BASEL LAND

Waldenburg

The Waldenburgerbahn has one steam locomotive used on public excursions on the 3rd Sunday of the month between Liestal and Walderburg.

BERN

Brienz

As detailed under the Brienz Rothorn Bahn, this railway still uses steam in regular service.

Burgdorf

The Emmental Burgdorf Thun Bahn has 2 steam locomotives used on occasional public excursions.

Huttwil

Eurovapor have 3 steam locomotives based at the VHB Depot used on occasional public excursions over the VHB/EBT network.

Laupen

The Dampfbahn Bern has 3 steam locomotives used on public excursions on the Sensetalbahn on the 1st Sunday of the month between Flamatt and Gümmenen.

Meiringen

Two steam locomotives are based at the SBB Depot, and used on occasional excursions on the SBB metre gauge line to Interlaken, and since 1996 also over the rack to Giswil and beyond.

Spiez

The Bern Lötschberg Simplon Bahn has 2 steam locomotives used on occasional public excursions.

Wilderswil

The Schynige Platte Bahn has one steam locomotive available for charter.

Worblaufen

Eurovapor have a metre gauge steam loco based here, and used on private excursions over the Regionalverkehr Bern Solothurn between Worblaufen and Worb Dorf or Solothurn on the 2nd Sunday of the month.

Zweilütschinen

The Berner Oberland Bahnen have one steam locomotive available for charter.

GRAUBUNDEN

Grono

The Associazione della Ferrovia Mesolcinese operate regular excursions over the surviving part (Castiglione-Cama) of the RhB Bellinzona-Mesocco line.
4 railcars.

Landquart/Samedan

The Rhätische Bahn has 3 steam locomotives used on occasional public excursions, usually between Landquart and Disentis, Landquart and Filisur, and St Moritz and Scuol Tarasp.

JURA

Pré Petitjean

La Traction have 2 steam locomotives, plus other stock, used on occasional public excursions over the CF de Jura metre gauge system.

LUZERN

Luzern

The National Transport Museum (Verkehrshaus) is located on the north side of Lake Lucerne, about 2 km from the station (take a No. 2 trolleybus). The lake steamers also call at a pier adjacent to the museum. Some of the exhibits are changed from time to time, so not all are on display.
17 steam, 15 electrics, 1 diesel, 9 railcars, 5 trams.

Triengen

The Sursee Triengen Bahn has 2 steam locomotives available for charter.

Vitznau

The Rigibahnen has 3 steam locomotives used on public excursions from Vitznau on the 1st & 3rd Sundays of the month. Other specials are operated from Arth Goldau.

NEUCHÂTEL

St Sulpice

The 'Vapeur Val de Travers' Society operate steam services on certain weekends over the Régional Val de Travers. Including the normally freight only St Sulpice-Fleurier section.
9 steam, 4 diesels, 1 railcar.

SOLOTHURN

Balsthal

The Oensingen Balsthal Bahn has 3 steam locomotives used on public excursions on the last Sunday of the month.

THURGAU

Sulgen

Eurovapor have ex DB 23.058 based here for use on occasional excursions over main lines.

Weinfelden

The Mittel Thurgau Bahn has one steam locomotive used on occasional public excursions.

TICINO

Capolago

The Ferrovia Monte Generoso has one steam locomotive used on occasional public excursions.

Mendrisio

The Club San Gottardo operate regular excursions on the closed Mendrisio-Stabio-Valmorea (Italy) line.
2 steam, 2 electrics, 1 railcar.

URI

Realp

The Furka Bergstrecke Society has restored part of the Furka Oberalp Bahn over the Furka Pass, abandoned when the Furka Base Tunnel was opened. Three steam locomotives have been restored, including two repatriated from Vietnam! The terminus at Realp is close to the FO station.
7 steam, 6 diesel, 1 railcar.

Visp

The Brig Visp Zermatt Bahn has one steam locomotive available for charter.

VAUD

Bouveret

'Trains de Rive Bleu' operate steam trains on Sundays between Bouveret and Evian les Bains (France) on the closed line along the south side of Lake Geneva. Diesel trains are operated at other times.

Chaulin

The Blonay Chamby metre gauge line is undoubtedly Switzerland's premier enthusiast-operated line, with excellent views over Lake Geneva. Operates at weekends using both steam and electric traction. Some of the stock is stored at other locations. Occasional excursions operated on the nearby Gruyère Fribourg Morat and Montreux Oberland Bernois lines.
12 steam, 3 electrics, 6 railcars, 10 trams.

Eschallens

The Lausanne Eschallens Bercher Bahn has one steam between Cheseaux and Bercher on public excursions.

Le Pont

The Compagnie du Trains à Vapeur de la Vallée de Joux has 2 steam locomotives used between Le Pont and Le Brassus on public excursions over the Pont Brassus Bahn.

ZÜRICH

Bauma/Uster

The Dampfverein Zürcher Oberland (DVZO) run steam trains over the normally freight-only SBB line between Bauma and Hinwil on the 1st and 3rd Sunday of the month. The DVZO depot is at Uster; locos are based at Bauma as required.
6 steam, 2 electrics, 1 diesel.

Zürich Giesshubel

The Sihltal Zürich Uetliberg Bahn has one steam locomotive available for charter.

NOTES

NOTES

SWISS RAILWAY SAGA BAHNPANORAMA SCHWEIZ/ SWISS RAIL REVIEW

THE SWISS RAILWAY SAGA is the official hardback book to accompany the 150 years jubilee of Swiss Railways. It contains chapters covering all aspects of Switzerland's Railway operations, plus over 600 illustrations reproduced on 328 large format pages. This magnificent publication is a must for all enthusiasts of Swiss Railways. TEXT IN ENGLISH ONLY. £49.95

Published and printed in Switzerland, **SWISS RAIL REVIEW** is a clear and readable account of Swiss Railways past, present and future. It contains 145 colour and 191 black and white photographs, which capture the true atmosphere of Switzerland's Railways. Includes some rare early photographic material, plus many spectacular scenic shots of mountain railways at work. Text is in German, English and French. £27.50.

LIGHT RAIL REVIEW

Over the past 15 years light rail transit has advanced considerably in the UK with the introduction of schemes like Manchester Metrolink and South Yorkshire Supertram, and further important developments are in the pipeline. Published annually, Light Rail Review takes a comprehensive look at current and future light rail schemes. The editorial content consists of topical articles by recognised authorities in the light rail field, concentrating on both UK and overseas developments. Much use is made of illustrations, a high proportion of which are in colour making Light Rail Review an informative source of reference which will appeal to both enthusiasts and transport professionals alike. Each book is A4 size and thread sewn.

ISBN 1 872524 44 3 Light Rail Review 4	**£7.50**
ISBN 1 872524 56 7 Light Rail Review 5	**£7.50**
ISBN 1 872524 67 2 Light Rail Review 6	**£7.50**
ISBN 1 872524 77 X Light Rail Review 7	**£8.95**

TRAM TO SUPERTRAM

Peter Fox, Paul Jackson & Roger Benton

The official publication to commemorate the opening of Sheffield's new Supertram light rail system, is a pictorial account of Sheffield's tramway development. Printed in colour throughout, the book illustrates the old street tramway which finally died out in October 1960 and contrasts this with the construction, development and operation of the new modern tramway network.

ISBN 1 872524 61 3. A4. 48 pages in colour. Saddle Stitched. £4.95

PLEASE SEE INSIDE FRONT COVER TO ORDER THESE TITLES